Celibacy, Culture, and Society

Celibacy, Culture, and Society

The Anthropology of Sexual Abstinence

Edited by

Elisa J. Sobo
and
Sandra Bell

THE UNIVERSITY OF WISCONSIN PRESS

The University of Wisconsin Press
1930 Monroe Street, 3rd floor
Madison, Wisconsin 53711-2059

3 Henrietta Street
London WC2E 8LU, England

www.wisc.edu/wisconsinpress

Printed in the United States of America

Library of Congress Cataloging-in-Publication Data
Celibacy, culture, and society : the anthropology of sexual
    abstinence / edited by Elisa J. Sobo and Sandra Bell
        284 pp.   cm
    Includes bibliographical references and index.
    ISBN 0-299-17160-4 (cloth: alk. paper)
    ISBN 0-299-17164-7 (pbk.: alk. paper)
    1. Celibacy.   2. Sexual abstinence.   I. Sobo, Elisa Janine,
    1963–   II. Bell, Sandra.   III. Title.
    HQ800.15 .C45 2001
    306.73′2 — dc21   00-010697

ISBN-13: 978-0-299-17164-3 (pbk: alk. paper)

Contents

Foreword

Several years ago a colleague, then researching the DNA of slime molds, shared with me the wisdom that her biological research had taught her. Life, she said, came down to feeding, fighting, and mating. Those were not, of course, her exact words, but close enough. They are also close to the ideas of Richard Dawkins quoted by Qirko in this volume. We are designed by our genetic code, he states, to love life and love sex.

These shards of neo-Darwinian philosophy are the more persuasive because they evoke not only contemporary biological thought but also an older, universal human commentary on experience — a commentary found as much in the prosaic conversation of the locker room or beauty parlor as in the bawdy wordplay of an Elizabethan dramatist or a Sinhalese exorcist. During the twentieth century this combination of earthiness and science has supported a continual flow of what might be called tight explanations of human nature: explanations that connect the doings of people tightly and directly to their physical, inherited endowments and urges. The logic and purported power of these explanations lie in their success in the wider living world. If it is supposed that sexual attraction or mating — or for that matter territoriality, male social privilege, or aggression — can be explained on plain neo-Darwinian principles for all other animal species, and if humans are but one animal species among others, then it must follow, as the night follows the day, that such explanations rule in the human as well as in the animal world. This style of explanation has sometimes gone under the title of "sociobiology" and most recently under the title of "evolutionary psychology."

Anthropologists have responded strongly to these forceful intellectual currents. Indeed, cultural anthropology is historically founded on a spirited opposition to such biologistic explanation. It was Franz Boas and his pupils who so energetically opposed what they regarded as the error of treating physiology — then often meaning skull shape, now meaning genetic code — as social and cultural destiny. Yet in fact opposition to biologism also meant a declaration of independence, such that human cultural and social arrangements deserve and require their own particular explanations, their own specific kind of descriptions. These descriptions lead not to comparisons between humans and other species but to comparisons among different societies or historical periods. We are free, in other words, to read the chapters of this volume as a celebration of human sociocultural creativity applied to even so basic a desire and activity as sex. We are free, too, to discover through comparing forms of celibacy the variety of specifically human reasonings that govern sexuality and its control. We discover not just that there are different reasons and reasonings for celibacy but also that there is an irreducible subtlety about these reasonings and a consequent demand for nuance in description, which is demonstrated across all the ethnographic chapters. To compare Mazatec ritual celibacy with the lifelong celibacy of Catholic priesthood, and these again with the life-cycle celibacy of an adolescent Moroccan female, is to compare not just kinds of celibacy (and sexuality) but also different ways of making a world.

Anthropologists are indeed free to take this logic even further. If we can describe Shaker, Hindu, or Buddhist views on celibacy, then we can also describe, as yet another way of making a world, contemporary Western evolutionary psychological views on the matter. For example, evolutionary psychologists stress individual partner choice, and ignore social constraints upon choice, to a degree which makes their conceptual world a very peculiar one indeed, especially as compared with all those other psycho-socio-sexual worlds that ethnographers meet around the globe. On these grounds we are free to declare, in fact, that a biological, universalizing description of sexuality and celibacy is no more or less powerful than any other local version of these matters.

I think that the significance of this book is not that it (implicitly) rejects biological reductionism but rather that it suggest a wider form of explanation that would embrace both biological and anthropological perspectives. The key to this reading is given by Bell and Sobo in their introduction. They note, first, that sexuality is a facet of human sociality and go on to observe that sociality, in this perspective, is a matter of a general human propensity for mutual engagement and mutual responsiveness, or, in a word, intersubjectivity. So far so good — or at least, so far, so challenging to narrowly biological explanation. Yet, as they and the other authors demonstrate, human sociality/sexuality is still far more complex and requires a deeper and more nuanced description than biologists usually expect to give.

Consider, for example, the facet of human sociality that Michael Cole, in his 1996 *Cultural Psychology: A Once and Future Discipline* (p. 185), has call *prolepsis*, "looking ahead." He uses the modest case (drawn from the observations of an obstetrician) of a mother who said, as she held her newborn daughter in the hospital for the first time, "I shall be worried to death when she's eighteen." The remark is a sort of miniature of the complexities of the human condition. First, it looks forward to a projected, predicted life cycle for the daughter. It shows, in other words, the extent to which a present moment is, for human beings, subject to considerations over a long term, indeed, over a lifetime. And of course the remark looks back as well, to the experience of the mother and her peers and forebears: the mother is (re)collecting her own and others' past to predict her daughter's future.

Note, too, that this combined retrospection and prediction take into account not just a broad temporal view but also a view across society, with its norms and arrangements. For example, within the Anglophone mating system, the daughter will face real social and psychic dangers — dangers embodied in cultural concepts such as "unmarried mother" and "unwanted pregnancy." In other human mating systems the dangers for the daughter's life chances may be even greater (as in the Moroccan case discussed here by Schlegel), or they may be less (as in African bridewealth systems). But in any case, each system will have its locally appropriate plans or scripts for coping with those dangers, plans which comprehend not only the daughter and her prospective sexual partners but many other persons in society as well. In the Anglophone case, these other persons may include peers of the daughter as well as teachers, the medical profession, perhaps the minister of a church, and so forth.

So any description of human sociality/sexuality requires a complexity of description and the inclusion of a range of mental and social facts that simply do not exist in the repertoire of other animal species. Consider another case: that of the Shakers, described here by Collins. To some, the Shakers have seemed to embody a biologically precarious, nearly miraculous, social arrangement, a society without sexuality or reproduction. Yet they have survived more than a century and a half — more than six biological generations — and still persist, though in a greatly diminished form, even today. How is this possible? One kind of answer might be the ingenious one put forward by Qirko here, stressing a sort of virtual or imagined kinship which leads individuals to consider themselves reproductively successful within a fraternal-sororal institution. There is ample ethnographic evidence for the creative use of fictitious kinship in celibate institutions. We would do well to consider that the Shakers are like the celibate monastic orders of the Christian and Buddhist worlds in other ways as well. For these monastic institutions, with their institutionalized means of controlling sexuality, are supported, provisioned, and crewed by a society as a whole. They comprise a group of religious virtuosi and have an active role as specialists of the long term and of the ends of life. Some societies, even in such austere circumstances as those of the Tibetan plateau, can afford both economically and procreatively to support such virtuosi in the long run. Against this background, the Shaker decline may be an inevitable result not of their biologically improvident sexual and moral rules but rather of a failure of Shakers and the larger society to find an enduring working relationship such that regular recruits join the Shaker communities. So a proper description of Shaker celibacy must perforce be one that takes a whole social formation into account.

In fact the theoretically rich, and theoretically varied, chapters in this volume suggest among them an even broader schedule of questions that might need to be asked of human sociality/sexuality than I have adumbrated here. The challenge — and I believe it is a challenge issued to biologists as well as anthropologists — is to develop a sufficiently nuanced and comprehensive set of questions to enable us to map the tremendous territory of diversity that humans have reserved for themselves among the stark and constricting necessities of provisioning, survival, and reproduction (feeding, fighting, and mating). However that challenge is taken up, the chapters of this volume show that human beings, in their deadly serious play with ideas and social arrangements about sexual comportment, are a prodigiously inventive species.

MICHAEL CARRITHERS

Celibacy, Culture, and Society

Sandra Bell and Elisa J. Sobo

Celibacy in Cross-Cultural Perspective
An Overview

Across times and cultures, individuals and groups of sexually mature people have been culturally defined and socially positioned as celibates on the basis of temporary or long-standing nonparticipation in certain kinds of sex. Celibacy per se is accompanied by a removal of oneself from the larger social world and/or an effort to alter that world, whether in an actively engaged fashion or through a self-centered or passive critique of it. This volume aims to explore, comparatively, examples of the occurrences, perceptions, and meanings of celibacy. Scrutiny of celibacy's diverse manifestations will help us to more fully understand sexuality, of which celibacy is one form.

Researching the Sexual Realm

As Abramson and Pinkerton argue, "If it isn't penile-vaginal intercourse, sans contraceptives, between two fertile individuals at the right time of the month, then it isn't procreative sex. Clearly then, very little sex is of the procreative variety" (1995: 17). If not procreation, then what is the unifying factor that underlies "the sexual" as a concept? It is not erotic pleasure; for many people, sex is anything but physically pleasurable. For some the absence of pleasure is a problem; for others, such as infibulated women, culture teaches that sex should not be pleasurable anyhow

3

(Boddy 1982). People may have sex neither for physical pleasure nor to procreate but rather to please a partner, bind a relationship, fulfill conjugal duties, and so forth. So, on the face of it, the sexual is anything but a unified, cohesive construct. However, it does have a core, and we believe that that core is sexuality's inherently social nature. With this volume, we seek to show that celibacy exists as a coherent sexual discourse in many different cultures. Moreover, these various expressions of celibacy are connected not merely through a shared negative feature (nonparticipation in sex) but also, and more important, through notions and experiences surrounding desire, power and control, social cohesion, social productivity, and the social good.

In order to demonstrate this, the ethnographic perspective must be considered in combination with structural perspectives on and bioevolutionary approaches to the nature of sex. Ethnography emphasizes the immense cross-cultural and transhistorical variation in human sexual expression; social anthropology focuses on the macrolevel functions of sexuality (and its control); evolutionary approaches take into account environmental and biological forces that help underwrite social and cultural diversity. Some may argue that each perspective is mutually exclusive, but the notion of impenetrable disciplinary walls is a very recent development in academia. We believe that diverse perspectives can inform each other and that *no* topic — let alone a topic so complex and multifaceted as sexuality — can be fully understood unless viewed through multiple lenses. By bringing together scholars who take a variety of approaches, our project strives to answer Tuzin's call to "deal conceptually with the serious, interactive play between phenomenal events and culturally constituted ideas," the need for which he identifies as a major deficiency in previous anthropological inquiries into sexuality (1995: 257).

Celibacy: A Sexual, Social Act

Sexuality comprises what Hearn and Parkin describe as "an aspect and part of an all-pervasive body-politics rather than a separate and discrete set of practices" (1995: 57).[1] Viewed in this way, sexuality cannot be satisfactorily explained as an ahistorical, essential quality inherent in the individual. At the same time, it is not reducible to a set of intangible, socially constructed discourses; while we acknowledge the value of social constructionist theories and the foundational work of Michel Foucault, too often in the process of deconstruction the object of study "seems to crumble as we look" (Connell and Dowsett 1993), weakening the analytic value of this approach.

Of course, local definitions of the sexual do vary. For example, when men in India walk along the street hand in hand, the gesture is not perceived by passersby as indicative of a sexual relationship. But in most parts of the United Kingdom or the United States, the equivalent action is likely to be read as an explicit assertion of sexual intimacy.

Just as we can expect to find immense variation in local understandings of sexuality, so can we expect to find different local definitions and applications of celibacy. For example, celibacy can differ in relation to *volition* (elected or imposed) and *temporality* (temporary or permanent). Further, what sex and celibacy mean, or are associated with, will differ cross-culturally and historically. Within heterogeneous cultural areas, as in the United States, these meanings are likely also to vary subculturally (for example, by gender, age, or religious persuasion).

While at the microsocial level the differences in the manifestations and interpretations of celibacy are so vast that we might be right to say that celibacy as a category is a falsely unified field, at a more general level of abstraction we can argue that an underlying core links various forms of celibacy across time and space. From this vantage point it is helpful to view sexuality itself as an elementary form of human sociality. Here we follow Carrithers in understanding sociality as a capacity resulting from our evolutionary history through processes of natural selection (Carrithers 1992). It is a capacity that endows human beings with a potential to create formidable variation in social forms, and can be defined as "intersubjectivity, an innate human propensity for mutual engagement and mutual responsiveness. Some of this propensity is cognitive or intellectual, some of it is emotional, but in any case human character and human experience exist only in and through people's relations with each other" (Carrithers 1992: 55). Sexuality is one specific example of sociality.

As a field for human interaction, sexual relationships contribute to the creation of cultural practices and ideals (e.g., certain gift-giving practices, hygienic practices, conjugal ideals, etc.). Some of these cultural forms are aimed toward society's management or cultural maintenance (e.g., gender-linked partnering rules; see Sobo 1997). Hence the relationship between sexuality and culture is a dialectical and dynamic one. And under certain circumstances and in certain situations, it induces withdrawal — voluntary or enforced, short term or permanent — from sexual activity, as illustrated by the various examples treated in this book's chapters.

Sexuality also involves bodies. When we view sexuality as a form of sociality and the body as inherently social, we see clearly the error of accepting the unexamined notion of biology as stable, universal, transcultural "fact" — as something to be contrasted with the historical and contingent realm of culture. This position already has been strongly challenged by anthropologists who question the uncritical acceptance of a rigid distinction between the analytic categories of biological sex and gender (e.g., Laqueur 1990).

So celibacy is worthy of anthropological attention not simply because it appears in various guises and numerous contexts and not simply because it would seem, on first glance, to contravene species' survival goals. No matter how much it may differ from place to place, and partly because it does so, celibacy provides a useful lens through which to reconsider the significance of the body and of desire as inherently social rather than as biological givens upon which social practices are inscribed. We hope that this book demonstrates that, so long as various perspectives are informed by this understanding, they may be applied effectively to illuminate the celibate realm.

Body as Bridge

In his reflections on the management of desire in Indian thought and praxis, Madan notes: "The human body is a key symbol which bridges nature and culture but does not by itself constitute the totality of being. Any effort to locate the body exclusively in either of these two domains is a bad choice, for it is bound to fail" (1987: 95). For one thing, as a social species, human beings engage interactively in bodily practices, such as sexual arousal and eating. Even an apparently solitary activity such as masturbation is likely to feature others, through fantasy or as represented in pornographic or erotic images and text. Though sexual arousal is *in* and *of* the body it is routinely mediated, managed, and created as an aspect of social life.

This is seen in sex-and-gender research among Gitanos (Spanish Gypsies). Gay-Y-Blasco (1997) describes her attempts to interpret the Gitanos' assertion that female virgins possess a tangible physical organ, the *honra,* that is removed during a ritual defloration ceremony conducted by married women prior to a wedding. Gay-Y-Blasco was reluctant to treat her informants' conviction in the biological reality of the *honra* as solely an abstraction, a disembodied discourse. She was therefore forced to conclude that her material did not permit either "a radical constructionist or a radical essentialist approach" (p. 530).

Instead, Gay-Y-Blasco elected to focus on "the concept of 'experience' " (1997: 530), especially in relation to Mauss's notion of body techniques. In his essay of that title, Mauss claims that even the most elementary acts — for example, the act of quenching thirst — are pursued in a series of what he terms "assembled actions": actions that are "assembled for the individual not by himself alone" (1979: 105). For Gay-Y-Blasco, then, understanding the Gitanos' body techniques in relation to the concept of female virginity and the *honra* meant expanding her inquiries to "what characteristics of the body people imagine, how the body relates to other practices and understandings, where its meanings come from, and how it intertwines with other aspects of social life" (1997: 530). Moreover, these questions were asked in pursuit of a theoretical agenda that seeks to reconceptualize sex and gender as categories of analysis by asserting the "cultural specificity of sex itself" (p. 519). Different groups of people may emphasize different bodily elements to distinguish biological sex, and doings associated with these distinctions forge key elements of social and personal identity.

Similar questions about sexuality's role in the embodiment of social realities are addressed by several authors in this volume. For example, in his chapter on ritual celibacy among the Mazatec Indians of southern Mexico, Duke (this volume) notes that being heterosexually celibate or closed off (*encerrado*) from the world of mutual obligations and social intercourse "allows the messiness and contingencies of everyday life to dissipate from the body." In Mazatec experience, heterosexual relations and their gendered attributes are intense. Sex entails potentially troublesome physical and social consequences. Withdrawal into abstinence is a necessary prelude and preparation for those who are about to undertake critical economic, medical, or spiritual exertions that will benefit the group as a whole or through helping members of it. So even in denying society, celibacy supports it.

Celibacy Communicates and Creates

Self-conscious abstinence from elementary human behaviors such as sleeping, eating, or having sex can contribute to the creation of a certain status or socially intelligible identity. Going without some or all of these three activities is a frequent feature of initiation and life-cycle rituals around the world (La Fontaine 1985) and constitutes an expression of piety in some ascetic religions. Jain laity, for example, often follow vows known as the 14 disciplines (*caudah niyam*). These include avoiding sexual relations, joking, and flirting as well as restricting diet, travel, bathing, and attire. Jain celibate ascetics sometimes fast slowly unto death through a process known as *sallekhana* (Laidlaw 1995). Among Jains and various other peoples, religious fasting and prohibitions about amounts and kinds of food are frequently intertwined with sexual abstinence and sometimes with restrictions on sleeping. The ideal form of asceticism as practiced by Theravada Buddhist "forest monks" entails rigorous restrictions on eating and sleeping as well as on sex (Tambiah 1984: 85).

Individuals or groups who refrain from sexual activity are, in addition to creating themselves after a specific fashion, communicating something about themselves in relation to others and so about their own standing in society. They are also often engaged in constructing and disseminating a coherent commentary on the nature of social life and a set of philosophic statements about what it means to be fully human. For example, the celibacy of Roman Catholic priests not only helps create and maintain the priest persona; it also (1) articulates a triangular relationship among the Church (represented by the priest), Church members, and God (Southgate, this volume) and (2) makes a statement about normative expectations and values among local church members (Aguilar, this volume). Similarly, celibacy among Shakers (Collins, this volume) is not only a performative part of being Shaker but also indicates a complex critique of asymmetric property relations and related gender inequalities within the surrounding ambiance of emergent capitalism.

Even when celibacy is imposed rather than chosen consciously, it can actively indicate values and attitudes. Measures taken by parents to ensure their daughters' virginity express a nexus of concerns surrounding the economics of sexual reproduction and the ordering of family life (Schlegel, this volume). Likewise, the denial of sexual activity to prisoners can express complex notions about individual rights and privileges (even while helping to create the prisoner identity and his or her prison-specific sexuality). Fleisher and Shaw (this volume) discuss how U.S. citizens view celibacy as a form of deprivation deservedly visited upon criminals as part of a prison sentence. This attitude, traceable to the Quaker approach to moral and social rehabilitation, also prevails in Britain, where there is near-universal opposition to the idea of conjugal visits for prisoners. Resistance to the idea that prisoners might be allowed sexual privileges is so strong in these societies that, on the rare occasion that it is acknowledged, prison sex is portrayed as coercive, bestial, and devoid of pleasure.

Imposed or elected, celibacy is always enacted (or feigned to be) as part of a complex configuration of ongoing negotiations regarding social values and cultural attitudes. Out of these negotiations come patterned gains and losses for each party. The religious celibate forswears sex but gains sacred status and, in many cases, economic support (e.g., Aguilar; Kawanami; Southgate; each this volume), generally while helping his or her community in some way. The "sworn virgin" in Albania relinquishes her female gender to become a man, thereby gaining access for her family to resources and for herself to traditionally male occupations and so to a higher social status than she could possess as a woman (Gremaux 1994; see also Phillimore, this volume; Young 2000). Anorexic women, too, may challenge the conjugal rights of potential or current partners, and thereby challenge mainstream conjugal norms, by withdrawing from sex as part of their efforts to retain control over their own bodies (Lester, this volume). In ways such as these, nonparticipation in sexual relations can be managed and even manipulated as a channel for cultural creativity and innovation, self-creation, social climbing, and communication.

Purity and Pollution

The proposition that the practice of celibacy can assist in the achievement of personally sought-after and culturally recommended goals suggests that celibacy is a potentially potent ingredient in the construction of identity. And this is most obvious in those not uncommon contexts where sexual conduct is incorporated into a discourse of purity and pollution. As Douglas explains, ideas about sexual pollution can be posed in very concrete terms: "There are beliefs that each sex is a danger to the other through contact with sexual fluids" (1966: 3). Avoiding contact with the powerful reproductive juices of the other helps one to maintain one's own purity. A buildup of one's own sexual fluids also can be polluting, as in Jamaica, where this is believed to lead to mental and physical illness (Sobo 1993).

The concrete nature of sexual culture notwithstanding, Douglas's main argument is that "many ideas about sexual dangers are better interpreted as symbols of the relations between parts of society as mirroring designs of hierarchy or symmetry which apply in the larger social system" (1966: 4). The body physical is often brought into analogous relations with the body social so that "sometimes bodily orifices seem to represent points of entry or exits to social units" (p. 4), and fluid interchanges represent social interchanges and obligations, such as those that ensue between sexual partners.

Persuasive evidence for Douglas's argument comes from Jamaica (Sobo 1993), where, for example, women whose primary or "inside" male partners work away from home part of the year (e.g., in the United States, harvesting crops) are expected to remain chaste while their men are away. But chastity is difficult to maintain because of the pressure of human sexual "nature" — and of other men. A woman who gives in to such pressures may develop physical problems, such as skin ulcers where the "outside" partner's body rubbed against hers (e.g., on her belly), or her vaginal shape may change as it gets "pushed around" by the outside man's penis. Her vagina can be thereby "ruined" for her inside partner. Further, the outside partner may decide to make unwelcome claims on her labor or money. His comings and goings in and out of her yard (bed, vagina) may lead to gossip and so damage her social position.

Contravention of the sexual taboo placed on the female partners of migrant workers entails danger. The threat of bodily sanctions that might reveal their infidelities can keep women from compromising their temporarily celibate state while the men who have legitimate access to them are away. The belief that unchaste women will be so marked functions to conserve the status quo in sex and gender relations against the disruptive comings and goings, exits and entries, related to male migration (and to penetrative sex itself). This may not always be acted upon or accepted as true, but its place in the explanatory scheme casts infidelity as harmful, and the purity of temporary celibacy offers a welcome alternate to the threatened disorder that ungoverned female sexuality, with its telltale disfigurement, may bring. And adherence to the regime of celibacy helps a woman to ensure that her absent partner will, upon his return, still be hers.[2]

The benefits of celibacy go beyond physical purity or the calm endurance of existing partnership arrangements, and chaste wives or girlfriends are not the only ones interested in the protection from danger that celibacy can produce. Celibacy among Mazatec ritual specialists and healers in Mexico (Duke, this volume) allows for the achievement of a sacred spiritual status that, although not always permanent, can be compared with that which is ascribed in a variety of cultures to monks, nuns, and priests. And abstinence helps Mazatec ritual specialists and healers to create within themselves the temperament or traits or conditions (cleanliness) necessary for the socially beneficial and productive performance of their ritual duties, just as celibacy helps the Catholic priest to become more charitable, Christocentric, and unconditionally loving (Southgate, this volume).

Interpretations of celibacy often involve speculation about its effect on the disposition of celibate persons or institutions. Especially in combination with notions about sexual danger, celibacy is often construed as a source of charisma in the individual, and this charisma can have a societywide impact. For example, Weber notes that "the permanent abstinence of charismatic priests and religious virtuosi derives primarily from the view that chastity [celibacy], as a highly extraordinary type of behavior, is a symptom of charismatic qualities and a source of valuable ecstatic abilities" (1978: 603).

Weber describes two basic religious positions that favor celibacy as an instrument of salvation. The first is "mystical flight from the world," for which celibacy is a "central and indispensable instrument" (1978: 603). The other is asceticism, which represents sex as inimical to "rational, ascetic alertness, self control and the planning of life" because it is conceived to be "ultimately and uniquely unsusceptible to rational organization" (p. 604). In actuality the two perspectives are often combined and, according to Weber, may operate simultaneously to generate hostility toward sexual conduct and related social intermingling, which, as Douglas (1966) demonstrates, can be associated with dangerous pollution.

In light of the foregoing, we might say that the kind of temporary celibacy discussed in relation to the Mazatec (above) customarily confers charismatic abilities on shamanic figures and other specialists whose services are deemed critical to the well-being of others. It has been argued elsewhere as well (Lindholm 1993) that the shaman should be understood as being in possession of charismatic qualities that equip him, or her, to cross otherwise impenetrable boundaries to mediate between spiritual worlds and between different social worlds (and see Bell 1998b).

The control of sexual energy is commonly regarded as an important technique in the generation and maintenance of socially beneficial shamanic powers. Sometimes it is through one's occupation of a sexually liminal social space that one actualizes this control; other times, a personal lack of interest in sex to begin with is capitalized on. The celibate spinster (*célibe*) of rural Mexico, described by Arnold (1978) and celibate for either of these two reasons, is allowed special ceremonial roles. Arnold interpets the *célibe*'s ceremonial function as providing "a link between the communal ritual of adult males and the familial ritual of adult females" (p. 53). The *célibe*'s sexual liminality and related practice of celibacy protects her when she crosses boundaries; her celibate status allows her to ignore categoric imperatives that others would need to apply.

Celibacy and Desire

The English term *celibacy* derives from the Latin *caelebs*, meaning "alone or single." In everyday English usage *celibacy* implies abstention from all sexual relations as well as from marriage. In this volume, the word generally signifies only the former (it may also entail the latter, when specified), because we take it for granted that the unmarried may engage in sexual activity and that married people may undertake celibacy. Indeed, Mahatma Gandhi famously advised that celibacy be beneficially practiced by married couples once they had completed their families (Caplan 1987: 280). The uncritical use of the term *celibacy* to mean "unmarried" has led to some very confused theorizing, for many authors have unthinkingly let normative assumptions lead them to conflate the unmarried state with that of the sexually abstinent, much as early incest theorists tended to confuse rules related to sex with rules related to marriage (Fox 1967: 55).

Further confusion comes from the historical use of the term *celibacy* in relation to the specifically heterosexual activities and heterosexual marriages of the biologically sexually mature. In Western societies the strength of the stigma attached to homosexual relations between men or between women was such that gay men and especially lesbian women were often perceived as (heterosexual) celibates.[3]

Where heterosexuality represents a hegemonic ideal and same-sex relations are negatively sanctioned, homosexual celibacy can scarcely be imagined by members of the heterosexual mainstream. This is true not only in western European history but in a portion of other societies as well. For example, a person who does have homosexual relations is still classified a celibate by the Mazatec Indians of southern Mexico (Duke, this volume), and Laidlaw observes that Jain rules about celibacy for renouncers "show no concern for the possibility of homosexual relations between them" (1995: 255 n.).

In any given society, we will find individuals who practice celibacy as individuals, and in many societies we will find individuals who practice celibacy as part of a cultural role entailing or defined by (whether partly or wholly) the denial of sexual desire, such as the role of the nun. Celibacy must, at least first, and at least conceptually, entail a denial of sexual desire. That is, simple asexuality—simply having no sexual drive—does not count (unless it has been instilled by celibate practices). One cannot abstain from what one has no appetite for doing. Notwithstanding this distinction between individual celibacy and asexuality, being asexual may predispose the individual to take up the *cultural* role of the celibate (Levy 1971).[4]

So, much for the same reasons as those we have described for homosexual men and women, children who do not have sex cannot be classed as celibate when culture does not attribute sexual desire to them to begin with. Under these conditions, children's nonparticipation in normative sexual relations is not construed in the same way as adult celibacy is.

Nevertheless, children's status in some cultures as presexual (deMause 1976) may be employed, through symbolic reversal, to denote celibacy in adults. Lang (1987) evokes a vivid example of this process in his description of medieval Europe, where, following a tradition established by the early Church, heaven was conceived as a sexless realm. In a 1440 Stefan Lochner painting of the Day of Judgment, the resurrected saints are portrayed as children "in order to emphasize their non-sexual status," whereas the damned are "adults who clearly retain their sexual features" (Lang 1987: 156). There are also indications that medieval female ascetics sought to conflate the presexual and the celibate in their efforts to recall the prepubertal state by suppressing menstruation through fasting (Bell 1985; Brown 1989).

Celibacy and Social Change

In a modern, secular context Lester (this volume) proposes that the rejection of food and sex by North American women diagnosed as anorexic represents their efforts to control the boundaries of the body and assert self-determination. A recovered anorexic interviewed by Woods described the transformations of self that she experienced through anorexia: "I felt like one of those early Christian saints who starved themselves in the desert sun. I felt invulnerable, clean and hard as the bones etched into my silhouette" (1981: 242). So although the modern female anorexic is medicalized and secularized, she may still resort to powerful religious images of self-control to convey her experience. This anorexic woman possesses a vivid, though highly selective, picture of early Christian asceticism, which she reconstructs in her own image. Similarly, de Munck's sexually abstinent college students (this volume) identify Christian monks and nuns as traditional exemplars of prototypical celibacy. These examples suggest a complicated relationship between the historicity of celibacy in the West and its reinvention within contemporary contexts.

De Munck suggests that in the United States celibacy is conceptually and motivationally linked to a schema of self that is, in turn, connected to cultural models of individualism and of romantic and platonic love. De Munck's research participants are concerned about the level of physical intimacy that can be permitted before celibacy, as they define it, is contravened. This suggests that recent debates and moral arguments about the value of sexual abstinence among the unmarried may be eliding the distinction between celibacy (abstinence from all sexual activity) and chastity (striving to abstain from unlawful or uncondoned sexual activity). Celibacy, for many of de Munck's participants, exists as a graded semantic category allowing for degrees of erotic contact — kissing, hugging, and holding hands — between heterosexual couples. It is not an all-or-nothing affair, nor is it necessarily a lifetime vocation.

In early and medieval Western Christianity, distinctions between the concepts of celibacy and chastity were more clear-cut. The Church expected all unmarried lay people to forgo both reproduction and erotic pleasure. The sexual conduct of the married laity gradually became the subject of canon laws, through which the Church sought to oversee lay chastity. Heterosexual intercourse, even within the marriage bed, was now to occur rarely and with the sole goal of conception. The crime of sodomy, as then defined, included all sexual excitations other than penetrative vaginal intercourse between woman and man (Brundage 1996: 43). Although unmarried lay people were supposed to avoid the temptations of erotic desire, they were potentially marriageable and therefore distinct from priests and members of religious orders, who were, ideally, perpetual virgins: childlike and therefore Christlike. In his discussion of the writings of John Cassian, composed in the early fifth century c.e. and "a classic without rival in the monastic west" (Knowles 1969: 15), Foucault underscores the contrast between lay and monastic chastity. The latter meant vigilance in "expelling for good everything impure or conducive to impurity" (Foucault 1985a: 24), including corruptions of the mind that might reveal themselves in erotic dreams and nocturnal emissions. The ideal monk thus departed from the virtuous lay person, whose chastity depended solely on obedience to canon law. Monastic celibacy, on the other hand, developed to a point that has "nothing to do with a code of permitted or forbidden actions but is a whole technique for analyzing and diagnosing thought, its origins, its qualities, its dangers, its potential for temptation and all the dark forces that can lurk behind the mask it may assume" (Foucault 1985a: 24).

This kind of self-analysis required what Foucault describes as "a permanent hermeneutics of the self" (1985b: 371), which he identifies as important to the genealogy of modern subjectivities. Others have also argued that elements of what came to be labeled Western individualism can be traced to certain psychological and social characteristics of Christian monastic life (Collins 1988).

In the end, for medieval monks and nuns, chastity entailed celibacy. For married people, however, chastity was a matter of conjugal fidelity and of refraining from certain kinds of sex; celibacy was not expected of them.[5]

During the Reformation in western Europe, the whole monastic enterprise came under attack. Parrinder describes how the Reformers attacked "clerical celibacy and monastic vows of continence. Marriage was exalted as a divine institution, for everybody, and celibacy was condemned as contrary to divine law" (1980: 230). As a result of the Reformation, the number of monks in Roman Christendom was almost halved (Knowles 1969). In England they disappeared altogether, and clerical marriage came to be approved by Protestants.

Lang suggests that widespread socioeconomic and cultural change during the eighteenth century, especially in relation to marriage, the family, and the domestication of Christianity, led to a further retreat from the charismatic noninvolvement with the world that characterized early and medieval Christianity. He writes:

The idea of choosing one's own partner while rejecting arranged marriage, the rejection of traditional Christian suspicion and hostility towards sensuality, and the glorification of sexuality for its own sake promoted the emphasis on romantic love, sexual privacy and domesticity. This surge of sentiment involves a new definition of human happiness, and hence of the human being. (1987: 162)

As the symbolic value of romantic love in Western societies has gained ever-greater currency during the twentieth century, so celibacy itself has become romanticized and eroticized. Jeremy and Mark, two young men discussed by de Munck (this volume) are virgins; they describe themselves as celibate, and both associate celibacy with freedom and life.

The notion that celibacy energizes is not unique to Jeremy and Mark. Although not all cultures subscribe to a hydraulic model of sexual energy, many do support the notion that sexual abstention makes energy available for other activities or pursuits. For example, as Alter explains, self-help literature promoting the "biomoral" benefits of celibacy (e.g., increased wisdom, stamina, power, etc., more of which later) has a wide circulation in North India (1997: 280). Or, as Southgate (this volume) notes for the male Catholic priesthood, "The celibate directs his generative energy to the daily seeking of this goal [union with God] through prayer, ministering to his community, and nurturing his friendships."

The conjunction of eroticism and celibacy discussed by de Munck also is not as extraordinary as it might first seem. Caroline Walker Bynum's (1991) careful scholarship on medieval piety refers to the "ecstatic, even erotic overtones" (p. 184) of ascetic spirituality that she detects mainly, but by no means exclusively, among celibate female saints, during the period between 1200 and 1500 c.e. Bynum relates the corporeal nature of medieval female asceticism with, among other things, the fact that female saints wrote not in scholastic Latin but in the vernacular of their various European mother tongues. They drew their vocabulary from available vernacular literature, predominantly "various kinds of love poetry and romantic stories" (p. 196). This suggests the existence of a strand in the history of European thought that is not at all inimical to the interpolation of the semiotics of romance, eroticism, and celibacy.

In contemporary contexts the conjunction of these three elements may be due to tensions arising from the extensive commoditization of sexuality, which promotes sexual permissiveness as well as anxiety about the consequences of this permissiveness for family stability and personal fulfillment. U.S. college students live in a society that lauds sexual (especially heterosexual) pleasure and romance, which is valorized in Hollywood movies, popular music, and other forms of mass culture (Lindholm 1998: 23). Young people who contemplate or attempt celibacy may therefore be prone to appropriate models of love to their schemas of self, as de Munck demonstrates. These young people are looking for ways by which love can be integrated with the ideal of abstinence. What emerges may appear more like virtuous chastity than celibacy, except for the accompanying discourse of self-analysis identified by Foucault (1985a) as a component of Christian asceticism.

The rise of interest in the self and in individual identities that marks the development of "high capitalism" (Giddens 1991) and the fetishization of intimate relationships is most compatible with Weber's "innerworldly asceticism" (1978: 541–556). This condition prompts a tendency toward the domestication of religious celibacy and away from its contemplative world-fleeing orientation (both are always present according to Weber).

As "high modernity" got underway in the Western world, an unusual range of options or alternative discourses became available (Giddens 1991). One such discourse was that of the sexologists, who championed orgasm for people of all sexual orientations (Béjin 1985). The cultural power of the discourse of celibacy is muted in such a context, but its symbolic value still may be appropriated for alternative understanding of erotic experience. In the process, celibacy may be secularized or medicalized (e.g., as an answer to AIDS), romanticized or eroticized (as in de Munck's examples), or even regenerated in a new religious guise. One such case is the recent introduction of Buddhist monasticism to Europe and the United States. However, in these contexts, unlike in Asia, the monks' charisma seems as dependent on their rejection of material wealth as on their abandonment of sexual gratification (Bell 1998a).

Although many Christians may welcome the emergence of the romanticized new celibacy, others have begun to question whether too much importance already has been ascribed to the practice. During the past few decades, an increasingly noisy debate for and against the introduction of married priests has been underway within and outside the Roman Catholic church. The debate is fueled by arguments claiming that married priests would be better adjusted and more able to understand the personal problems of their sexually active constituents. The recent emergence of a number of cases of serious sexual misconduct by Catholic clergy, past and present, has provided an increased sense of urgency for many who are engaged in the debate. (See Southgate, this volume; see also, e.g., the *Independent* [London] June 27, 1998, and June 18, 1999).

Meanwhile, since the deliberations of the Second Vatican Council in 1965, there has been a trend in Roman Catholic religious orders to dismantle clergy-community barriers and to stress agapic love and service for all (Ebaugh 1977). These moves also indicate a shift from Weberian world-fleeing religious commitment to a more innerworldly orientation (Weber 1978: 541–556).

Celibacy as Resistance

Evidence that the style and interpretation of celibacy is contingent upon historical processes also comes from the Indian subcontinent (Khandelwal; Phillimore; each this volume). Gandhi's reinvention of the classical Hindu institution of brahmacharya (celibacy), making sexuality a site of resistance during the colonial era, has been well documented (Caplan 1987). The hermeneutics of brahmacharya during the postcolonial period has recently begun to receive attention too; Alter has written repeatedly on the topic, with particular reference to its impact on notions of masculine identity and forms of nationalism in North India (1994, 1997).

In its classical Vedic formulation (Khandelwal, this volume), Hindu brahmacharya is associated with the four ashramas, or stages of life, that male members of Brahman, Kshatriya, and Vaishya castes go through. Sexual abstinence and other ascetic practices are prescribed for the stage following a young man's initiation as a genuine student of the Vedic text. Formal sexual abstinence also is practiced for short, intermittent periods by married men or women in the householder stage of life to ensure their purity as sponsors of rituals, on the undertaking of vows, or during a pilgrimage.[6] Still, a long tradition acknowledges that some men may reject the householder stage altogether and practice lifelong celibacy as a sannyasi. A sannyasi enhances his physical and mental vitality through the retention of semen, and after a 12-year period of this he spontaneously achieves his spiritual goal (Caplan 1987: 275).

Alter's interest is in the contemporary reinvention of male sexual abstinence as a therapeutic lifestyle conferring immunity from all manner of semen loss, including by unconscious processes, and eventual immunity from sexual desire. Numerous yoga teachers and naturopaths promote celibacy for all men directly, in their teaching and through a body of popular literature; both means of dissemination have increased significantly over the past 70 years (Alter 1997). In these contexts, male celibacy is presented as a means to achieving "seminal truth" (p. 275), which is viewed not so much as a moral virtue but more as a physiological and psychological advantage, a duty to oneself as a man and, ultimately, to the nation (Alter 1994).

According to Alter, those who propagate this modern discourse on brahmacharya do so because of a feeling of "impending powerlessness and disintegration" (1994: 54). They believe that "postcolonial India is enslaved by its 'freedom' to develop and Westernize; enslaved not so much to sex itself — although certainly that — as to the idea that power is a function of potency, and virility the coefficient of modernization" (p. 57). By these lights, brahmacharya is an embodied, masculine tool with which to crush "the discourse of postcolonial desire that afflicts contemporary society" (p. 63).

Modern brahmacharya in North India represents an attempt to diffuse the celibate ideal throughout the body politic, whereas celibacy in the nineteenth-century United States was more often practiced by people opting out of the body politic as a whole. Celibacy was undertaken by members of intentional communities, for which it served as a form of resistance to existing structural arrangements. We have already mentioned the Shakers, who, in the early stages of their development as a society, advised sexual abstinence on religious grounds. They later came to adopt a more secularized and politicized rhetoric of abstinence with the development of communal living and the advent of Shaker villages. By this stage, both sex and marriage were to be avoided because "private property is based on the family and on inheritance. . . . In order to abolish the cause of greed and violence one needs to abolish . . . the traditional family" (Collins, this volume). Celibacy and communal living served, at least in the villages in which they were practiced, to correct for economic maldistribution, gender inequality, and overpopulation.

Not only the Shakers expressed organized opposition to existing economic and political arrangements through the formation of an intentionally celibate community. Another mixed-sex celibate group, the Koreshian Unity, formed in the mid-1880s in Chicago. The group acquired land in Florida and migrated there to build the "New Jerusalem." Like the Shakers, the Koreshians promoted female economic and political rights. So did the Women's Commonwealth, a single-sex, celibate society that became an official community in Texas in 1890. Also known as the Sanctified Church, this group included many women who had left their husbands. Court documents, interviews, and the church's constitution reveal a commitment to the social and economic independence of women from men (Kitch 1989: 11–15).

These and other intentional communities adopted celibacy in reaction to a social structure they did not support, a social structure that was maintained in part by the sexual relations it constituted. Celibate individuals might have had idiosyncratic motivations to join, but their groups had a suprapersonal agenda of resistance and even revolution.

When joining a group is not possible or desirable, celibacy can provide a tool for individual resistance. Schlegel (this volume) discusses how, within the family itself, adolescents may opt for celibacy over marriage in order to subvert parental control through dissent and disobedience (see also Gutschow, this volume). Schlegel provides examples from among communities of early Christians and nineteenth-century silk workers and shows how adolescents' "celibacy can backfire on dominating parents." This is especially so in societies where virginity and celibacy are held in high esteem, because in such social contexts parents cannot cast out defiant girls who in the end prefer celibacy to marriage. The politics of gender are deeply implicated in the practice of celibacy.

The Political Economy of Female Celibacy

Kinship systems often contain some requirement for absolute celibacy among certain categories of persons. For example, in India, especially among high-status castes or those who are competing for higher status, widows are frequently not permitted to remarry or to engage in sexual relationships on the grounds that they must remain faithful to their deceased husbands (Khandelwal, this volume). In Nepal, if a widow fails to remain chastely celibate she forfeits her share of her husband's estate (Agarwal 1994: 246). Her chastity is watched over by remaining kin (and village gossips). The virginity of unmarried daughters may be closely guarded too.

In these cases, celibacy exists to preserve forms of symbolic capital or stock, such as honor and purity, which are essential for the status of the family as a whole within the wider society. The relationship among the symbolic value of virginity, the regulation of reproduction, and the flow of material resources, traced by Schlegel (this volume), explains why most societies that impose sexual abstinence on adolescent girls also have the family of the bride make presentations to the family of the groom. In these societies the girl is not only a potential wife but also an heiress expected to attract a good match in her husband. The point of sexual restriction here is to prevent the girl from becoming pregnant with an unsuitable suitor who will then have grounds to press claims on her, her child, her future children, and her dowry. (It also prevents her from acquiring a reputation as a potential cuckolder, which has similar implications for the proper flow of wealth through affinally linked lineages.)

The preservation or increase of resources in a family, or among a group of families, may lead to the imposition of lifelong celibacy on some members. Hager (1992) has charted how families were benefited by female religious claustration in Europe from ca. 400 to 1300 c.e., when the founding of convents by lineages provided a means of controlling land, conserving wealth, and creating alliances with the Church. Families that endowed a convent usually placed several daughters or other female relatives in it, "even in subsequent generations" (p. 393). Such fidelity "gave the family a secure place to sequester females consistently over several generations while probably increasing the chances a member of that family would attain the abbacy" (pp. 393–394). This mattered because abbesses, "particularly those of the larger and wealthier convents and double [dual-sex] monasteries" (p. 395), played an important role in ecclesiastic politics. Even an abbess of nonroyal blood might attend kings' councils in England and Germany and advise the high nobility, thereby increasing her lineage's prestige and influence.

Families retained control of the land attached to convents that they endowed, and they also profited if widows of their lineage retired to convents on the death of their husbands. When a widow used part of her dowry or patrimony to enter the convent, this meant a "small immediate loss to her husband's lineage but a large gain in resources in the long run by preventing remarriage and the possibility of conflict of interest between her former husband's kin" (Hager 1992: 392). Where sexual access does not imply ownership, this kind of arrangement might never emerge.

Notwithstanding, in the later Middle Ages, when landed resources grew scarcer and nunneries were a fixture, existing convents still functioned as repositories for excess daughters, but the nobility were inclined to detect fewer benefits in founding new convents. This tendency for institutions featuring celibacy to rise and decline according to particular historical conditions indicates the flexibility and creativity with which celibacy may be deployed as a social strategy for the maintenance and allocation of resources. In his discussion of the institutionalized practice of women living masculinized and celibate lives (sadhin) among the Gaddis of the Indian Himalaya, Phillimore (this volume) allows us to see how such responses might effloresce and degenerate across a relatively brief time-span. The Gaddis draw on Hindu and Buddhist teachings concerning asceticism and the regulation of female sexuality to manufacture a cluster of symbolic references that locate the sadhin within a set of discernible cultural frames, even though the women do not live particularly religious lives.

Phillimore (this volume) points out that it is hard for us to imagine celibacy "divorced from striving for a religious goal." Notwithstanding, an example from the Balkans demonstrates that celibacy does not necessarily require justification as a means to religious ends. The declining, but still extant, institution of the sworn virgin — the previously mentioned virilized celibate transvestite female — is documented by Gremaux (1994) among mountain-dwelling Montenegrins and Albanians where the "localized patrilineages typically failed to provide women with full social rights," including rights to inheritance. Gremaux goes so far as to describe women of these societies as "social outsiders" (p. 243) when in the feminine guise. The opportunity for a greater degree of inclusion is open to a woman raised from childhood as a son or one who, when young, renounces her given gender and constructs herself anew as a man. The occupational and life choices available to the sworn virgin appear relatively varied according to the case studies presented by Gremaux. Access to land was but one possible outcome; the sworn virgins he studied also became teachers and soldiers and pursued male crafts such as carpentry. Each clearly enjoyed a higher status and degree of autonomy than she would have enjoyed as a woman (see also Young 2000).

Versions of female celibacy occupy a continuum of sorts, ranging from a total affiliation between perpetual virgins and sacred institutions, represented by medieval nuns (we might also include chaste widows), through an ambiguous affiliation, as with the Gaddi sadhin, to a lack of institutional affiliation, as demonstrated in Montenegro and Albania. One explanation for this might be a link between the degrees of respect and the rights to property that are accorded to women in the different societies. Among the European nobility, women did possess rights to property. As Hager points out, "The practice of female claustration is thought to be tied to the tradition of partible inheritance, particularly when it is bilateral" (1992: 401). Where women could inherit land, claustration of females helped to prevent "the alienation of property from a particular kin group" (p. 402). Further, it may be that the possibility for conferring religious status on celibate women correlates with the range of roles and options that are available to women in the secular domain and, at least in patriarchal societies, depends on there being religious status for celibate men to begin with.

This last point is reinforced by Gutschow and by Kawanami (each this volume). Each author explores the consequences for women when male models of celibacy are afforded priority and predominance. Gutschow, who discusses Buddhist nuns in Zangskar, dwells on the opposition and subordination of female renouncers to their male counterparts, relating the source of asymmetry to prevailing gender relations, expressed through the exchange of women. Nuns do not escape the patriarchal economy of the family because, unlike monks, they remain active in the productive and reproductive world of the kinship system. For example, they assist their families with seasonal agricultural tasks, helping to maintain and to reproduce the kin unit with inputs of food. Moreover, nuns actively support monks' nonproductive roles by serving them, and parents receive the religious merits that accrue from their daughters' piety.

Kawanami, who examines the position of Theravada Buddhist nuns in Burma (now Myanmar), describes how their status in the religious domain remains lower than that of monks, despite the education of and respect for Buddhist nuns in Burma, unlike in Thailand and Sri Lanka. Burmese kinship is matrilocal and bilateral. Women enjoy considerable economic independence, hold property in their own right, and enjoy relative equality with their husbands in marriage. Kawanami argues that in Burma the subordination of Theravada nuns to monks is premised on ambiguities inherent in dominant images of the feminine as a vessel for procreation and object of desire, rather than on structural factors per se.

Celibacy, Altruism, and Kin

As well as conferring benefits on one's kin or one's social network, celibacy benefits individuals (or is thought to benefit them, in cases where it is imposed). Kin and close relations receive symbolic capital (e.g., merit for having donated a daughter or son), material capital (e.g., land or other riches), physical capital (e.g., donations from the celibates, who have no households of their own, of domestic and productive labor), and spiritual capital (e.g., through celibates' prayers for the well-being or salvation of kin). Qirko (this volume) argues that people also may benefit genetically; that is, celibacy may aid in species survival.

Celibacy that directly benefits kin can be explained, says Qirko (this volume), in terms of the bioevolutionary theory of inclusive fitness, which argues for the persistence of genetically driven traits that confer survival advantages to others who do not share that trait. That is why some insect species persist in producing nonreproducing worker castes. Cultural evolution sometimes occurs along similar lines: learned traits that confer a survival advantage can be selected for.

Celibacy in culture-bearing *Homo sapiens* is not amenable to a reductionistic, *post hoc* explanation based on a supposed genetic predisposition. But, as Qirko shows, social theories regarding celibacy can be enhanced through the thoughtful integration of certain key bioevolutionary concepts (and vice versa). Indeed, the fruitful juxtaposition of biological and social theory has a long history in anthropology (see Langness 1980). Using such a framework, Qirko shows that society-preserving altruism (e.g., self-sacrifice through nonreproduction or through the redirection of energies from the household into the community) can be induced through "manipulated altruism," in which kin-recognition mechanisms are manipulated so that altruism benefiting the larger social group is evoked. Qirko shows that many forms of institutionalized celibacy make use of this tactic. For example, certain celibate groups make use not only of kin terms (e.g., *sister, brother*) but also of visual cues that encourage "false phenotypic matches" such as uniform clothing and hairstyles and the disavowal of individuating decoration.

Complex Topic, Complex Approach

Whether elected or enforced, permanent or temporary, celibacy entails removing (or attempting to remove) oneself from the larger social world or attempting to alter that world, whether in an actively engaged fashion or through a self-centered or passive critique of it. So celibacy entails more — much more — than simple personal sexual inaction. It can improve or alter one's personal status, perpetuate or change (or at least represent an effort to change) one's society, and further one's own and one's family's social, material, symbolic, spiritual, and even genetic fortunes.

The chapters that follow aim to explore, comparatively, examples of the occurrences, perceptions, and meanings of celibacy in various times and places. Such a complex topic cannot be understood from one viewpoint alone, so this collection weaves together a wide range of approaches, including the biological, cognitive, ethnographic, historical, psychological, and structural. Each perspective offers its own important insights. By drawing them together and using them in ways that highlight the social aspects of sexual abstinence, we can achieve a more powerful and intellectually satisfying understanding of celibacy.

Notes

1. The extent of sex, the impact of sexuality, and the full range of meanings that attach to the sexual domain are hard for researchers to assess because much is likely to be concealed from the gaze of observers, ethnographers included (Tuzin 1995: 264). Further, people may actively lie about sexual matters and also have genuine problems with recall (Harris 1995; Kelly 1998: 31). If collecting reliable and representative data for contemporary people is difficult, historical sexuality research is even harder; historians must rely on sources that may be heavily gender biased (Bullough 1996: 9) and class biased as well.

2. Male migration for farm work abroad is by no means the norm, and the pattern described provides just one example of the ways in which pollution beliefs come into play in Jamaican gender relations and sexual life. For a broader description and more detailed analysis of gender and sex in Jamaica, see Sobo 1993.

3. In 1921 British members of Parliament refused to endorse an amendment to a parliamentary bill that sought to inflict legal penalties for "gross indecency between female persons." They did so on the grounds that sexual relations between women were so alarming that legislation would draw attention to such conduct and introduce the idea to otherwise innocent women, thereby possibly corrupting them. The best weapon was silence, which would contribute to the desired effect of rendering lesbianism invisible (Jeffreys 1985: 114). Unmarried women could be assigned to what was considered the sexually arid zone of spinsterhood.

4. Where homosexuality is not condoned, homosexual individuals might opt out of heterosexuality by joining gender-specific celibate institutions such as con-

vents or by adopting a culturally available celibate role such as that of the sworn virgin, available in the Balkans (Gremaux 1994; Young 2000) and described earlier in this chapter.

5. Records show the laity being subjected to humiliating public confessions and whippings as well as the imposition of fines for breaking chastity rules. But accounts of canonic tribunals and evidence for the institutionalization of female prostitution by municipal authorities suggest that transgressions continued (Brundage 1996: 43–45).

6. Celibacy is also enjoined for the final stage of male life, when a man ideally renounces his duties as a householder in order to cultivate religious knowledge.

References Cited

Abramson, Paul, and Steve Pinkerton. 1995. *With Pleasure: Thoughts on the Nature of Human Sexuality.* Oxford: Oxford University Press.

Agarwal, Bina. 1994. *A Field of One's Own.* Cambridge: Cambridge University Press.

Alter, Joseph S. 1994. Celibacy, Sexuality, and the Transformation of Gender into Nationalism. *North India Journal of Asian Studies* 53: 45–66.

Alter, Joseph S. 1997. Seminal Truth: A Modern Science of Male Celibacy in North India. *Medical Anthropology Quarterly* 11(3): 275–298.

Arnold, Marigene. 1978. Celibes, Mothers and Church Cockroaches. In *Women in Ritual and Symbolic Rites,* ed. J. Hoch Smith and A. Spring, 45–53. New York: Plenum.

Béjin, André. 1985. The Influence of the Sexologists and Sexual Democracy. In *Western Sexuality: Practice and Precept in Past and Present Times,* ed. Philippe Ariès and André Béjin, 201–217. Trans. Anthony Foster.

Bell, Rudolph, M. 1985. *Holy Anorexia.* Chicago: University of Chicago Press.

Bell, Sandra. 1998a. British Theravada Buddhism: Otherwordly Theories, and the Theory of Exchange. *Journal of Contemporary Religion* 13: 149–170.

Bell, Sandra. 1998b. "Crazy Wisdom": Charisma, and the Transmission of Buddhism in the United States. *Nova Religio* 2(1): 55–75.

Boddy, Janice. 1982. Womb as Oasis: The Symbolic Context of Pharonic Circumcision in Rural Northern Sudan. *American Ethnologist* 9: 682–698.

Brown, Peter. 1989. *The Body and Society: Men, Women and Sexual Renunciation in Early Christianity.* London: Faber.

Brundage, James, A. 1996. Sex and Canon Law. In *Handbook of Medieval Sexuality,* ed. Vern L. Bullough and James A. Brundage, 33–50. New York: Garland.

Bullough, Vern, L. 1996. Sex in History: A Redux. In *Desire and Discipline: Sex and Sexuality in the Premodern West,* ed. Jacqueline Murray and Konrad Eisenbichler, 3–21. Toronto: University of Toronto Press.

Bynum, Caroline Walker. 1991. *Fragmentation and Redemption: Essays on Gender and the Human Body in Medieval Christianity.* New York: Zone Books.

Caplan, Pat. 1987. Celibacy as a Solution? Mahatma Gandhi and Brahmacharya.

In *The Cultural Construction of Sexuality,* ed. Pat Caplan, 271–295. London: Routledge.

Carrithers, Michael. 1992. *Why Humans Have Cultures: Explaining Anthropology and Social Diversity.* Oxford: Oxford University Press.

Collins, Steven. 1988. Monasticism, Utopias and Comparative Social Theory. *Religion* 18: 101–135.

Connell, R. W., and G. W. Dowsett. 1993. Introduction. In *Rethrinking Sex: Social Theory and Sexuality Research,* ed. R. W. Connell and G. W. Dowsett, 49–75. Philadelphia: Temple University Press.

deMause, Lloyd. 1976. The Evolution of Childhood. In *The History of Childhood,* ed. Lloyd deMause, 1–73. Reprint ed. London: Souvenir. Original publication: N.p.: Psychohistory Press, 1974.

Douglas, Mary. 1966. *Purity and Danger: An Analysis of Concepts of Pollution and Taboo.* London: Routledge and Kegan Paul.

Ebaugh, H. R. F. 1977. *Out of the Cloister: A Study of Organizational Dilemmas.* Austin: University of Texas Press.

Foucault, Michel. 1985a. The Battle for Chastity. In *Western Sexuality: Practice and Precept in Past and Present Times,* ed. Philippe Ariès and André Béjin, 14–25. Trans. Anthony Foster. Oxford: Basil Blackwell.

Foucault, Michel. 1985b. Sexuality and Solitude. In *On Signs,* ed. Marshall Blonsky, 365–371. Oxford: Basil Blackwell.

Fox, Robin. 1967. *Kinship and Marriage: An Anthropological Perspective.* Harmondsworth: Penguin Books.

Gay-Y-Blasco, Paloma. 1997. A "Different" Body? Desire and Virginity among Gitanos. *Journal of the Royal Anthropological Institute,* n.s., 3: 517–535.

Giddens, Anthony. 1991. *Modernity and Self-Identity in the Late Modern Age.* Stanford: Stanford University Press.

Gremaux, René. 1994. Woman Becomes Man in the Balkans. In *Third Sex, Third Gender,* ed. Gilbert Herdt, 241–281. New York: Zone Books.

Hager, Barbara. 1992. Get Thee to a Nunnery: Female Religious Claustration in Medieval Europe. *Ethnology and Sociobiology* 13: 385–407.

Harris, Helen. 1995. Rethinking Heterosexual Relationships in Polynesia: A Case Study of Mangaia, Cook Island. In *Romantic Passion: A Universal Experience?* ed. William Jankowiak, 95–127. New York: Columbia University Press.

Hearn, Jeff, and Wendy Parkin. 1995. *"Sex" at "Work": The Power and Paradox of Organizational Sexuality.* New York: St. Martin's.

Jeffreys, Sheila. 1985. *The Spinster and Her Enemies: Feminism and Sexuality 1880–1930.* London: Pandora.

Kelly, Gary. 1998. *Sexuality Today: The Human Perspective.* Boston: McGraw-Hill.

Kitch, Sally. 1989. *Chaste Liberation: Celibacy and Female Cultural Status.* Urbana: University of Illinois Press.

Knowles, David. 1969. *Christian Monasticism.* Toronto: McGraw-Hill.

La Fontaine, Jean S. 1985. *Initiation: Ritual Drama and Secret Knowledge across the World.* Harmondsworth: Penguin Books.

Laidlaw, James. 1995. *Riches and Renunciation: Religion and Economy among the Jains.* Oxford: Oxford University Press.

Lang, Bernard. 1987. The Sexual Life of Saints: Towards an Anthropology of Christian Heaven. *Religion* 17: 149–171.

Langness, L. L. 1980. *The Study of Culture.* Novato, Calif.: Chandler and Sharp.

Laqueur, Thomas. 1990. *Making Sex: Body and Gender from the Greeks to Freud.* Cambridge Mass.: Harvard University Press.

Levy, Robert. 1971. The Community Function of Tahitian Male Transvestitism: A Hypothesis. *Anthropological Quarterly* 44(1): 12–21.

Lindholm, Charles. 1998. The Future of Love. In *Romantic Love and Sexual Behavior: Perspectives from the Social Sciences,* ed. Victor de Munck, 17–32. New York: Praeger.

Madan, T. N. 1987. *Non-renunciation: Themes and Interpretations of Hindu Culture.* Delhi: Oxford University Press.

Mauss, Marcel. 1979. Body Techniques. In *Sociology and Psychology: Essays by Marcel Mauss,* 95–120. Trans. Ben Brewster. London: Routledge and Kegan Paul. Original French publication: Paris: Presses Universitaires de France, 1950.

Parrinder, Geoffrey. 1980. *Sex in the World's Religions.* London: Sheldon.

Sobo, Elisa J. 1993. *One Blood: The Jamaican Body.* Albany: State University of New York Press.

Sobo, Elisa J. 1997. Love, Jealousy, and Unsafe Sex among Impoverished Inner-City Women. In *The Political Economy of AIDS,* ed. M. Singer, 75–103. Amityville, N.Y.: Baywood.

Tambiah, Stanley. 1984. *The Buddhist Saints of the Forest and the Cult of Amulets.* Cambridge: Cambridge University Press.

Tuzin, Donald. 1995. Discourse, Intercourse, and the Excluded Middle: Anthropology and the Problem of Sexual Experience. In *Sexual Nature, Sexual Culture,* ed. Paul Abramson and Steven Pinkerton, 257–275. Chicago: University of Chicago Press.

Weber, Max. 1978. *Economy and Society: An Outline of Interpretive Sociology.* Edited by Guenther Roth and Claus Wittich. Berkeley: University of California Press.

Woods, J. 1981. I Was Starving Myself to Death. *Mademoiselle,* May, 200–201, 242–248.

Young, Antonia. 2000. *Women Who Become Men: Albanian Sworn Virgins.* New York: Berg.

PART I

CELIBACY, KINSHIP, AND SOCIAL ORGANIZATION

1 *Peter Phillimore*

Private Lives and Public Identities
An Example of Female Celibacy in Northwest India

In many parts of the world, celibacy expresses religious values, in which beliefs about self-denial and self-discipline mesh with beliefs about the refinement, salvation, or elimination of the self. Among Hindus this link is elaborately developed in the religious concept of brahmacharya (usually glossed as "absolute chastity"). Sexual abstinence, whether of short or long duration, either inside or outside marriage, is for Hindus generally motivated by religious ideals, expressed through individual transcendence of worldly desires and obligations in pursuit of salvation (Burghart 1983a, b; Dumont 1970; Ghurye 1964; Narayan 1989; O'Flaherty 1973; van der Veer 1987, 1989). To be celibate is a corollary of ascetic ideals, and it is hard to imagine celibacy and chastity entirely divorced from striving for a religious goal.

The ethnography discussed here explores a somewhat anomalous case, however, where there is a tension between ascetic and mundane (in its literal sense of "worldly") interpretations of celibate choices. The case concerns a small group of women in northwest India, and one of the issues raised is the extent to which a quasi-ascetic idiom is central to the identity of these women. For it may instead be a "dressing up" of a more or less secular celibacy in the interests of cultural legitimacy and local respectability.[1] This itself leads to a consideration of the very different circumstances and connotations of female and male celibacy in Hindu society.

29

In 1976 I started fieldwork in Kangra, a district of Himachal Pradesh, among one of the main groups of pastoralists in the region, named Gaddis. I soon came across a couple of women in the village where I settled whose outward appearance was deliberately masculinized.[2] They dressed in a version of male clothing, modified according to individual taste: they kept their hair cut short and covered with a man's cap, and they wore trousers. I learned that there were five such women in the village, the oldest being around 90 years old. No other village in the area had more than one or two of these women, if it had any at all, and by chance the village I had chosen to work in was seen locally as the center of this particular custom. In due course, I came to know four of these women in my village, met or saw a further five in the wider area, and had reliable reports of eight more. With few exceptions, all were of the Gaddi caste, or belonged to castes associated with the Gaddis,[3] and were to be found in a cluster of villages on the southern slopes of the main mountain range of the area, the Dhaula Dhar, on the northeastern fringe of Kangra. The practice was therefore extremely localized, to the extent that people living a few miles away were generally unfamiliar with it. Moreover, by all accounts it was not an old practice but a comparatively recent one, the woman of 90 being regarded as its initiator.

These women were known as sadhins. Though the majority were of high caste, a couple belonged to low castes. They were celibate, having rejected marriage and sexual activity. They took this step in principle before puberty and certainly before they were to be married. The status of sadhin was indeed the one recognized alternative to marriage for a woman, and it entailed lifelong chastity. Their distinctively male appearance outwardly marked their difference from other women, and their name (a feminine form of *sadhu,* the most common generic term for a male ascetic) associated them at the same time with the wider Hindu ascetic tradition.

Yet these women by no means necessarily portrayed themselves as ascetics or quasi-ascetics. More often it was fellow villagers who glossed their status in that way. An alternative depiction, often favored by sadhins themselves, played down themes of renunciation and emphasized instead the mundane or secular character of a sadhin's daily life, and paradoxically (bearing in mind that it was highly unusual) the very ordinariness of living as an unmarried woman in the natal home, with parents or alongside brothers. A summary of the ethnography will help to show how much scope existed for such alternative local constructions of what it meant to be a sadhin.

Living as a Sadhin

Whether the ascetic aspect of a sadhin's status was stressed or muted, invariably speakers emphasized that it was the girl herself who chose to follow this path, often against parental wishes and certainly in defiance of the powerful convention that girls were destined to become wives and mothers (Altekar 1956; Leslie 1989; Wadley 1994, 1995). One of the women I knew said that she had decided to become a sadhin at the age of six; the father of another stated that his daughter had become a sadhin at about that age too. More commonly, the approach of arrangements for marriage seems to have been the spur for girls to make the decision never to marry. The three women I knew best said that they had become sadhins because they did not wish to marry and had convinced parents and other kin of their determination in this regard.

Whatever her age, a girl who becomes a sadhin must be a virgin (*kanyā* or *kūmarī*), a condition that is fulfilled by limiting the adoption of this status to young girls, preferably to those who have not reached puberty. Entering this new status requires no public ceremony marking an initiation. There is no community of sadhins to join. In keeping with a choice that flies in the face of conventional expectations for girls, the transition is marked in as low key a way as possible, simply by putting on male clothing, specifically trousers of some kind. Only the barber's services are required, as the girl's head is shaved and then covered with a cap. The unostentatious form of this personal rite of passage is deceptive, however, for there is no escaping the magnitude of the step that has been taken: the event signifies a lifelong commitment, entered into at a very young age.

A sadhin thereafter dresses in this manner for life, keeping her hair close cropped. But in other respects there are few requirements. No special diet is expected of a sadhin, for example, other than to avoid meat. However, her new identity offers her the liberty to act "like a man" in a variety of contexts. For instance, a sadhin may choose to sit with male kinsmen or neighbors if she wishes to smoke (either a hookah or cigarettes) during an interlude in a wedding or to pass a few minutes in the course of everyday routines. Equally, she may undertake tasks usually considered as being for men alone, such as plowing or sowing crops. There have also been instances of a sadhin taking a flock of sheep and goats on the migratory cycle followed by Gaddi shepherds, an activity which requires her to enter the male world of shepherding to an extent which has no counterpart in the village-centered tasks of agricultural cultivation.

Yet this adoption of male characteristics does not imply a social reclassification as male. A sadhin is not seen as male, even if she is seen in certain respects to be like a male. Her gender is unchanged by her new status: a sadhin retains her personal name, suffixed with "Devī" like all female names, and she is referred to by female pronouns or kin terms. Being a sadhin is thus a female role, albeit an unusual one.[4] This is illustrated by a sadhin's continued performance of all the agricultural and domestic tasks done by the other women among whom she lives. In effect, the sadhins I knew lived as women but could at their convenience or from necessity step outside the conventional gender division of labor. Moreover, although I knew a couple of sadhins who smoked, from my observations they all preferred to remain with other women on occasions when the sexes were clearly separated, especially at large events, the individuals concerned acknowledging that they felt more comfortable doing so. In general, they were shy and self-effacing, but emphatically respected, women. Neither individually nor collectively had they any public role to play in village life, in either a political or a religious context; nor were they credited with special powers that could be put to the benefit of others as healers. In short, they lived outside the limelight, though not out on the margins of village life. At the same time, it would be fair to say that a sadhin gained for herself a considerable degree of autonomy in daily life, the kind of autonomy typically reserved for men.

Although the step a woman takes in becoming a sadhin is said to be irrevocable, she does not make the equally irrevocable decision typically made by Hindu ascetics to abandon home and the relationships associated with it as one of the first steps in renouncing the claims and desires of the social world.[5] Living as a sadhin entails remaining in the familial home. In addition, her status also gives her certain property rights denied to women by custom, even though not by law. At her father's death or at partition of the family property, a sadhin's right to claim a share of the inheritance on equal terms with any brothers is broadly accepted. This right is not always exercised, and most sadhins continue to live with brothers or brothers' sons after their parents' deaths. I do not know how much direct or tacit pressure may be applied to discourage the exercise of such rights. I knew only one sadhin with brothers who inherited a full share of her father's property — land, flock, and house — and in due course she sold first her flock and then her land back to her brothers. However, in two other cases of sadhins inheriting a house and land, significantly there were no brothers to press any claim for their exclusive rights to inheritance. In one of these cases, the sadhin was an only child; in the other, she was the youngest of three sisters.

Where there are no sons in a family, there is a clear economic rationale for keeping at least one daughter at home, and one of the two sadhins just mentioned told me that the lack of brothers was an important consideration behind her decision not to marry. Such a decision also has potential religious benefits for a man with no son. As his heir, his sadhin daughter may take on the son's role after his death, making necessary offerings (at rites known as sraddha) for the well-being of his spirit and its integration with the ancestors. Because the sadhin has no children herself, however, the spiritual benefit lasts no more than the one generation.

The best illustration of a sadhin fulfilling a son's role upon the death of a father, in fact, concerned a sadhin who had brothers. Bhujalo Devi was at home when her father died, while her two brothers, both younger than she, were away with the family flock. In their absence, senior kinsmen agreed that it would be acceptable for her to take the part of her father's chief mourner, usually reserved for the eldest son, lighting the funeral pyre and making the appropriate offerings. Bhujalo herself saw this as an exceptional but appropriate solution to the dilemma posed by a son's absence at his father's death. However, her role also continued after the day of the cremation, when she took over the responsibility for disposing of her father's ashes and traveled to the holy center of Haridwar to immerse them in the river Ganges. These events provided Bhujalo with the one occasion, she maintained, in which she had won an ochre *kurta-pyjama* (loose-fitting trousers and top) in her village and then subsequently at Haridwar. Yet the clothing poses a puzzle in this case. By dressing as she did, Bhujalo seems to have used her ascetic qualifications to legitimize her unorthodox role at her father's funeral. However, the "true" Hindu ascetic would in theory have no part to play at the funerals of others, least of all as chief mourner, for by renouncing all social and ritual obligations, he becomes dead to the world. Perhaps the implication of Bhujalo's approach to her role was that she felt that her quasi-ascetic clothing helped to affirm her fitness, auspiciousness, and purity as a surrogate for one of her brothers.

While in Haridwar, Bhujalo met an ascetic who, she said, had become her spiritual guide, or guru. But seeking a tie with a guru was by no means the rule. The turn of events at Haridwar seems to reflect Bhujalo's individual religiosity rather than a consensus that a relationship with a spiritual teacher was something to which a sadhin should aspire. In any case, the relationship Bhujalo described was short-lived and may even have existed in her eyes alone. I say this because there was no initiation to mark her entry into one of the sectarian traditions of Hinduism; indeed, how could there have been when a sadhin does not fulfill some fundamental criteria for such a tie (Burghart 1983a, b; Denton 1991). The relationship implied here between teacher and disciple was altogether more informal, even though Bhujalo cast it in the idiom of the ascetic guru-chela (teacher-disciple) tie.[6]

A second sadhin, Napali, had likewise established a link with an ascetic guru for a while, also after her father's death. She suggested that while her father had been alive she had served him, but once he died, establishing a relationship with a guru helped her to "justify" her position. But other sadhins saw neither the personal religious need nor the social necessity to legitimize their status in this way. In a couple of cases I was told that individual Brahman priests acted as a kind of alternative to a guru, but it was hard to know how far this was a defensive gesture to placate potential skeptics and how far it was a purposeful search for spiritual guidance and nourishment.

Similar ambiguities surrounding their ascetic status also became apparent at the time of the death of the oldest, and apparently the original, sadhin. Prabhi Devi was around 90 years old when she died in the late 1970s, and the event sparked off some discussion as to the most appropriate manner to dispose of her body.[7] Prabhi was in fact cremated in conventional fashion, as might have been anticipated. But a minority view expressed by some men was that samadhi, the practice of burial in an upright posture reserved for ascetics, would have been appropriate in the case of a quasi-ascetic like a sadhin (and particularly such a pathbreaking and venerable one as Prabhi). Prabhi's death provided an occasion when tacit assumptions about the character of this institution came to the surface and were articulated. There was no great dissension. Instead, it was a case of uncertainty in the absence of obvious precedents to follow. Nevertheless, discussion set the pragmatic realities of sadhins' lives against an ascetic ideal. The view that prevailed and led to Prabhi being cremated emphasized that a sadhin did not renounce home, family, and property, but simply marriage. Moreover, she could not be considered a renouncer because she did not dress as one. The counterargument placed less emphasis on these visible signs and more on assumptions about the inner intention and spiritual achievement of a sadhin. By invoking respected Hindu ideals of brahmacharya and tapasya (ascetic austerity), those suggesting samadhi dwelled on the sadhin's commitment to lifelong celibacy. This was acknowledged as an authentic mastery of self, a recognizably ascetic achievement.[8] To have departed from the conventional practice of cremation, however, would have been a major and undoubtedly controversial step. Not surprisingly, the less contentious path was taken, even if questions were raised for which there was no straightforward answer.

If Prabhi's death brought to the surface questions that were largely latent in day-to-day life, so too did the one occasion when a sadhin abandoned her commitment to chastity and celibacy and eloped with a lover. One of the more explicit conventions surrounding the practice of becoming a sadhin is that there is no reversing the decision. As one man put it, a sadhin "resolves to lead a pure life"; in the words of another, "She can't go and have relations with every third man." Only once was convention defied, and defied in a way that was still recalled vividly more than 20 years after the event. Premi, a Seok who came from a village close to the one where I worked, had been a sadhin for some 20 years when it became impossible for her to conceal the fact that she was pregnant. For a long time she had kept horses as pack animals and was often away from home. At the first public inkling of her pregnancy, Premi had apparently fled her village, crossing the mountains to Chamba with her Gaddi lover, a man who also kept horses and with whom she had worked. They eventually returned to Kangra years later, after they had become married, and settled some distance from their earlier homes.

By fleeing on short notice, Premi was gone before any formal attempt to deal with her could be initiated. But her former covillagers clearly regarded her as expelled for what she had done; one person used the English word *boycott* to me to describe their response. Though at the time of my fieldwork she lived within easy reach of her old village, she had never returned, nor had she been expected to do so.

It would be misleading to suggest that becoming a sadhin has been the invariable outcome for Gaddi women who do not marry. However strong the cultural imperative may be for women to be married — and it is certainly very strong in Kangra (Parry 1979) — there is bound to be the odd occasion where marriage arrangements fail to materialize and a girl is left unmarried. One such woman I knew worked as a servant for a family with two sons who had not at that stage married; she fulfilled many of the tasks their wives would eventually undertake. Her unmarried status was seen locally as a consequence of her marriage prospects having always been slight because she was without any close kin and was also deaf from birth. No one suggested that she might have become a sadhin or that it would have been more respectable if she had done so. It was simply accepted that she would never marry. But such cases, where circumstances conspire to limit opportunities to marry, are quite different from those where a deliberate decision is made to depart from the conventional expectation that women will marry (see Gutschow, this volume). It is this intentionality which has created — and, I would argue, necessitated — the identity of sadhin.

Celibacy and Sexuality

Here, then, is an identity which has drawn on some of the idioms and symbolism of Hindu asceticism while in other respects presupposing behavior that has little to do with the codes and conventions of ascetic sects.

The question of sexual abstinence is central to an understanding of the way in which this unusual identity has developed and to the alternative ways in which it has been construed locally. The denial of the senses and the transcendence of physical appetites, especially sexual desire — expressed by Wadley as the "sublimation of digestive powers to internal powers" (1994: 45) — is at the heart of Hindu asceticism (Alter 1992, 1997a; Narayan 1989; O'Flaherty 1973). The sadhin's lifelong commitment to chastity and celibacy has thus been readily acknowledged as an ascetic achievement, which has made it possible to associate sadhins with other kinds of Hindu ascetics, as their name itself proclaims.

In making this association, sadhins were never identified with ascetic women but were invariably identified with ascetic men. There was no local acknowledgment that some Hindu ascetics in India are women. On the other hand, Buddhist asceticism did furnish such a parallel. I was struck during fieldwork that while sometimes sadhins were described to me as being a kind of sadhu, on a number of occasions they were compared with celibate Buddhist women, nuns or nunlike individuals known as "*jomo*" (*chomo*). A large number of Gaddis were familiar with *jomo* in Lahul, Spiti, or Kinnaur, on the northern edge of Himachal Pradesh, whom they had seen or learned about during annual migrations to high-altitude pastures with their flocks of sheep and goats. Ethnographic accounts from Kinnaur (Kumar 1963) and more especially Ladakh (Grimshaw 1992) and Zangskar (Gutschow, this volume) illustrate why this comparison may seem an apposite one to Gaddi shepherds. These "nuns" commonly remain closely involved in, if not necessarily resident in, their natal home and in several areas provide an example of home-based celibacy that accords closely with the way that sadhins live.[9] In appearance, too, the desexualizing androgyny which Gutschow mentions evokes the sadhin's case. I am not suggesting that the identity of sadhins should be seen as a cultural appropriation of a Buddhist model. But *jomo* nonetheless offered a reference point when those people I knew contextualized their own practice in answer to my questions. In short, if one of the local ways to place sadhins was to refer to celibate Hindu men, an alternative was to refer to celibate Buddhist women.

The lack of awareness of Hindu traditions of female asceticism among the Gaddis I knew is not particularly surprising. Women ascetics are comparatively few in number in India and much less visible than their male equivalents. Moreover, a widespread reluctance to acknowledge a place for such women fosters this invisibility. These androcentric attitudes found an echo in the neglect of female ascetics, until recently, in academic writing on Hinduism and Hindu society. Over the last two decades, however, this oversight has been challenged by several ethnographic accounts that have focused upon the lives of women ascetics within Hinduism (Babb 1984; Bradford 1983; Denton 1991; Khandelwal 1996, 1997; Ohja 1981, 1988; also King 1984). This literature allows us to see where sadhins fit in this larger canvas. A number of observations are relevant to this end.

Denton (1991), for example, in distinguishing alternative forms of Hindu female asceticism, illustrates the varying levels of detachment from the mundane world presupposed by different ascetic paths, just as Burghart (1983b) and van der Veer (1987, 1989) have observed in relation to different groups within the male Ramanandi tradition. Not all traditions imply complete abandonment of domestic ties. Celibate students (brahmacharinis), Denton notes, "are in many ways still very much 'of the world' in that they accept the ritual categories characteristic of householdership. They work within the system, so to speak" (1991: 229).

One of the sadhin's most distinctive features is her male dress and masculinized appearance. This does not appear to imitate a general practice among Hindu women ascetics. Both Denton (1991) and Ojha (1981, 1988) mention plain saris as the most commonly worn dress among ascetic women in Varanasi, though some do adopt the ochre robes of the male sannyasis. Yet male dress is not unknown as a mark of the ascetic woman. In Karnataka, in southern India, for example, certain female devotees of the goddess Yellamma are described as *jōgamma* (Bradford 1983). The more "overtly ascetic" among these *jōgamma* are often distinguished by their male dress. Bradford mentions turban, jacket, and dhoti in this regard (1983: 318). This, he argues, is not about a transformation of gender. Instead, he interprets "their wearing of male dress as an indication of asceticism" and suggests that "the limited male characteristics they take on . . . are an indication of asexuality and coolness" (p. 318). The adoption of male characteristics thus serves as one possible way to make visible a female ascetic identity.

However, Khandelwal (1997; this volume) cautions that to see female renunciation as no more than an anomalous variant of an essentially male path is to see the practice only through a patriarchal lens. Arguing for "the specificity of a renunciant female voice" (1997: 104), she makes a persuasive case that "*sannyasa* is sometimes gendered feminine" (p. 86). She suggests that alongside acknowledgment of the obstacles facing them as ascetics on account of their gender there is also a sense that "certain feminine qualities are thought to have great spiritual significance in that they make renunciation easier for women" (p. 88). At the same time, as Khandelwal (this volume) also argues, there is no evading the fact that a young virgin making a lifelong renunciation of sexuality profoundly challenges both Brahmanic and patriarchal conceptions of social order, through asserting an autonomy that is subversive in its implications.

All this suggests that in appearance and conduct sadhins are less an anomaly as ascetic women than may seem to be the case at first sight, however few in number they may be. Yet there are a number of paradoxes that require closer consideration. In the first place, the language of renunciation in key respects implies a self-denial that is misleading in the case of the sadhins I knew. A celibate, unfettered by the obligations of marriage, life seems to have been a preference rather than a test, more blessing than self-transforming discipline. In that sense, to assimilate sadhins with lifestyles predicated on radical selflessness and detachment is to go too far. Spared the emotional ordeal of being uprooted from her natal household upon marriage and instead given title to property denied to women following a more conventional path, a sadhin acquired one more freedom in the sexual restraint enjoined upon her. Men may have made occasional ribald remarks about the self-discipline required for a sadhin to follow a celibate life, but such comments underline a difference between the way that others (particularly men) preferred to view these women and the way that they viewed themselves. What an ascetic and a more secular construction of the sadhin's celibacy both share, however, is the principle that this is a purposeful path (see Khandelwal, this volume), with implications for an understanding of the autonomy and human agency of these women.

Yet whatever emphasis is placed on the sadhins' own understanding of the choice they have made and on their autonomy in making this choice, there is another side to sexual abstinence which cannot be overlooked. An extensive literature documents the "dangers" thought to be associated with women's sexuality in rural India, the disruption to the social order that it threatens, and the necessity of controlling it (Bennett 1983; Parry 1979; Raheja and Gold 1994; Wadley 1994). As Wadley (1994: 41) has suggested, women are thought to have greater sexual power than men. If marriage channels and regulates this sexuality, remaining unmarried connotes sexuality uncontrolled. The sadhin's celibacy needs to be seen therefore as the cornerstone of the wider social (public) regulation of her sexuality, the only way to accommodate her unattachment through marriage, and the key to permitting her social visibility. The social control of a sadhin's sexuality is subtly reinforced in ways which proclaim her status to be not simply nonsexual (in the sense that she refrains from sexual activity) but asexual (in the sense that the possibility of a sexual persona is categorically denied). Through the convention that a girl becomes a sadhin before puberty (or at least before marriage) and cannot reverse her decision throughout her lifetime, a direct transition from presexual immaturity to asexual maturity is constructed, without the intrusion of any intervening expression of sexual potentiality. The boycott of Premi, described above, reflects the challenge her sexuality made to the ideology of asexual celibacy, around which this identity is built. Most visibly, the sadhin's male clothing serves to desexualize her: the masculinizing of her appearance aids the desexualizing of her identity.[10] While this has an ascetic connotation, of being without desire, as Bradford (1983) argued, it also has a connotation of social control, of desire ruled out. In this perspective, it is not the autonomy of the sadhin but her dependency that is to the fore.

All this suggests that the chastity of the sadhin and the chastity of the male ascetic are not precisely equivalent. For the latter, past sexual actions are irrelevant to his goal of transcendence, which implies detachment not only from the desires of the world but from its dualities of sex and gender differentiation also (Burghart 1983a, b; Das 1977; Thapar 1981; van der Veer 1987, 1989). For a sadhin, by contrast, past sexual activity would be incompatible with a status that entrenches her in a scheme of sexual classification rather than serving as a means for her to rise above it. In short, she is at least as much a prisoner of the definitions of others as she is the architect of her own purposeful self-definition.

Public and Private

It would be hard for a life of celibacy in rural India ever to be a purely private affair, however retiring or self-effacing the individual. Even though no public rite of passage marks the decidedly low-key transition from girl to sadhin, thereafter she is marked out, her appearance and career setting her apart from the other women among whom she lives. In a locality where marriage has not necessarily meant the bride moving to another village,[11] there has not been quite the split between outgoing daughters and incoming sons' wives to be found where village exogamy was expected. As a consequence, an adult woman living in her natal village has not been exceptional. On the other hand, only a sadhin continues to live in her natal home, which does distinguish her from other women.

Yet I would argue that some of the differences in emphasis discussed earlier concerning the sadhin's identity and behavior arise from an implicit tension between public constructions and private understandings of this unusual life choice. As mentioned, the very name sadhin permits association with a wider ascetic tradition and is one of the keys to the public legitimacy and respectability of the status. For most of the sadhins that I knew, however, there seemed to be something slightly uncomfortable about this ascetic emphasis, as if it put them in cultural clothing they would rather not wear. I would say that they saw themselves as celibate women leading ordinary day-to-day lives. Their narratives were not glossed with claims about their special status or achievement. The ordinariness stemmed from the routine agricultural and domestic tasks they performed, the web of social relationships they were part of, and the everyday pleasures they enjoyed, such as smoking the hookah. Others too, and not only other women, tacitly accepted this more prosaic version of what it means to be a sadhin. Yet part of this ordinariness has been a degree of autonomy in daily life which is, paradoxically, far from ordinary for women.

Among the sadhins that I knew, only one, Bhujalo Devi, clearly projected a different and more overtly religious self-image, her ties with a guru, her visit to Haridwar after her father's death, and her ochre clothing reinforcing her account of how much she saw her position in terms of a kind of asceticism. Yet Bhujalo was also one of the minority of sadhins to have exercised her right to inherit a share of her father's property, a distinctly worldly action for the most ascetic of these women. There may have been others who saw themselves in a similarly ascetic light, but not among those I knew; indeed, one of them made it plain to me that Bhujalo's choice was not for her.

To understand the public construction of this life choice, it is useful to return to two points mentioned at the beginning of the chapter: namely, that this identity does not have a long history and that it is known in a fairly small area, centered on northeast Kangra. What circumstances could account for the emergence of this practice, albeit on a very small scale, at a particular time and in a particular place? And what might be the factors that have helped it to continue?

Gaddis had migrated in large numbers to Kangra from Chamba, farther to the north across the Dhaula Dhar mountain range, since the mid-nineteenth century. The chief attraction was the market in land that opened up after the British imposed direct control over Kangra in 1848, while Chamba remained under the rule of its raja (and without a market in land) for another century, till after Indian independence. Both necessity and choice drew Gaddis (and similar groups in the mountains, like Seoks) to settle on the slopes of the Dhaula Dhar rather than down in the valley itself, placing them physically as well as socially apart from the wider Kangra society. I say necessity because the fertile Kangra Valley was, even in the nineteenth century, densely populated (Parry 1979); further, acquiring the more desirable irrigated land as newcomers was not easy. I say choice because the mountain slopes offered rights of grazing in extensive tracts of forest or so-called *waste* which were of particular value to migrant grazers. My initial supposition was that becoming a sadhin was a "traditional" practice that was more common in Chamba but that lingered on in Gaddi communities in Kangra. I was surprised to find that in Chamba as well as in Kangra the reverse was the case: the fringes of the Kangra Valley were regarded as both the center and the source of the practice.

As I see it, the position of sadhin probably emerged as a consequence of the immigrant Gaddis' settlement in Kangra. Parry's (1979) study of Kangra's high-caste Brahmans and Rajputs illuminates the fairly rigid conventions surrounding marriage and the status of women which were still subscribed to at the time of his fieldwork in the late 1960s. In such a context, where the ethos of hypergamy (condensed in the idea that brides should marry bridegrooms of higher status) served to accentuate status consciousness, it was in theory unthinkable for the high castes to leave daughters unmarried. We lack comparably detailed evidence from Chamba; nevertheless, few hill regions of the Indian Himalaya seem to have placed quite such a strong emphasis on hierarchy as Kangra did, manifested most visibly in expectations surrounding women's behavior and marriage (Parry 1979; Sharma 1980).

It is against that background that the creation of the role of sadhin makes most sense. A woman choosing to be celibate or not to marry became an issue only when Gaddis came increasingly into contact with the stricter codes surrounding women in the wider Kangra society. The result has been an accommodation with dominant values. To make such an action respectable, these women were assimilated within the one framework which provided any alternative to a woman's role and duties as wife, that of the Hindu ascetic. Once the precedent was set, this status evolved into a recognizable option in the locality of my fieldwork for a small minority of Gaddi and Seok women.

If the practice has a fairly short past, it may well have an even shorter future. I knew of few young sadhins, and I share the local judgment that even fewer girls will be drawn to this identity in the years ahead.[12] I suspect that it answered a need and provided a convenient cultural niche during one particular period, for reasons outlined above. Mass education for girls as well as boys, shifts in women's expectations about their own roles, and a weakening of traditional hierarchic values in the larger Kangra society may all be serving to diminish both the attraction and the necessity for this life path to be adopted nowadays.

As suggested in the previous section, a balance has to be struck between election or choice, on the one hand, and imposition or compulsion, on the other, in understanding the practice of being a sadhin. These contrasting emphases both seem to me to be present, lending an ambiguity to the position of these women that I do not think is only in my mind as an observer. Private and public are in some respects at odds here. The private construction of what it means to be a sadhin promotes personal preference as the primary consideration and implies some degree of individual autonomy, with the language of self-denial a minor matter. Yet if this were simply a voluntary matter, why publicly regulate it? Public discourse brings into the foreground precisely this language of self-denial and ascetic self-control, behind which, I suggest, lies an enduring preoccupation with the social regulation of female sexuality. If no such preoccupation were to exist, it would be hard to explain why a woman who wishes to live a celibate life should need to become a sadhin in order to follow her preference.

In this context I return to some of the different connotations of celibacy for Hindu women and men in India. For men, sexual abstinence, focused on the protection of semen (Alter 1994, 1995, 1997a; Khandelwal, this volume; Narayan 1989; O'Flaherty 1973), enhances their powers, yielding benefits which are not only religious and spiritual but resonate in other spheres of individual and collective life also, from personal health to politics.[13] This preoccupation underpins the notion that "the entire construct of *brahmacharya* is conceived of in male terms" (Alter 1994: 53).

Yet Khandelwal's ethnography (this volume) challenges such an exclusive ideology, and it has become increasingly clear that women have not in practice been wholly excluded from the benefits of brahmacharya. As Denton (1991) has shown, women have been readily accommodated within its compass. At one level, the status of sadhin provides another variant on the same theme — a variant from the margins rather than at the center of Hindu practice. Yet the danger here lies in conveying a picture of the sadhin's life that accepts the voluntarism of her choice uncritically. Lifelong celibacy may be chosen, but it is assuredly also compelled. The crux of this is that a sadhin's sexuality is denied, removed from her at the moment she adopts her new identity. In this sense, the idiom of brahmacharya that was occasionally used by my informants conveniently masks the straightforward exercise of social control over female sexuality, even as it legitimizes that control, in a manner that has no counterpart in discourses around male asceticism.

Notes

I should like to acknowledge the helpful ideas and critical advice of Elisa Sobo, Sandra Bell, Meena Khandelwal, and anonymous referees.

1. In the context of secular celibacy, Alter is illuminating. His writing on celibacy among wrestlers (1992, 1995) and members of a modern yoga society (1997a, b) highlights urban North Indian examples of male celibacy in which the secular and the ascetic intersect. The absorption of self-consciously ascetic principles within everyday secular lives provides a useful reference point in trying to understand the quite different social milieu of the women whom I discuss here.

2. Fieldwork took place in Kangra (and to a lesser extent in neighboring Chamba) between 1976 and 1978, and again in 1980, with brief visits in 1987 and 1997. I have written elsewhere (Phillimore 1991) about the women who are the subject of this chapter. This account places more weight on the contrast between public and private representations of what it meant to be a sadhin. Some of the personal names are pseudonyms.

3. Strictly, "Gaddi" has been a caste name, referring to a localized Rajput caste. In the upper reaches of the Ravi River in Chamba and in the higher villages along the Dhaula Dhar in Kangra, the Gaddis live alongside small numbers of Brahmans and three low castes (Sipis, Riharas, and Halis). These are often described by outsiders as Gaddi castes, and indeed the name "Gaddi" seems increasingly to be used in a generic sense regardless of caste, however much this is disapproved by those who would preserve the narrower definition. For convenience I use the name generically from now on. In smaller numbers, members of another localized Rajput caste, named Seok, share the mountain fringes of the Kangra Valley with the Gaddis. A minority of the women described in this chapter are Seoks.

4. Some of the ethnography on "third gender," dual gender, or transgender identities shows parallels with the identity of sadhin: for example, Gremaux's (1994) account of "sworn virgins" in Albania and adjoining areas of the Balkans. See also Goulet's (1996) enlightening deconstruction of the much-discussed category of berdache, or two-spirit, in North American ethnography. However, the parallels should not be pushed too far. I would emphasize that a sadhin is not a transgendered individual, despite the play on male characteristics and masculinity that adoption of this status requires (clothing) or permits (smoking the hookah, inheriting property). The status of sadhin utilizes some of the imagery often associated with a third gender without actually being conceptualized in those terms. The same issue arises in Bradford's (1983) account of the cult of the goddess Yellamma in South India, in the contrast between *jōgappa* and *jōgamma* (discussed in the next section).

5. In practice, as Burghart points out, "different sects have different rules concerning which social relationships must be severed in order to obtain release from transience" (1983a: 643). See also Denton 1991 with reference to women, and Khare 1984 with reference to Chamar ascetics. This plurality of practices makes fertile ground for disputing who counts as a "real" ascetic. I pick up this point again in the next section.

6. Khandelwal (this volume) mentions that the cohesiveness of sects is not what it used to be, with the growing popularity of independent gurus unaffiliated with any sect.

7. Although her death occurred during my fieldwork, I was not in the village at the time and learned of these events later.

8. When those I spoke to referred to brahmacharya, they usually prefixed it with *bal* (denoting childhood), apparently to underscore that this was a commitment made at an early age.

9. Grimshaw, for example, introduces the subject of *jomo* in these words: "I

was told that she was a *chomo*. This meant she had not taken formal monastic vows, but she lived a celibate life, shaved her head and wore red clothes (but not robes). . . . They were a common sight in the Himalayas and the majority lived in the household of their parents or brothers where they were treated more or less as domestic servants. Occasionally these women were attached to monasteries" (1992: 12). The picture of *jomo* at the mercy of many people's demands, emphasized also by Gutschow (this volume), who notes that *jomo* can be used to refer to ordained nuns too, is one feature that is not reflected in the case of sadhins. While they may be retiring and self-effacing as individuals, I never sensed that they were put upon. The respect they were held in saw to that.

    10. I recognize that we may also view their dress as an effective way of neutralizing unwelcome sexual attention. The dual and apparently contradictory connotations of the sadhin's male clothing, as emblem of both freedom and constraint, echo observations in the literature on veiling (*ghungat*) and seclusion (purdah) in South Asia (Harlan and Courtright 1995; Sharma 1978).

    11. In the Gaddi villages I knew, a sizable minority of marriages linked families resident in the same village (Phillimore 1982).

    12. A brief visit in 1997 reinforced this view. No girl in the vicinity has opted to become a sadhin for about a quarter of a century now.

    13. Discussing the "political salience" of brahmacharya, Alter has recently argued that "it is part of a larger, more ambiguous discourse in which sex, health and politics blur together" (1994: 45).

References Cited

Altekar, A. S. 1956. *The Position of Women in Hindu Civilisation.* 2d ed. Banaras: Motilal Banarsidass.

Alter, Joseph S. 1992. The Sannyasi and the Indian Wrestler: The Anatomy of a Relationship. *American Ethnologist* 19: 317–336.

Alter, Joseph S. 1994. Celibacy, Sexuality, and the Transformation of Gender into Nationalism in North India. *Journal of Asian Studies* 53: 45–66.

Alter, Joseph S. 1995. The Celibate Wrestler: Sexual Chaos, Embodied Balance and Competitive Politics in North India. *Contributions to Indian Sociology,* n.s., 29: 109–131.

Alter, Joseph S. 1997a. Seminal Truth: A Modern Science of Male Celibacy in North India. *Medical Anthropology Quarterly* 11: 275–298.

Alter, Joseph S. 1997b. A Therapy to Live By: Public Health, the Self and Nationalism in the Practice of a North Indian Yoga Society. *Medical Anthropology* 17: 309–335.

Babb, Lawrence A. 1984. Indigenous Feminism in a Modern Hindu Sect. *Signs: Journal of Women, Culture and Society* 9: 399–416.

Bennett, Lynn. 1983. *Dangerous Wives and Sacred Sisters: Social and Symbolic Roles of High-Caste Women in Nepal.* New York: Columbia University Press.

Bradford, Nicholas J. 1983. Transgenderism and the Cult of Yellamma: Heat, Sex, and Sickness in South Indian Ritual. *Journal of Anthropological Research* 39: 307–322.

Burghart, Richard. 1983a. Renunciation in the Religious Traditions of South Asia. *Man*, n.s., 18: 635–653.

Burghart, Richard. 1983b. Wandering Ascetics of the Ramanandi Sect. *History of Religions* 22: 361–380.

Das, Veena. 1977. *Structure and Cognition: Aspects of Hindu Caste and Ritual.* Delhi: Oxford University Press.

Denton, Lynn Teskey. 1991. Varieties of Hindu Female Ascetisim. In *Roles and Rituals for Hindu Women*, ed. I. Julia Leslie, 211–231. London: Pinter.

Dumont, Louis. 1970. World Renunciation in Indian Religions. In *Religion, Politics and History in India*, 33–61. Paris and The Hague: Mouton.

Ghurye, G. S. 1964. *Indian Sadhus*. Bombay: Popular Books.

Goulet, Jean-Guy. 1996. The "Berdache"/"Two-Spirit": A Comparison of Anthropological and Native Constructions of Gendered Identities among the Northern Athapaskans. *Journal of the Royal Anthropological Institute*, n.s., 2: 683–701.

Gremaux, Rene. 1994. Woman Becomes Man in the Balkans. In *Third Sex, Third Gender*, ed. G. Herdt, 241–281. New York: Zone Books.

Grimshaw, Anna. 1992. *Servants of the Buddha: Winter in a Himalayan Convent.* London: Open Letters.

Harland, Lindsey, and Paul B. Courtright. 1995. Introduction: On Hindu Marriage and Its Margins. In *From the Margins of Hindu Marriage: Essays on Gender, Religion, and Culture*, ed. L. Harlan and P. Courtright, 3–18. Oxford: Oxford University Press.

Khandelwal, Meena. 1996. Walking a Tightrope: Saintliness, Gender, and Power in an Ethnographic Encounter. *Anthropology and Humanism* 21(2): 111–134.

Khandelwal, Meena. 1997. Ungendered Atma, Masculine Virility and Feminine Compassion: Ambiguities in Renunciant Discourses on Gender. *Contributions to Indian Sociology*, n.s., 31: 79–107.

Khare, R. S. 1984. *The Untouchable as Himself: Ideology, Identity and Pragmatism among the Lucknow Chamars.* Cambridge: Cambridge University Press.

King, Ursula. 1984. The Effect of Social Change on Religious Self-Understanding: Women Ascetics in Modern Hinduism. In *Changing South Asia: Religion and Society*, ed. K. Ballhatchet and D. Taylor, 69–83. London: School of Oriental and African Studies.

Kumar, C. 1963. A Village Survey of Kothi (Kalpa Sub-Division, District Kinnaur). *Census of India 1961*, vol. 20: *Himachal Pradesh*, part 6, no. 1. Simla: Government of India Press.

Leslie, I. Julia. 1989. *The Perfect Wife: The Orthodox Hindu Woman according to the Stridharmapaddhati of Tryambakayajvan.* Delhi: Oxford University Press.

Narayan, Kirin. 1989. *Storytellers, Saints, and Scoundrels: Folk Narrative in Hindu Religious Teaching.* Philadelphia: Univeristy of Pennsylvania Press.

O'Flaherty, Wendy Doniger. 1973. *Asceticism and Eroticism in the Mythology of Siva.* Delhi: Oxford University Press.

Ojha, Catherine. 1981. Feminine Asceticism in Hinduism: Its Tradition and Present Condition. *Man in India* 61: 254–285.

Ojha, Catherine. 1988. Outside the Norms: Women Ascetics in Hindu Society. *Economic and Political Weekly* (April 30): 34–36.

Parry, Jonathan P. 1979. *Caste and Kinship in Kangra.* London: Routledge and Kegan Paul.

Phillimore, P. R. 1982. Marriage and Social Organisation among Pastoralists of the Dhaula Dhar (Westsern Himalaya). Ph.D. thesis, Anthropology, Durham University.

Phillimore, Peter. 1991. Unmarried Women of the Dhaula Dhar: Celibacy and Social Control in Northwest India. *Journal of Anthropological Research* 47: 331–350.

Raheja, Gloria Goodwin, and Ann Gold. 1994. *Listen to the Heron's Words: Reimagining Gender and Kinship in North India.* Berkeley: University of California Press.

Sharma, Ursula. 1978. Women and Their Affines: The Veil as a Symbol of Separation. *Man,* n.s., 13: 218–233.

Sharma, Ursula. 1980. *Women, Work and Property in North-West India.* London: Tavistock Publications.

Thapar, Romila. 1981. The Householder and the Renouncer in the Brahmanical and Buddhist Traditions. *Contributions to Indian Sociology,* n.s., 15: 273–298.

van der Veer, Peter. 1987. Taming the Ascetic: Devotionalism in a Hindu Monastic Order. *Man,* n.s., 22: 680–695.

van der Veer, Peter. 1989. The Power of Detachment: Disciplines of Body and Mind in the Ramanandi Order. *American Ethnologist* 16: 458–470.

Wadley, Susan S. 1994. *Struggling with Destiny in Karimpur, 1925–1984.* Berkeley: University of California Press.

Wadley, Susan S. 1995. No Longer a Wife: Widows in Rural North India. In *From the Margins of Hindu Marriage: Essays on Gender, Religion, and Culture,* ed. L. Harlan and P. Courtright, 92–118. Oxford: Oxford University Press.

The Women Who Refuse to Be Exchanged
Nuns in Zangskar, Northwest India

> Why exchange women? Because they are "scarce [commodities] . . . essential to the life of the group" the anthropologist tells us.
> —Luce Irigaray, *The Sex Which Is Not One,* on Lévi-Strauss

While Buddhist doctrine proclaims phenomenal reality to be empty of absolute or independent existence, in practice both gender and sexuality appear to be inescapable and absolute conditions of the monastic existence. Buddhist nuns may renounce the act of sex and desire, but they cannot transcend the sex-gender system that constrains their monastic vocation.[1] Nuns can no more escape the eternal dialectic of desire between the sexes than they can flee the mundane gender roles that enmesh them. Even those intrepid nuns who successfully maintain the celibate life remain complicit with a central premise of the sex-gender system: the exchange of women.[2] While daughters are exchanged in marriage, nuns are traded for merit. Monks regulate this traffic in women, for they reserve the right to control the admission, confession, and absolution of nuns. These privileges date back to the founding of the nuns' order, when the Buddha apparently gave the monks considerable control over nuns.

For Buddhist nuns, domestication has been achieved at the expense of liberation. In the Tibetan Buddhist regions of the northwest Indian Himalaya, the narrow path to female celibacy is strewn with obstacles through which only the hardiest souls may persevere. Along the way, nuns must engage in everyday forms of resistance in order to evade the demands and desires made by their families, acquaintances, and monastic brethren for assistance or succor. Even as their shorn heads and sexless maroon robes signal a lofty intent to renounce the worldly life, nuns remain tied to sex and gender roles in ways that monks are not. Nuns are expected to toil selflessly in the gardens, fields, and kitchens of both village and monastery while forgoing their own meditations. Their status as dutiful daughters constrains their efforts at becoming sacrosanct celibates while ensuring the agrarian prosperity essential to both household and monastic economies. Classical Buddhist injunctions against renunciates working in the fields are ignored by both villagers and monks, who eagerly recruit nuns prized for their altruism. In theory, nuns' compassion is supposed to be applied universally; in practice, it may be exacted along lines dictated by custom and kinship.

The Law of the Buddha and the Domestication of Nuns

The Buddha's initial ambivalence about founding the nuns' order was based not on women's lack of spiritual qualification but on a perceived threat to the male monastic order.[3] Legend has it that the Buddha established the nuns' order only after being accosted by his aunt, Mahāpajā-patī, and his closest disciple, Ānanda. After considerable hesitation, he relented but warned that the entry of women into the order was as dangerous as mildew on a rice crop or rust on a sugar cane field. Furthermore, the Buddha allowed women to ordain on one condition: that they henceforth adopt the so-called Eight Chief Rules (*Garudhammā*). These rules specify that nuns may never censure or admonish monks, that the most senior nun must respectfully prostrate before a freshly ordained monk who may be decades her junior, and that all nuns must take their ordinations, bimonthly confessions, rainy season retreats, and penances in the presence of monks. While these baneful rules may never have been spoken by the Buddha, as some scholars claim, they positioned the nuns' order as subordinate to the monks' order from the start.[4]

The cumulative effect of these rules was to give monks the right to discipline and punish the nuns while ensuring that the monasteries overshadowed the nunneries in terms of wealth and power. Centuries of regularized repetition of subservience led the nunneries to become economically and spiritually dependent on monasteries. Because nunneries never gained as much patronage and political power as monasteries did, the nuns' order eventually died out in many regions. By the eleventh century, women could no longer seek full ordination throughout South, Southeast, and Central Asia.[5] Since only novice ordination was transmitted to Tibet and the Indo-Tibetan realm, nunneries never held the same status, wealth, and power that monasteries did. While monks still receive rich dividends from their monastery's vast endowments in land and livestock, nuns in the Buddhist Himalaya still work on their relatives' farms in exchange for their daily bread.[6] Additionally, nuns have been disqualified from teaching or transmitting esoteric practices and knowledge. Thus, female students have been forced to supplicate themselves in front of male teachers, a posture that has grave potential for abuse.

Nuns are domesticated by monks, for whom they perform menial tasks, just as a wife might for her husband. Although such tasks are strictly forbidden by the monastic discipline, or Vinaya, I have seen and helped nuns wash and sew clothes, collect dung and firewood, weed and water fields, roast barley, bake bread, and perform countless other chores for monks in the Tibetan Buddhist region of Zangskar.

Officially, only monks can manage a woman's passage into celibacy and the monastic order. In Zangskar, only fully ordained monks can officiate the first tonsure ceremony, which signals the initial commitment to celibacy, and the ordination ceremony, when a nun formally joins the monastic order.[7] The officiating monk must be sufficiently pure and ritually advanced in order to transform the latent and manifest symbolic content of these rituals. Hair is a potent symbol of sexuality; its removal signifies a rejection of femininity and fertility.[8] Because long and glossy braids are markers of a woman's fertility, their absence may be mourned inwardly. The ritual offering of hair and jewels during the tonsure rite during ordination expresses a symbolic exchange in which forgone sexuality is traded for future merit. Yet monks reserve the right to regulate this traffic in merit making.

This chapter focuses on the nun's life in Zangskar, a region which lies tucked among the folds of the Greater Himalaya, in the Indian state of Jammu and Kashmir. Three staple crops — barley, peas, and wheat — along with large herds of yaks, cows, goats, and sheep guarantee most houses self-sufficiency in basic foodstuffs. This livelihood is essential in a region cut off from vehicular traffic for at least seven months because of heavy snows.[9] Marriage and inheritance patterns are changing rapidly, although vestiges of polyandry and polygyny remain. Until recently, marriage and residence patterns were flexibly oriented toward a single goal: keeping household landholdings intact. A melange of patrilocal and matrilocal monogamy and polygamy contributed to an economy where household fortunes might rise and fall, yet landholdings remained fairly stable over generations.[10]

Primogeniture is still customary. While the oldest son inherits the house and fields, younger sons may either join their brother's marriage or become monks, homesteaders, or outmarrying husbands. Daughters either marry out or inherit their father's estate in the absence of sons. Zangskari households are still linked by the exchange of women. Bridewealth payments consist of silver coins left over from the Raj, as well as cash, grain, and livestock, although brides also receive substantial dowries to take to their husband's home. Conspicuous wedding feasts culminate the lengthy marital negotiations, which may be drawn out over the better part of a decade. Overall, marriage maintains the symbolic capital of Zangskari culture: generosity, reciprocity, and hospitality.

Zangskar, where 95 percent of the population practice a local variant of Tibetan Buddhism, has an extraordinarily high number of nunneries.[11] Although the absolute number of monasteries and nunneries is roughly equal, the ratio of nuns to monks (two to five) is far higher than in neighboring areas of Tibet and Ladakh.[12] It may constitute the highest such ratio in the Indo-Tibetan realm. While most nuns and monks in Zangskar are monastic celibates in the Gelugpa and Drugpa Kagyud orders, some of the members of the latter order are married meditators (*sgrub pa*) practicing Tantra. This chapter examines one of Zangskar's largest nunneries, which supports 20 novice nuns (*dge tshul ma*), who come mostly from the village of Shun (population 440) and other nearby villages in the region's mandala-shaped central valley.

The Narrow Path to Nunhood

The path to religious renunciation is long and tortuous in both life and literature. These two realms may even merge when a narrative staged as a drama becomes ground for embodied experience. When the famous Tibetan folktale of Nangsa Obum was performed during the course of the annual Gustor (*dgu gtor*) Festival in Shun one year, the play became a participatory performance and identifying narrative for local actresses.[13] Several weeks before the performance, members of the all-female cast appeared to take up the play as an allegory for the difficult choice between the religious and the married life. At rehearsal parties, which lasted far into the night, the young actresses confided their own deepest fears of marriage and dashed dreams for the celibate life. Palkyid admitted that, as an oldest daughter, she was destined to marry, thereby destined for joy in this life but suffering in the next. Kesang said she had wanted to join the nunnery rather than be sent off as a slave to an unknown husband but had cared for her sick and aging parents instead of studying religion (*chos*). Lobsang recounted that when she divorced her husband after just a week of marriage, she had tried to become a nun but had been unable to master the archaic scriptures. Although other actresses had not sought out the celibate life, most identified with the play, a Tibetan *Bildungsroman* of a woman who seeks to renounce worldly life in spite of nearly insurmountable obstacles.[14]

Nangsa Obum: The Girl Who Would Renounce

Once upon a time in a Tibetan village, there lived an elderly couple who were devoted Buddhists.[15] Though they were very aged, one night the wife had a vision of the Tibetan goddess Tārā in her sleep. Indeed, nine months later she gave birth to a daughter, whom they named Nangsa Obum. When Nangsa grew into a beautiful maiden, suitors came from many lands, but her parents refused them all, saying she wanted to become a nun. One year when she went to religious festival, the lord of Rinag saw her and decided she must marry his son. When he called her over to propose, she protested that she was not fit to be a nobleman's wife. The arrogant lord persisted, placed a turquoise on her head, and declared that he would kill any other man who dared marry her. The next day the lord appeared at her parents' doorstep, announcing that he had come to make the bridewealth payments. When he left, Nangsa wailed that she would rather meditate until she died than marry. Her parents replied that the lord might kill them all. In the end, Nangsa was married and a bore a son after a year.

Nangsa was terribly unhappy at her husband's palace, where her sister-in-law, an unmarried and perhaps sexually frustrated spinster, never gave Nangsa keys to the storeroom and generally made life difficult. One day, two religious mendicants came to visit the palace while Nangsa was in the fields harvesting barley. Because she had no access to the storeroom, Nangsa could offer them only grain straight from the fields. The jealous sister-in-law struck Nangsa for her insolent and impromptu generosity and complained to her brother. Nangsa's husband then beat his wife, breaking three of her ribs. Nangsa bore her pain in silent resignation. Shortly thereafter, another religious mendicant (her future teacher, in disguise) came to the palace. When he sang a parable about the suffering that beautiful women experience, Nangsa was deeply moved and, for lack of anything else to offer, gave him the jewels from her breast.[16] The lord, who had been listening at the door, entered the room in a fury. The beggar leaped out the window, but the lord beat Nangsa senseless, inadvertently killing her. When the lord called in an astrologer, he warned them not to burn Nangsa's body, because she would come back from the dead in seven days' time. As foretold, she came back to life a week later, declaring her intention to take up the celibate life.

When Nangsa's in-laws pleaded and her son begged her not to abandon him, she relented. Still miserable, she went to visit her parents and told them of her wish to become a nun. Her mother told Nangsa how ridiculous she was to ignore her husband and his fine palace and yearn for celibacy. After feuding with her mother, Nangsa ran off to the mountains to search for her teacher. Wandering for days, she found his hermitage, where she requested religious instruction. The teacher flatly refused and said she was not ready. In response, she pulled a knife from under her skirt, threatening to plunge it into her breast. He relented and initiated her into Tantric practices. Eventually, Nangsa's husband came to recapture her with an army. Killing many meditators, the soldiers captured her teacher and insulted him:

> You are an old dog that has seduced our snow lion! . . .
> Why did you try to rape this white grouse? . . .
> Why did you pull out her feathers and wings?
> You are an old donkey living in a dirty stable.
> Why did you rape our beautiful wild horse?
> Why did you cut off her mane?
> You nasty old bull, why did you have sex
> with our beautiful white female yak?
>
> (from Allione 1984: 122)

The Tantric master reached out, moved the mountains, and brought his dead disciples back to life. In response to the soldiers' taunts, Nangsa levitated, mocking their attempts to tame her or own her. When the soldiers saw her flying above them, they dropped their arms, and all were converted to the religious life, including her husband and the vicious sister-in-law.

Even as a miraculous practitioner, Nangsa is traded like a commodity between men. After her parents give her away to a pestering suitor, she is pursued to the hermitage by the Rinag clan like an animal who has gone astray. She represents an object of exchange that has been seduced and defiled by the Tantric teacher. Because Nangsa's true nature is wild, she protests their attempts to domesticate her. Nangsa can pierce through the delusions of the Rinag clan, yet such a success is far less likely for nuns in Zangskar. The contradictions between intense spiritual ambition and social constraints overwhelm many women who set out to be nuns. The themes of Nangsa's story—domestic abuse, harsh in-laws, jealous spinsters, and the urge to flee the worldly life—both draw and derail the Zangskari woman's quest for celibacy.

The Struggle for Celibacy in Zangskar

Attaining and maintaining celibacy is a long and difficult battle with one's own family as much as one's conscience. While some girls are chosen by their parents to serve as future nuns, others must fight to leave home and clandestinely join a nunnery. The words of a charismatic teacher, a propensity for religious study or devotion, and childhood hardship or abuse, all may influence the choice to take up celibacy. The only women who almost never become nuns are oldest daughters destined for marriage. While there is no single factor that determines monastic celibacy in Zangskar, a few patterns emerge. Some nuns are illegitimate children or partial orphans, and many have lived away from home during their childhood. They may have learned the self-abnegation, stoicism, and self-restraint that are essential to the celibate life. Yet for every orphaned or illegitimate girl who arrives at the nunnery, there are many other such girls who do not choose the nun's life.

Palmo is a nun who has told me of her unlucky childhood as an illegitimate daughter. Her mother's informal liaisons with two married men caused Palmo much suffering. Since her mother was only a mistress but never a wife, Palmo was sent to live with her father shortly after her mother had weaned her.[17] Palmo's father took her to his new home in Shun, where he had been forced to marry his older brother's widow after the brother's death. Palmo was an outsider twice over in her stepmother's house. Her father was a second husband who could never fill his older brother's shoes, and Palmo was a constant reminder of his past indiscretions with his mistress. Since her father now lived matrilocally in his wife's house, he had no permanent inheritance rights. As the unwanted child of another woman, Palmo was treated worse than a servant girl. She ate last from the leftover scraps which others had neglected.

Palmo lost count of how many times she ran away to her mother's village, only to be discovered by her enraged father, who beat her soundly and took her back to Shun. Her father's abuse may have stemmed from the rage he felt as a powerless and henpecked husband in a house he would never call his own. With no prospects for a properly arranged marriage, Palmo vowed to become a nun and never wind up a spurned mistress like her mother. After having her head shaved and memorizing the required texts, Palmo begged her father to allow her to join the nunnery.[18] Her father and stepmother stalled until Palmo threatened to kill herself if they did not allow her to join the assembly of nuns. Although her father and stepmother relented, they soon forgot their promise. When Palmo remained adamant, her father took her to the nunnery and petitioned the male abbot that she be admitted to the nuns' assembly. Palmo's father and stepmother never built her a cell and still scold her when she is absent from household duties while attending ritual services.

An elderly nun, Deskyid, told me how she grew up, the second of six children in a poor household. Because her parents could not afford to feed all their children, they sent her away to live with two of her father's sisters, who were both married to the same man and childless to boot. Deskyid's aunts treated her terribly, perhaps because they too were victims of abuse at the hands of a husband who mocked them for their sterility. She recalls "not being allowed to finish a single cup of tea without getting up for nine different chores." She had no shoes, hardly any clothes, never enough to eat, and often slept without a blanket. Her sadistic aunt once cracked her ankle with the fire prongs, cutting her to the bone, and her uncle once beat her unconscious. She still bears the traces of a childhood marred by misery and abuse.

The first time Deskyid tried to run away, she was thrashed until she fainted. Her aunt told Deskyid she would drown her slowly in the river by dipping her in and out. Deskyid was so frightened that she didn't run away again until she was 19 years old. During her second attempt, she was caught by two men on the open desert plain just outside her aunt's village. On her third attempt a year later, she forded the river on horseback with a young man who saved her life, she still says. When she reached her parents' house, she vowed never to return to her aunts' house again. She began to memorize religious texts with her brother, a monk, and begged to have her head shaven. Her family replied that she was too old to learn all the required texts. Yet her diligence impressed an elder nun who took her on as a student, and some years later Deskyid took a seat at the nunnery.

Drolma was sent to take care of her sister's children in a distant village. Until she returned home at age 16, when her wedding negotiations went into full swing, Drolma studied religious texts with her friend Chosnyid at the home of a neighboring doctor (*am chi*). When a learned monk (*dge bshes*) from Ladakh came to give the precious Kālacakra teachings in Zangskar one year, Drolma and Chosnyid went to be initiated. Dressed in their finest silk brocade vests, tie-dyed shawls, and jewelry, the two maidens were oblivious to the stares of young men and older folks who whispered about Drolma's imminent wedding. When the monk finished his sermon, they were so overwhelmed that they decided to take up the religious life as soon as possible. Explaining her motivations for renunciation on the next day, Drolma told the monk, "To be enmeshed in delusion is nothing but endless suffering. When the lama shaves my head, he cut the ties of worldly sorrow." After Drolma returned home with a shorn head, her parents began to cry because she was their youngest daughter. Yet Drolma saw how unhappy two of her sisters were in their marriages with abusive husbands. She told me she prefers the nunnery, where she enjoys quiet evenings reading scripture rather than cooking for ungrateful men.

Chosnyid had far greater difficulties, for she was an oldest daughter who flagrantly disobeyed both her parents and society. When she did not return home after the teachings, her father came looking for her. When he saw her shorn head and her neck bereft of jewelry, he was livid with rage. In a sober voice that would admit no counterarguments, he told her that he had drunk the asking beer of her engagement over the last five years. Quite simply, it was too late to turn back the wedding. He then tied her onto the horse in front of him like a child and took her home. Although he hastened to conclude the marriage negotiations, his daughter outwitted him and fled back to the nunnery. Again, her father came to fetch and berate her. For a year, Chosnyid and her father were engaged in this tedious game of hide and seek until she could bear it no longer. When the snow melted, she fled over the passes to Ladakh and went to Dharamsala, where she settled in a hermitage near the Dalai Lama's exile residence. She has never returned to Zangskar, although 25 years have passed.

Celibacy and Its Discontents

Celibacy is an essential aspect of monasticism in the Gelugpa order, and it is literally defined as "purity" or "perfection" (*gtsang ma, tshangs ma*) in Tibetan idiom. When I asked nuns how difficult it is to maintain celibacy, they equivocated or laughed. By the time most nuns join the nunnery, they have been celibate for years. While most nuns confessed to having no carnal knowledge from their youth, some lay people differed on this point. Zangskari lay people generally treat nuns with great respect and rarely recite the Tibetan folktales about Aku Tonpa and Drukpa Kunley, filled with bawdy references to sexually frustrated nuns.[19] However, in Tibetan, there are more words for abandoning celibacy (*mi tshang par spyod pa, log g.yem, 'khrig pa, grong pa'i chos*) than for maintaining it.

Many have asked me if there are lesbian relations at the nunnery, but I never saw or even heard evidence of this. Locals may joke about the homosexual activity in monasteries, but they demur when asked about nunneries. How do nuns sublimate their sexuality? Perhaps a degree of physical proximity and the lifelong companionship of nuns substitute for sexual intimacy. Since most nuns are engaged in higher Tantric meditations intended to subdue the passions of the body, they follow well-established methods of sublimation. Even so, a younger nun once quipped, "If you bring us a few husbands the next time you come from America, will they follow obediently or will you put rings through their noses like we do with our calves?" Many of the nuns I interviewed were pleased to be single because they had a chance to pursue their religious studies. Some recited a common proverb:

> Rang dbang thams cad dge ba yin
> Gzhan dbang thams cad sdug bsngal yin.
>
> (Everything by your own will is blessed happiness,
> Everything by another's will is suffering.)

In my observations, lapses from celibacy usually occurred while outside Zangskar on pilgrimage and resulted in immediate disrobing for nuns, although not always for monks. Monks seem to get away with an occasional village tryst, since no witness may be found for the monk to be formally charged with sexual misconduct. I have heard of monks protesting their innocence years after most of the village is sure of their guilt. In contrast, women often bear an undeniable marker of their indiscretions: pregnancy.

Nuns and monks who lose their celibacy are rarely ostracized by villagers, although they are punished by their respective orders.[20] Rather than shame, families express a deep sadness over the lost karmic potential, for a defrocked monk or nun can never join a Tibetan order again in this lifetime.[21] I have seen mothers weep decades after their child's disrobing.

Although there are probably as many defrocked monks as nuns, nuns usually are blamed for the lapse of celibacy. With folktales extolling women's dangerous and insatiable desire, many villagers are not surprised when a young woman takes a "wrong turn" before reaching the nunnery. To be and to become a nun involve subtle but continuous resistance to the domestic demands and physical desires of those who claim a share of a nun's time or her body.[22] Nuns may renounce sex but remain vulnerable to unwanted advances. Long after they take vows of celibacy and homelessness, they may be called back into productive and procreative roles.

Like several other nuns whose stories I heard, Yangdrol was seduced back into the mundane realm of village life. After she joined the nunnery, her father became completely bedridden, and so she began to live with her parents in the village. Although Yangdrol had become a nun in hopes of getting on in life and escaping domestic servitude, it seemed her destiny was to grow old and single in her parents' house. Her neighbor, who had been observing her from afar when she went to fetch water each day, eventually propositioned her. When he asked if she wanted to join him on a pilgrimage to attend the Dalai Lama's teachings in Sarnath, she jumped at the chance. Although her mother and her friends warned her about the neighbor's lecherous ways, she had higher dreams. After the pilgrimage, she returned pregnant and has since had two more children by the same man, who bears no responsibility for their children.

Why Are There Relatively Few Nuns?

The decision to give up a child to the nunnery is rarely an issue of having one fewer mouth to feed, although this may be a contributing factor. If motivation for celibacy were purely economic, one would expect to find a far greater percentage of nuns and monks in Zangskari society. The paucity of nuns suggests that daughters may be too valuable to be "given away" to the nunnery, despite a promise of increased merit. To treat the monastic vocation as an economic solution to the problem of feeding one's children is to reduce social actors to a Parsonian rationality which neglects affective and irrational aspects of human nature and fortune.[23] Many Zangskari parents cry when a daughter leaves home for the nunnery because they are losing a child even while gaining merit. Mothers may bemoan the loss of companionship with daughters who forgo the roles of mother and wife, and siblings may envy the sisters who spend increasing amounts of time studying and practicing the monastic life. Over time, family members must accept that monasticism is premised upon the erasure of social and affective bonds between an individual and the family.

There are not only psychological costs but also material costs in sending a daughter to the nunnery. Even a family that cannot afford to feed its children may find it cheaper to send a daughter to a relative or to keep her home as a spinster than to send her to a nunnery. After joining the nunnery, a nun may ask her family to provide the labor and materials to build her cell. She will also call upon her parents and relatives to sponsor numerous rituals for which she is nominated steward. However, although her parents lose some of her labor when she begins to live at the nunnery, parents do not lose a daughter to the nunnery in the same way that they lose a son to the monastery. The relatively high ratio of nuns noted earlier may be related to the unique source of adult labor power that female monasticism provides in Zangskar. Because they seek their daily bread from home rather than from their monastic institution, nuns remain at the mercy of their relatives who call them to work. Yet renunciation superimposes a web of chores owed to the monastic collective. Many nuns find themselves in a double bind, with duties to their fictive kin at the nunnery as well as to their real kin in the village.

Only rare and intrepid souls dare undertake a journey to lifelong celibacy, which demands considerable perseverance. A nun does not land in her position by accident because her parents cannot afford a wedding. Nuns are not the ugly ducklings who failed to find husbands by middle age; such women remain spinsters and rarely master the classical Tibetan required for the monastic profession. Many Zangskari women agree that the nun's life is the most difficult to attain but the most rewarding in the end. Yet these Zangskari women speak less of making their own life choices and more of responding to a destiny they call karma. Older women see their situation as largely determined by birth order, household wealth, and status. A handful of younger Zangskari women have become nurses, teachers, and medical orderlies, but such roles were unthinkable a generation ago. Traditionally, the nunnery was the only haven for exceptional women with intellectual or spiritual aspirations.

Many nuns have told me that celibacy is a karmic boon earned in a previous lifetime. Such nuns believe they accumulated enough merit in prior lifetimes to have achieved a rebirth in which they were able to become nuns. Karma provides a theodicy but allows room for agency as well, because every action is also a choice for which the individual must bear ultimate responsibility. Adversity thus forges rather than erodes individual determination. While nuns may recognize the hardships or, as Durkheim (1965: 351) would have us believe, the painful wounding of their maternal instincts, they find compensation in the karmic philosophy which underlies their action. One nun, Lhaskyid, when asked if she missed not having her own children, replied, "We nuns are lucky; we are every child's mother. We do not rejoice or grieve over only our own."

The Impossible Refusal of Exchange

For nuns, celibacy and renunciation are more about resistance than release, more about struggle than liberation. In Zangskar as elsewhere in the Tibetan realm, nuns are domesticated by the social and cultural construction of sexuality that places them in subservience to both families and monks.[24] I propose that the subordinate position of nuns rests upon a deeper impossibility of allowing them to be equal to monks. A radical egalitarianism between male and female celibates would threaten the traditional and inviolable hierarchy of male over female. In practice then, Buddhist monasticism maintains sexual difference even at the expense of doctrine. If nuns were free to transcend their sexuality, they would stand radically outside their society's sex-gender system. Because monasticism is bound to the very roots of the society upon which it depends, sexual hierarchy appears inevitable.[25]

Questioning the assumption of obligatory heterosexuality in Lévi-Strauss's 1969 theory of kinship, Irigaray writes: "Women, signs, commodities, and currency always pass from one man to another; if it were otherwise, we are told, the social order would fall back upon incestuous and exclusively endogamous ties that would paralyze all commerce. . . . *But what if these 'commodities' refused to go to the 'market'?*" (1985: 192, 196; emphasis in original).[26]

Female celibacy may threaten the principles of kinship and exchange, yet its negation of both sex and gender runs more directly counter to these principles. A nun's refusal of marriage and motherhood opposes the principles of alliance and reciprocity. While nuns are permitted to relinquish responsibilities to forgone husbands, in-laws, and children, they cannot deny their roles as daughters and sisters. In the end, nuns cannot avoid the symbolic exchange for merit and the promise of filial service. They may elude the patriarchal economy of desire, but their refusal to be exchanged cannot be fulfilled. Nuns can attempt, but cannot maintain, the refusal to be exchanged. Monks are not casual bystanders but operate the exchange of women between the secular and the sacred realms. As noted, monks retain the sole authority to admit, admonish, advance, or expel nuns within their own order. The monk's order upholds the principle of exchange when they receive one more dutiful servant whose spirituality does not challenge but sustains their fundamental ritual and economic superiority. Although Buddhist doctrine preaches an ultimate escape from the dualism of sex and gender, this message is quite gender specific. Nevertheless, when nuns cease to be simply at the mercy of others' desires, the utopian ideals of Buddhist celibacy may be fulfilled.

Notes

I thank many Zangskari nuns for their infinite patience, compassion, and hospitality over the past years. Heartfelt thanks to M. Aris, S. Bell, D. Donahue, H. Havnevik, A. Kleinman, S. Levine, R. Norman, E. Sobo, J. Willis, and N. Yalman for comments on earlier drafts. The Jacob Javits Foundation, the Mellon Foundation, and the Harvard Department of Anthropology funded my research between 1991 and 1997.

1. Rubin uses "sex/gender system" to denote "the set of arrangements by which a society transforms biological sexuality into products of human activity, and in which these transformed sexual needs are satisfied" (1975: 159). Caplan's (1987) introduction to a book on the cultural construction of sexuality addresses the relations among the terms *sex, gender,* and *sexuality.*

2. Rubin notes, " 'Exchange of women' is a shorthand for expressing that the social relations of a kinship system specify that men have certain rights in their female kin, and that women do not have the same rights either to themselves or to their male kin" (1975: 177).

3. See Sponberg's (1992) and Falk's (1980) insightful analyses of the social context and subtle shifts in the attitudes toward women during the early Buddhist era.

4. Falk (1980), Gross (1993), Horner (1930, [1952] 1992), Paul (1985), and Willis (1985) describe the impact and nature of the Eight Chief Rules (in Pali, *Garudhammā;* in Sanskrit, *Gurudharma*).

5. Falk (1980) describes the decline of the nuns' order in Asia, whereas S. Levine (forthcoming) and Tsomo (1988, 1996) discuss campaigns to reinstate full ordination for nuns in South Asia.

6. Aziz (1976), Fürer-Haimendorf (1976), Grimshaw (1983a, b, 1992), and I

(Gutschow 1997, 1998), Havnevik (1990), and Willis (1989) describe the economic situation of Buddhist nuns in the Nepalese and Indian Himalaya.

7. In Tibet before 1959, charismatic nuns may have officiated at tonsure ceremonies, as Havnevik (n.d.) notes.

8. The connections between hair and sexuality are analyzed in Eilberg-Schwartz and Doniger 1995; Hershman 1974; Leach 1958; and Obeyesekere 1981. Cixous (1981) explores the connection between decapitation and castration.

9. In the winter, the frozen Zangskari River is the main route in and out of Zangskar, for it is sunk deep within a gorge and protected from the fiercest storms. The 1980 completion of a 250-kilometer dirt road from the neighboring district capital of Kargil has altered local economies of supply and demand in terms of rations, foodstuffs, construction materials, and consumer items.

10. In 1992, I conducted a rough kinship survey which included some 398 marriages, of which 26 (7 percent) were polyandrous and 30 (8 percent) were polygynous. The marital and residence patterns found in Zangskar, Ladakh, and the Tibetan Himalaya are summarized in Crook and Osmaston 1994; Gutschow 1995; N. Levine 1988; and Phylactou 1989. Klein 1985 describes the exchange of women in Tibet.

11. Buddhism was introduced to Zangskar from Kashmir in the early part of the first millennium and from Tibet after the tenth-century Buddhist renaissance in western Tibet.

12. In Tibet before 1959, the ratio of nuns to monks was one to nine, according to Shakabpa (1967). In a 1994 census, Zangskar's nine nunneries housed a total of 116 female celibates (2.3 percent of the female population), and its seven monasteries housed 297 monks (5.6 percent of the male population). The number of monastics appears to be declining: Cunningham (1854) and Ramsay (1890) reported that roughly 15 percent of the Ladakhi population were monastics.

13. Rosaldo (1986) and Steedly (1993) describe how narratives shape lived experiences.

14. Nangsa Obum's tale belongs to a didactic genre known as 'das log (literally, "returned from beyond"). Such stories tell of individuals who have died and returned to life to teach a religious message. See Epstein 1982; Havnevik, n.d.; and Pommaret 1989.

15. In the Zangskari version of the folktale, Nangsa becomes a nun rather than a Tantric yogini, as in the Tibetan tradition. The Tibetan folktale is translated in Allione 1984 and Waddell 1895.

16. Faure (1998: 20) notes that while beauty may be a blessing for monks, it is a curse for women who seek to become nuns. Consider the Zangskari variant of the famous story of Gelongma Palmo, in which the tenth-century Indian nun prays for leprosy so that she might be disfigured enough to become a nun and avoid the marriage her parents had negotiated. Her story and the popular fasting ritual she has inspired are described in Gutschow 1999; Ortner 1978, 1989; and Shaw 1994.

17. Customarily, an illegitimate child (nal bu) is raised by the mother for the first few years and then sent to the father's house. Illegitimate daughters usually become spinsters in their father's home.

18. Joining the nunnery (*ri la 'jug byes;* literally, "to dwell on the cliff") requires the permission of one's parents in theory, although this may be overlooked in practice.

19. Dorje (1975) and Dowman (1998) have translated the tales of these legendary rascals.

20. In the past, defrocked monks were covered with ashes and exiled from the village while seated backward on a donkey. Nowadays, defrocked nuns must pay fines up to 10,000 Rs ($250), and defrocked monks pay between 5,000 and 10,000 Rs, each to their respective monastic assembly.

21. Tsomo's translation of the nun's disciplinary code (*Bhikṣuṇī Prātimokṣa*) from the Dharmagupta canon states: "Just as a person whose leg is injured is unable to walk; Similarly those who have broken the precepts cannot be reborn as a god or a human" (1996: 25).

22. Ortner (1995) reviews the mushrooming literature on resistance following the 1985 publication of Scott's book on peasant resistance, and Abu-Lughod (1990) warns of the dangers of romanticizing the resistance, which is so eagerly sought after by ethnographers. While Ortner castigates the subaltern school for having dissolved the subject as the nuns attempt to recuperate agency, I try to foreground how nuns have had a central role in founding and shaping their own monastery's social and ritual activities (Gutschow 1997, 1998).

23. Yalman (1962) posits that in Sri Lanka, young boys are sent to the monastery so that poor families may have fewer mouths to feed and may earn merit as well. I have described how nuns are embedded in Zangskar's economy of merit (Gutschow 1997, 1998).

24. For a comparison of how female renouncers are constrained by Hindu cultural and social norms, see Khandelwal 1996, 1997, and this volume; and Phillimore, this volume.

25. Lévi-Strauss (1962) theorized that every society must have at least three types of communication: women, goods and services, and messages. In other words, kinship, economics, and language were simply variations on a universal theme: exchange.

26. Irigaray's (1985) brilliant deconstruction of the exchange of women finds a utopian escape in the lesbian women who refuse to "go to the market." Lévi-Strauss's position is further challenged in Butler 1990; Irigaray 1994, 1987; and Rubin 1975.

References Cited

Abu-Lughod, Lila. 1990. The Romance of Resistance: Tracing Transformations of Power through Bedouin Women. *American Ethnologist* 17(1): 41–55.

Allione, Tsultrim. 1984. *Women of Wisdom.* London: Arkana.

Aziz, Barbara. 1976. Views from the Monastery Kitchen. *Kailash* 4(2): 155–67.

Butler, Judith. 1990. *Gender Trouble: Feminism and the Subversion of Identity.* New York: Routledge.

Caplan, Pat. 1987. *The Cultural Construction of Sexuality.* New York: Tavistock Publications.

Cixous, Helen. 1981. Castration or Decapitation? *Signs: Journal of Women, Culture and Society* 7: 41–55.

Crook, John, and Henry Osmaston. 1994. *Himalayan Buddhist Villages.* New Delhi: Motilal.

Cunningham, Andrew. 1854. *Ladak: Physical, Statistical, and Historical, with Notes of the Surrounding Countries.* New Delhi: Sagar Publications.

Dorje, Rinjing, comp. and trans. 1975. *The Tales of Aku Tonpa: The Legendary Rascal of Tibet.* San Rafael, Calif.: Dorje Ling.

Dowman, Keith, trans. 1998. *The Divine Madman: The Sublime Life and Songs of Drukpa Kunley.* Middletown, Conn.: Dawn Horse.

Durkheim, Émile. 1965. *The Elementary Forms of the Religious Life.* New York: Free Press.

Eilberg-Schwartz, Howard, and Wendy Doniger. 1995. *Off with Her Head: The Denial of Women's Identity in Myth, Religion, and Culture.* Berkeley: University of California Press.

Epstein, Lawrence. 1982. On the History and Psychology of the 'Das-log. *Tibet Journal* 7(4): 20–85.

Falk, Nancy. 1980. The Case of the Vanishing Nuns: The Fruits of Ambivalence in Ancient Indian Buddhism. In *Unspoken Worlds: Women's Religious Lives,* ed. Nancy Falk and Rita Gross, 207–224. Cambridge: Harper and Row.

Faure, Bernard. 1998. *The Red Thread: Buddhist Approaches to Sexuality.* Princeton: Princeton University Press.

Fürer-Haimendorf, Christopher von. 1976. A Nunnery in Nepal. *Kailash* 4(2): 121–54.

Grimshaw, Anna. 1983a. Celibacy, Religion, and Economic Activity in a Monastic Community of Ladakh. In *Recent Research on Ladakh: History, Culture, Sociology, Ecology,* ed. Dieter Kantowsky and Reinhard Sander, 121–134. Munich: Weltforum Verlag.

Grimshaw, Anna. 1983b. Rizong: A Monastic Community in Ladakh. Ph.D. thesis, Department of Anthropology, Cambridge University.

Grimshaw, Anna. 1992. *Servants of the Buddha: Winter in a Himalayan Convent.* London: Open Letters.

Gross, Rita. 1993. *Buddhism after Patriarchy: A Feminist History, Analysis, and Reconstruction of Buddhism.* Albany: State University of New York Press.

Gutschow, Kim. 1995. Kinship in Zangskar: Idiom and Practice. In *Recent Research on Ladakh Nos. 4 and 5: Proceedings of the 4th and 5th International Colloquia on Ladakh Studies,* ed. Henry Osmaston and Philip Denwood, 337–348. London: School of Oriental and African Studies.

Gutschow, Kim. 1997. Unfocussed Merit-Making in Zangskar: A Socio-Economic Account of Karsha Nunnery. *Tibet Journal* 22(2): 30–58.

Gutschow, Kim. 1998. An Economy of Merit: Women and Buddhist Monasticism in Zangskar, Northwest India. Ph.D. dissertation, Department of Anthropology, Harvard University.

Gutschow, Kim. 1999. The Smyung Gnas Fast in Zangskar: How Liminality Depends on Structure. In *Recent Research on Ladakh No. 8: Proceedings of the 8th*

International Colloquium on Ladakh Studies, ed. Martijn Van Beek and Kris Bertelsen, 154–174. Aarhus: Aarhus University Press.

Havnevik, Hanna. N.d. Jetsun Ani Lochen's Biography or *rnam thar.* Unpublished manuscript.

Havnevik, Hanna. 1990. *Tibetan Buddhist Nuns.* Oslo: Norwegian University Press.

Hershman, Paul. 1974. Hair, Sex and Dirt. *Man,* n.s., 9: 274–298.

Horner, Isabelle. 1930. *Women under Primitive Buddhism.* London: George Routledge and Sons.

Horner, Isabelle, trans. [1952] 1992. *The Book of the Discipline (Vinaya Pitaka).* Vol. 5: *Cullavagga.* Oxford: Pali Text Society.

Irigaray, Luce. 1985. *The Sex Which Is Not One.* Ithaca: Cornell University Press.

Irigaray, Luce. 1987. *Sexes and Genealogies.* New York: Columbia University Press.

Irigaray, Luce. 1994. *Thinking the Difference: For a Peaceful Revolution.* New York: Routledge.

Khandelwal, Meena. 1996. Walking a Tightrope: Saintliness, Gender, and Power in an Ethnographic Encounter. *Anthropology and Humanism* 21(2): 111–134.

Khandelwal, Meena. 1997. Ungendered Atma, Masculine Virility, and Feminine Compassion: Ambiguities in Renunciate Discourses on Gender. *Contributions to Indian Sociology* 31(1): 79–107.

Klein, Anne. 1985. Primordial Purity and Everyday Life: Exalted Female Symbols and the Women of Tibet. In *Immaculate and Powerful: The Female in Sacred Image and Social Reality,* ed. Clarrissa Atkinson, Constance Buchanan, and Margaret Miles, 111–138. Boston: Beacon.

Leach, Edmund. 1958. Magical Hair. *Man* 88: 147–168.

Levine, Nancy. 1988. *The Dynamics of Polyandry.* Chicago: University of Chicago Press.

Levine, Sarah. Forthcoming. At the Cutting Edge: Theravada Nuns in the Kathmandu Valley. In *Swimming against the Stream: Innovative Buddhist Women,* ed. K. L. Tsomo. London: Curzon Press.

Lévi-Strauss, Claude. 1962. Social Structure. In *Anthropology Today,* ed. S. Tax, 321–350. Chicago: University of Chicago Press.

Lévi-Strauss, Claude. 1969. *The Elementary Structures of Kinship.* Boston: Beacon.

Obeyesekere, Gananath. 1981. *Medusa's Hair: An Essay on Personal Symbols and Religious Experience.* Chicago: University of Chicago Press.

Ortner, Sherry. 1978. *Sherpas through Their Rituals.* New York: Cambridge University Press.

Ortner, Sherry. 1989. *High Religion: A Cultural and Political History of Sherpa Buddhism.* Princeton: Princeton University Press.

Ortner, Sherry. 1995. Resistance and the Problem of Ethnographic Refusal. *Society for Comparative Study of Society and History* 37(1): 173–193.

Paul, Diana. 1985. *Women in Buddhism: Images of the Feminine in Mahayana Tradition.* Berkeley: University of California Press.

Phylactou, Maria. 1989. Household Organisation and Marriage in Ladakh-Indian Himalaya. Ph.D. thesis, London School of Economics.

Pommaret, Françoise. 1989. *Les Revenants de l'Au-dela dans le monde tibetain.* Paris: Centre de Reserche Scientifique Nationale.

Ramsay, Henry. 1890. *Western Tibet: A Practical Dictionary of the Language and Customs of the Districts Included in the Ladak Wazarat.* Lahore: W. Ball.

Rosaldo, Renato. 1986. Ilongot Hunting as Story and Experience. In *The Anthropology of Experience,* ed. V. Turner and E. Bruner, 97–139. Urbana: University of Illinois Press.

Rubin, Gayle. 1975. The Traffic in Women: Notes on the "Political Economy" of Sex. In *Toward an Anthropology of Women,* ed. Rayna Reiter, 157–210. New York: Monthly Review.

Shakabpa, Tsepon. 1967. *Tibet: A Political History.* New Haven: Yale University Press.

Shaw, Miranda. 1994. *Passionate Enlightenment: Women in Tantric Buddhism.* Princeton: Princeton University Press.

Sponberg, Alan. 1992. Attitudes toward Women and the Feminine in Early Buddhism. In *Buddhism, Sexuality, and Gender,* ed. J. Cabezon, 3–36. Albany: State University of New York Press.

Steedly, Mary. 1993. *Hanging without a Rope: Narrative Experience in Colonial and Post-Colonial Karoland.* Princeton: Princeton University Press.

Tsomo, Karma Lekshe. 1988. *Sakyadhita: Daughters of the Buddha.* Ithaca: Snow Lion.

Tsomo, Karma Lekshe. 1996. *Sisters in Solitude.* Albany: State University of New York Press.

Waddell, L. A. 1895. *The Buddhism of Tibet, or Lamaism.* London: W. H. Allen and Co.

Willis, Jan. 1985. Nuns and Benefactresses: The Role of Women in the Development of Buddhism. In *Women, Religion, and Social Change,* ed. Y. Haddad and E. Findly, 59–85. Albany: State University of New York Press.

Willis, Jan. 1989. *Feminine Ground: Essays on Women and Tibet.* Ithaca: Snow Lion.

Yalman, Nur. 1962. The Ascetic Buddhist Monks of Ceylon. *Ethnology* 1(3): 315–328.

3 *Hector N. Qirko*

The Maintenance and Reinforcement of Celibacy in Institutionalized Settings

Vows of lifelong sexual abstinence are difficult to understand from an evolutionary perspective. Richard Dawkins (1995: 2) has said that we "love life and love sex and love children" because we each come from an unbroken line of ancestors who were able to survive and reproduce. Darwinian evolutionary theory is predicated on a drive for reproductive survival, and behavior favored by selection should be that which leads to individual reproductive success (Archer 1991). Therefore, a decision, conscious or unconscious, by normal, healthy individuals to forgo reproduction seems to makes no sense. Yet it is a decision individuals often make. Sometimes the choice is temporary, as with a young American choosing to remain chaste until marriage (Wyatt, Peters, and Guthrie 1988) or a Cheyenne initiate of the Dog Soldier warrior society pledging celibacy for seven years (Moore 1990). In other cases, however, as in many monastic orders, the decision is made for life.

There are many culture-specific rationales for lifelong vows of celibacy. These include the demonstration or test of religious faith and the acquisition of personal strength, luck, purity, status, power, or material success. There is also variability, at both individual and group levels, in attitudes toward sexuality and reproduction. Demographic, historical, and perhaps even ecological (Reynolds 1986) processes affect the presence or absence of celibate institutions in particular societies. However, from a

65

Darwinian perspective, lifelong celibacy should be rare and difficult for individuals to sustain.[1]

One might argue that lifelong sexual abstinence is in fact rare. In the early sixteenth century, Martin Luther claimed that only "one in a thousand" priests actually kept his vows (Ozment 1972: 39). A recent survey of North American Roman Catholic priests, nuns, and laity found that only half of the priests and a third of the nuns support mandatory clerical celibacy (Rosetti 1994). However, Wynne (1988) demonstrates that religious rules (including ones pertaining to celibacy) have generally been adhered to in Catholic monastic orders throughout their history. This also appears to be the case for many Buddhist orders (e.g., Bunnag 1973), Hindu branches (e.g., van der Veer 1987), and other celibate institutions, including the Shakers (Kitch 1989). It is therefore reasonable to conclude that voluntary lifelong celibacy has been faithfully followed for centuries by many healthy men and women all over the world.

One might also argue that celibates, because of idiosyncratic variability with respect to sexual desire, do not find vows particularly difficult. Celibate institutions may simply be aggregations of those individuals who exhibit little or no interest in sex. However, this is unlikely. Factors other than individual sexual inclination clearly influence membership in celibate institutions. For example, because of primogeniture, most Tibetan recruits to lamaseries are second sons (Durham 1991: 71 n.). And many recruits to Christian monasteries in the Middle Ages were sent by their parents at early ages (Knowles 1963), well before their level of future sexual interest could be known.

The best reason to question the relevance of idiosyncratic variability is that so many have described the extreme difficulty of maintaining vows of celibacy. Members of many religious orders report that adhering to vows of celibacy is the most demanding aspect of their discipline (e.g., Pfanner 1966: 84). Celibacy has historically engendered a great deal of controversy in both Buddhism (Wei-hsun Fu and Wawrytko 1994) and Christianity (Wynne 1988) because of the difficulties it entails. Many branches and sects have been formed specifically either to escape or to reinforce adherence to celibacy.

In sum, celibacy is a relatively common, if difficult, choice that appears to run counter to Darwinian expectations. This chapter explores the possibility that induced or manipulated altruism may be associated with the maintenance and reinforcement of celibate vows in nonkin, institutionalized settings. Lifelong sexual abstinence is often a sacrifice performed for others, and Darwinian evolutionary theory predicts that individuals may sacrifice themselves for the benefit of genetic relatives. However, because humans generally recognize kin only by means of indirect cues, these cues may be manipulated so that individuals behave altruistically for the benefit of nonkin. Thus nonkin institutions that demand celibacy from their members may, through cultural means, manipulate psychological mechanisms pertaining to kinship recognition in order to maintain and reinforce altruistic behavior. The following pages present a research model designed to test these notions more rigorously, after which follows a brief summary of historical and ethnographic data that support the model's central prediction (see Qirko 1998 for expanded discussion).

Celibacy as Altruism

Altruism, or "self-denying or self-destructive behavior performed for the benefit of others" (Wilson 1987: 10), has a strict Darwinian definition: the sacrifice must involve fitness or reproductive success (Williams 1981). That is, in evolutionary terms, altruism is an act which results in a loss of reproductive potential for one organism and a gain for another, measured either with reference to the viability of the individuals ("somatic effort") or in terms of reproduction itself (Alexander 1979: 114).

Individuals of many species often behave altruistically to assist siblings or other close relatives. In many cases they play important roles in raising young, in the process often delaying or forgoing their own reproduction (Emlen 1984). Humans appear to behave nepotistically as well. Kin receive more unreciprocated help than nonkin, and close kin more than removed kin (Cunningham 1985–1986; Essock-Vitale and McGuire 1980, 1985; Piliavin and Charng 1990). This help can include forgoing reproduction, as in the case of an older sibling who remains single and childless to help raise younger siblings or care for parents (Kiernan 1988).

In some cases, younger siblings may forgo procreation so that their kin will benefit from the conservation of scarce resources. For example, the common Tibetan practice of sending second sons to Buddhist monasteries, previously discussed, appears to benefit reproductively typically polyandrous families (Durham 1991: 71–72; see also Messenger 1971). Therefore, along with contraception, emigration, and infanticide, celibacy can be a strategy that removes potential drains on a family's reproductive and material resources. The influence or wealth that celibates accrue as teachers and priests may also indirectly benefit relatives (Alexander 1979: 80).

Celibacy often benefits nonkin as well. Celibates devote time and energy to the furtherance of organizations by performing duties requested of them. In some cases, as in celibate military units, these duties entail risk of injury or death. In religious institutions, duties can include the maintenance of communal quarters, care for fellow members, and the performance of religious functions. Reproduction, time, and energy are sacrificed, not for offspring and other close kin, but for unrelated others, including not only institutional leaders and members but also abstract entities and supernatural deities.

A second benefit of celibacy for institutions is the control of wealth and other resources. Celibate members have fewer conflicts of interest with respect to acquiring resources for family members, and the legal transfer of property and wealth to family members does not, in general, occur (Balch 1985). In many cases celibate members donate their resources to the organization for the furtherance of its goals.

Thus, celibacy is often an altruistic act, especially in organizational settings. In Christian monasticism, for example, "there is a vast body of [incontrovertible] evidence about the remarkable hardships and sufferings which many order members voluntarily accepted on behalf of the church and their orders" (Wynne 1988: 47). Although this sacrifice comes in many forms, the loss of reproduction certainly qualifies. Indeed, "celibacy may be one reason for the extended longevity of monasteries as social systems — perhaps communes can generally be handled no other way" (Hillery 1992: 102).

Biological Altruism

In evolutionary terms, traits promoting altruism should not persist in a population except under three circumstances: where they increase fitness of close relatives, where return benefits exceed the costs of sacrifice, and where they are forced or manipulated by others (Trivers 1985: 41–52).[2] *Inclusive fitness* (or kin selection) theory, first formally proposed by Hamilton (1964), is based on the differing degrees to which individuals share copies of their genes, depending on the extent to which they are related. Therefore, any genetically driven trait can spread in a population if that trait confers an advantage to more individuals sharing it than are lost because of instructions (for example, one person dies to keep several of his brothers or sisters alive). This simple notion, with its attendant mathematical formulations, has helped explain many of the apparent paradoxes of the natural world, including nonreproducing worker castes of social insects (Wilson 1975: 193–196). As discussed earlier, it is becoming increasingly clear that humans often behave altruistically in accordance with the predictions of inclusive fitness theory.

In the case of *reciprocal altruism,* an apparently altruistic act can be selected for if it yields a return benefit larger than its cost. The necessary conditions are repeated interactions between individuals and a "significant" delay between the benefit received and the return act (Piliavin and Charng 1990; Trivers 1985: 48). For example, if a man jumps into icy waters to save a drowning unrelated child (a risky, but not a suicidal, act), there are direct and indirect benefits which can accrue to him as "hero" if he is successful (Wilson 1975: 58). Of course, "we must remain alive to receive the return effect. There is always some chance that we will not survive to enjoy the return benefit, and this chance of mortality will lead us always to devalue future effects when compared to present effects" (Trivers 1985: 49).

As with inclusive fitness, there is evidence that humans behave in accordance with predictions based on reciprocal altruism theory (Schroeder et al. 1995). Reciprocity can operate alongside kinship to promote altruism. In fact, in humans, although there appears to be a tendency to reciprocate more often and more strongly toward kin than toward nonkin, even close kin who fail to reciprocate are eventually abandoned (Essock-Vitale and McGuire 1980).

A third circumstance under which altruism can occur is *manipulated altruism,* where "the recipient *induces* altruism that would normally be directed elsewhere or not displayed at all" (Trivers 1985: 49; emphasis in original). What is important is that "all systems of altruism are vulnerable to parasitism in which individuals pretend a degree of relatedness they do not possess or a degree of reciprocity they will not express" (Trivers 1985: 52). Thus, manipulated altruism can take the form of kinship deceit, or the manipulation of kin-recognition mechanisms, to elicit nonkin altruism, which is relatively common in nonhuman species (Conner 1995). Cowbirds and cuckoos, for example, lay their eggs in other species' nests. When the foreign egg hatches, the chick is fed by its new "parents," which are fooled into caring for nonkin by the location and, perhaps, the behavior of the nestling. Conner reports that adult white-winged chough birds often "kidnap" unrelated young for the help they can later provide in raising true offspring. The young, apparently fooled by the kidnappers' feeding behavior, perceive them as kin. As will be discussed, induced altruism may relate to the reinforcement of nonkin altruism in humans.

Psychological Altruism

Proximate, psychological mechanisms are also likely to be important in human altruistic behavior. That proximate mechanisms, such as sexual pleasure, have led humans to perform acts that lead to greater reproductive success is a "central hypothesis in evolutionary biology" (Alexander 1987: 26).

In the case of human altruism, various proximate mechanisms have been proposed. One category relates to the pleasurable feelings that can accompany altruistic acts, ranging from a "warm glow" of self-satisfaction

(Andreoni 1990) to narcissistic ego gratification (Rappoport and Kren 1993).

The human capacity for empathy can also account for altruistic behaviors (Hoffman 1981; MacDonald 1984). For example, Batson (1990) conducted experiments where college students were told that some of their fellows were receiving mild electrical shocks. Many offered to receive the shocks instead, although they refused to take their colleagues' places when the shocks were perceived as clearly painful. Another possibility, related to reciprocal altruism, is that having an "altruistic behavioral disposition" gives an individual a reputation that results in payoffs over the long term, even though costly in any particular instance (Sesardic 1995: 152).

The most plausible mechanisms for human altruism, particularly relevant for cases that appear to run counter to evolutionary expectations, are related to human social learning and conformity. Humans are easy to instruct and convince (Bandura 1980; Campbell 1983), and it is quite possible that altruistic behavior can be learned. While it is clear that much altruism conforms to the expectations of kin selection and reciprocal altruism, human malleability could account for behaviors that have deleterious outcomes in terms of fitness (Fialkowski 1990; Sesardic 1995). For example, MacDonald (1984) attempts to integrate tendencies to imitate with the affective environment of the developing child, because children appear to be more altruistic if exposed to generous, as opposed to selfish, models (Piliavin and Charng 1990).

In addition, "the altruistic tendency could well be justified simply by our seeming necessity to achieve social acceptance" (Cela-Conde 1990: 148; see also Alexander 1987). Some work has been done around a conformity mechanism, or what Simon (1990) calls "docility," and its implications regarding the acceptance of fitness-reducing cultural traits (Boyd and Richerson 1985: 204–240; Logan and Qirko 1996). The logic is simply that accepting traits under certain conditions (e.g., the most frequently encountered, the status of the donor, traits encountered in the developmental process, etc.) is more likely, given our bounded rationality, than cost-benefit assessments of single traits. This could account for the perpetuation of maladaptive traits, of which certain altruistic behaviors could be one category.

Celibacy and Manipulated Altruism

How do celibate vows fit into these theoretical frameworks? At first glance, not too neatly. Where celibacy directly benefits kin, it can be explained in terms of inclusive fitness. But that explanation cannot apply where celibacy appears to benefit primarily nonkin, such as in many celibate organizations. Even if indirect benefits accrue to the celibate's family by his removing himself from its material and reproductive concerns, the daily maintenance of vows in nonkin settings requires additional explanation.

In the case of reciprocal altruism, celibate vows belong to a class of altruistic behaviors that may be called terminal. If one forgoes sex (and thus reproduction) for a lifetime, one cannot personally incur any fitness benefit that will outweigh the resulting loss; nor can one obtain reciprocal benefits at a later date.

Further, the resulting reproductive sacrifice is direct and obvious. As I explain later, human rationality is shaped and constrained by natural selection, but it is unlikely to be so shaped that it overlooks consciously chosen maladaptive traits such as the sacrifice of life or lifelong reproduction. Therefore, psychological mechanisms such as empathy, while perhaps appropriate for lower-cost acts, should not apply. Even the theories involving altruistic behavioral disposition and docility, which potentially explain a wide variety of sacrificial acts, assume eventual gains that are not possible if the actors forgo the ultimate biological currency, reproduction, for a lifetime.

However, the notion of induced altruism through kinship deceit does provide a possible means through which celibacy can be maintained and reinforced in nonkin settings. Johnson (1986, 1989; and Johnson, Ratwick, and Sawyer 1987) has suggested that altruism can be elicited through socialization by the manipulation of the means through which humans identify kin, because it is not kinship itself that humans recognize but rather "environmental cues that have typically been highly correlated with kinship" (Johnson, Ratwick, and Sawyer 1987: 158). Johnson lists association, phenotypic similarity, and the use of kin terms as the cues most likely to be utilized by humans in kin recognition and suggests that patriotic volunteerism, risking one's life in combat, and altruistic suicide are often elicited through the manipulation of these cues.

Similarly, McGuire, Fawzy, and Spar (1994) discuss six "trait signaling-recognition systems" that relevant literature suggests have been selected for in humans. These systems facilitate the transmission and encoding of information around individual "identity, motives, values, and emotional states" with respect to potential altruism and reciprocity-related behavior (p. 301). Three of these pertain specifically to the identification of kin: context (close proximity, e.g., parent–child relationships); association (identification through social learning, including kin terms and behavioral rules); and phenotypic matching.

Significantly, "how others are recognized and the categories (kin, non-kin) to which they are assigned have important consequences. If kin are recognized, one set of altruistic decision-making rules is likely to apply (invest in kin, do not expect immediate payback). A different set of rules is likely to apply to non-kin (invest cautiously and await a payback before investing further)" (McGuire, Fawzy, and Spar 1994: 304). It is easy to see the benefits for an unrelated individual to be recognized as kin by a potential altruist.

In small groups where kin-relatedness is to be expected and there is little institutional control of individuals (e.g., nonstratified societies), the need to induce altruism is likely to be unnecessary. But where groups of generally unrelated individuals are brought together in activities for which a willingness to sacrifice oneself is desirable, inducing and maintaining altruism can be effective and efficient for institutions.

Balch (1985) has discussed the historical control of reproduction, labor, and resources in nonkin organizations through abduction, enslavement, castration, and forced celibacy. Organizations (more properly, leaders of organizations) attempt to minimize the disruptive effects of familial obligations by destroying or preventing family attachments and by attempting to substitute themselves as kin. Balch, too, refers to kinship recognition cues such as association, familiarity, and the use of kinship-evoking language and symbolism as mechanisms that can facilitate accomplishing these goals.

Although his emphasis is on the forcible manipulation of recruits, Balch's logic also applies to organizations that rely on voluntary sacrifice such as vows of celibacy. In fact, attempts to replicate familial environments and relationships may be more important where force is not an option. In such organizations, the nature of relations between members is likely to be more important than in involuntary institutions, where the coercive relationship between the institution and its members maintains stability (Wynne 1988: 39–40).

Balch's work also suggests that attention should be paid to the developing nature of nonkin altruistic relationships. Humans have lived in small kin-groups for most of their history as a species (Ike 1987), and mechanisms for recognition of genetic relatives presumably evolved in that context. Therefore, frequent interaction with nonkin is a novel introduction, a consequence of increased population sizes and concomitant nonkin interactions. Where asymmetric power relationships and a lack of "liberal scruples" (Balch 1985: 316) have permitted forced altruism, it has apparently occurred. Where sensibilities have changed, less brutal means of obtaining organizational loyalty have developed (Salter 1995).

Kinship Recognition Mechanisms

Relevant literature on kin recognition mechanisms appears to support the possibility of manipulated human altruism. Across species, "kin recognition of one kind or another has been implicated in most kinds of social behavior" (Wilson 1987: 9). In humans, in addition to visual identification at birth, mothers are soon capable of identifying newborns through olfactory and auditory cues (Piontelli 1995; Porter 1991). There is mounting evidence that infants, even before birth, can recognize their mothers through the same means (Hepper 1991; Porter 1991). After the first few months of life, however, and for nonmaternal relationships, less direct cues are typically utilized, and individual recognition is less certain. Spatial distribution (if you're here, you're kin), association (familiar individuals, especially during development, are kin), and phenotypic matching (where a "template" is formed and those who match it are kin) are the traditional mechanisms described in the literature.[3]

These kin recognition mechanisms can work in combination with each other (Hepper 1991) and appear to do so in nonhuman primates (Bernstein 1991). In humans, phenotypic matching and association are the most likely to apply (Wells 1987), since spatial distribution requires the predictable distribution of kin (Sherman and Holmes 1985). The human brain appears particularly endowed to discriminate among human faces, which supports the importance of phentoypic similarity in kin recognition (Wilson 1987). In addition, humans may use mannerisms, habits, and speech patterns to help identify relatives (Alexander 1990: 273). Some support for the importance of association is found in studies of Israeli *kibbutzim* (Talmon 1964) and Taiwanese arranged marriages (Wolf 1995), where the practice of rearing children together and forcing them to marry often results in sexual dissatisfaction. Less direct evidence is available for other societies (Brown 1991: 118–129; Wolf 1995: 423–438; but see Scheidel 1996).

All humans also clearly categorize relationships through language and other symbolic referents. As summarized by Daly, Salmon, and Wilson (1997), all societies exhibit ego-centered kinship terminology based on parent-offspring relationships, and all distinguish between genders, generations, and degree of relatedness. In addition, kin relationships are often communicated through a wide variety of insignias and forms of adornment. Among the Kayapo, for example, girls wear crocheted arm and leg bands that signify membership in their immediate families (Turner 1987: 99). Knowledge of ancestors and the ability to trace descent are also cues to kinship; thus a stranger is often accepted as kin if he or she can provide the appropriate genealogy (van den Berghe 1981: 28).

Anthropologists have long discussed the presence of fictive kinship in societies and its role in forging and cementing alliances between unrelated (or only distantly related) members (Keesing 1975). For some, the ubiquity of fictive kinship terminology and the variability in kinship systems indicate a lack of relationship between cultural and biological notions of kinship (e.g., Sahlins 1976). However, individuals appear to be generally aware of the genetic relationships that are presumed to underlie kin nomenclature (Alexander 1979: 197–202; van den Berghe 1981: 27). For example, Chagnon (1988) finds that Yanomamo males often manipulate kinship classifications for female kin to increase the number of potential mates and, regardless of kinship terminology, favor closer biological relatives in village fissioning (Chagnon 1981). Heider (1976) notes that while New Guinea Dani children sometimes confuse social and biological kinship categories, the adults never do. Thus, while in all societies kin terms are extended "for evocative and propagandistic purposes" to apply to nonrelatives and even abstract entities (Daly, Salmon, and Wilson 1997: 287), kin recognition theory suggests a reason why this practice may be effective in reinforcing or manipulating desired behavior.

In addition, human development suggests two associated factors relevant to kin recognition. Human learning appears to involve sensitive periods during which learning in particular domains is greatly facilitated. The most well-understood example is language acquisition (Hurford 1991), but children's sensitivity to early social environments and relationships has a similarly powerful effect on later behavior (Draper and Harpending 1988; MacDonald 1988). This sensitivity, particularly in terms of human attachment, does not disappear at a particular age but instead slowly stabilizes with time. Further, "the intensity of environmental stimulation can overcome declining plasticity" (MacDonald 1988: 135). This suggests that individuals are most susceptible to kinship manipulation during childhood, although it can occur, to some degree, at later ages.

Also, it seems reasonable to suggest that new attachments are easier to make if old ones do not persist to confound them. Certainly new, stable attachments can replace severed ones. Ainsworth (1977) suggests that an individual may make several attachments during the course of development, and children separated from their parents can successfully form substitute attachments with others. Bowlby found that British children separated from their parents during World War II were able to form new, stable relationships (in Cole and Cole 1989: 228–229). Data suggest that separation from real kin would not preclude, and may even facilitate, the formation of artificial kinship ties (Dontas et al. 1985; Sagi et al. 1985).

Human Cognition

Can people really be fooled into seeing nonkin as kin? Deceit and its identification are fundamental aspects of human relationships, and "entire institutions in human cultures are predicated upon deception," including games, folklore, warfare, and the socialization of children (Anderson 1986: 333; see also Cronk 1995; Mitchell and Thompson 1986).

Also, human cognition appears to involve a variety of evolved mechanisms through which the "practical problems of living" can be solved but which can lead to mistakes and manipulation (Flohr 1987: 195). A good example of an innate mechanism is, again, language acquisition (Pinker 1994). However, in the areas of sexual attraction, mate choice, habitat selection, parental reproductive strategies, social categorization, and prejudice, humans may operate as much through evolved tendencies as through rational, cost-benefit calculations (Barkow, Cosmides, and Tooby 1992; Wright 1994). In addition, evolutionary theory predicts that an ability to discern degrees of relatedness will be crucial. For this reason, Tooby and Cosmides suggest that a "kin oriented motivation module" is likely to exist (1992: 113). Daly and his colleagues similarly propose that kinship may be "a special domain with its own rules," for children "acquire an understanding of kinship terminology in ways that cannot be accounted for by the hypothesis of domain-general inductive processes" (1997: 289). It is not farfetched that rules pertaining to kinship recognition can, particularly in novel environments, invite errors and manipulation. Complete fooling of humans with respect to kin, furthermore, is not necessary for kin manipulation to take place. Evolved tendencies can operate in concert (and in conflict) with rational decision making. The manipulation of kin cues might elicit behaviors even among individuals who know perfectly well who their kin are and are not, particularly if reinforced by conditioning and enculturation (Fialkowski 1990).

Research Model

On the basis of the preceding arguments, several identifiable traits are likely to lead to manipulated kinship recognition (and, as a consequence, to the reinforcement of desired altruistic behavior) in organizations. Manipulators should encourage:

- close associations that replicate natural kin contexts (particularly parent–child and sibling relationships),
- the use of false phenotypic matches (uniforms, emblems, hairstyles, etc.),

• the use of linguistic and other symbolic kin referents.

In addition, manipulators should:

• prefer young, impressionable recruits,
• discourage association with actual kin.

The following prediction can be made: Where voluntary vows or decisions of lifelong celibacy occur in the context of direct benefits to nonkin (even if there are indirect benefits to kin), the manipulation of kinship recognition mechanisms (as cited above) should occur as well.

Celibacy in Christianity

In light of this model, a review of the literature on Christianity is revealing. Since its early history, the Christian Church has been characterized by one form or another of mandatory sexual abstinence (see Southgate, this volume). The first written law on abstinence for priests appears to have been issued by the Council of Elvira in A.D. 305 (de Valk 1990). Roman Catholic priests are required to observe "total and irrevocable" celibacy (Napier 1989). In the Eastern Orthodox Church, priests can be married before ordination but must swear abstinence as a prerequisite to clerical duty. Bishops and those who take monastic vows must be chaste. The current debate over marriage for priests emerged at least twice in the Christian Church's early history, but the Gregorian reform in the eleventh century and the Council of Trent in 1563 reaffirmed the commitment to celibacy.

One major goal of demanding sexual abstinence from members has been to benefit the organization and its leaders (including supernatural figures), thus rendering celibacy an altruistic act. Saint Paul is often quoted with reference to the apostolic origins of Christian celibacy: "The unmarried man is busy with the Lord's affairs, concerned with pleasing the Lord; but the married man is busy with this world's demands and occupied with pleasing his wife" (Cholij 1989: 201). This passage is an invitation to devote one's life to "immediate service of the Church and to avoid the more immediate concerns of family life" (p. 201).

Cardinal Stickler reviewed explicit motives for celibacy in the early Church. An important one was organizational loyalty: "[Priests] must be completely free from any other occupation or stable commitment, especially that of a family of their own, in order to be able to dedicate themselves completely to the sacred ministry in its various exigencies and obligations. To serve the People of God it is necessary to belong exclusively to God" (Stickler 1972, quoted in de Valk 1990: 4).

This service was envisioned in material as well as in spiritual terms, for the early decrees were apparently in large part designed to prevent priests from diverting Church resources to kin (Balch 1985; Lea 1932). The Church's desire to control its wealth was often cited as a reason for its insistence on celibacy, especially by early Protestant reformers (Ozment 1972). Even presumably ascetic monasteries were, in a sense, business ventures. They often controlled great wealth (Dickinson 1961), demanded additional produce and rent from their tenants (Knowles 1963: 100–103, 441–444), and elicited contributions from pilgrims who came to view holy relics (Hunt 1971).

Manipulation of kin recognition mechanisms clearly appears to be present in monasteries. Although there is some variability among orders, the general pattern has consisted of immature recruits, averaging 14–15 years of age (although often much younger), who are separated from blood relatives to live with other recruits and members. Orders are characterized by uniform clothing, hairstyles, and accouterments that are used even where there is no contact with outsiders and social identification is not an issue. The use of kin terms and other symbols of kinship permeates all aspects of daily life (Wynne 1988).

This pattern can be illustrated by the European monasteries of the central Middle Ages (900–1200), epitomized by Cluny, the most influential monastery of a strongly religious age (Brooke 1974; Hunt 1971). Recruits, separated from real kin upon entering the monastery, were often infants whose parents "dedicated" them to lifelong service (Knowles 1963: 417–422). Ritually stripped of their clothes and dressed in novice habits, they were permitted only the company of other initiates and the "master" who oversaw them. At age 15 (and thus, often, after many years of initiation), boys could be admitted as novices. At this point individuals who wished to enter the monastery from the outside world could join initiates in being shaven, stripped, and uniformly attired. Novices spent most of their time learning rules of behavior. At the end of this learning period, usually a year, they petitioned to enter the order and, if accepted, took their formal vows. They received uniform robes, cowls, and capes. Members were clean-shaven and wore identical tonsured hairstyles. The new "brothers" were continually followed "to see that their conduct was in every detail in accordance with the usages of Cluny" (Evans 1968: 49). Abbots were referred to as fathers. Kin terms were similarly applied to abstract entities ("Mother Church," "Our Holy Father") and occurred frequently in the prayers and music that were a daily part of monastic life.

An example from modern times shows that this historical pattern remains. Hillery (1992), utilizing ethnographic techniques, researched American Trappist-Cisterian abbeys and monasteries in the 1970s and 1980s. He found that candidates were usually young men who remained in the monastery for four to six weeks and, if accepted, remained as postulants for an additional six weeks to six months. They then took temporary vows and were novices for two to five years. Monks had only limited contact with the outside world. Both novices and monks or nuns wore distinctive uniforms. Although most members had some contact with their families, "the biosocial family is absent from the communal organization in the monastery [and] certain insitutions must be substituted" (p. 97). Kinship models (including the terms *father, brother,* and *sister*) were an integral part of the monasteries' social structure.

A review of historical and ethnographic literature suggests that this pattern of kin recognition manipulation also applies in a wide variety of celibate organizations where the pool of recruits is based primarily on nonkin (Qirko 1998). These organizations include monastic orders in Buddhism, Hinduism, and Jainism, dervish groups in Islamic societies, Christian religious-military orders such as the Templars, Hospitallers, and Teutonic Knights, and various Christian separatist sects, such as the Shakers and the Harmonists. Significantly, most of these organizations are characterized by the organizational control of wealth and resources.

Cross-Cultural Survey

An analysis of cross-cultural ethnographic data also suggests that celibacy in nonkin settings is associated with the manipulation of kin recognition cues. Murdock and White's (1969) Standard Cross-Cultural Sample was utilized for this analysis. This sample consists of 186 societies chosen from 1,250 societies in the *Ethnographic Atlas.* Murdock and White selected sample units on the basis of geography, linguistics, subsistence economies, social organization, depth of ethnographic coverage, and other factors. Societies are identified with respect to time and place, and the names of authorities for each sample are provided.

Of the 176 societies for which there are adequate data for my research question, 32 exhibit celibacy in 41 institutional settings. In 26 of these settings, permanent abstinence is directly related to nonkin altruism. Eighteen of these relate to Christian and Buddhist monasticism and appear to conform to the pattern previously described.

The other eight cases of permanent abstinence in nonkin, altruistic settings are: the Bektashi celibate dervishes in northern Albania (Birge 1937); the so-called Amazons of the kingdom of Dahomey around the turn of the century (Skertchly 1874); priestesses of Babylon around 1750 B.C. (Driver and Miles 1952, 2: 365–367); vestal virgins of Rome around A.D. 100 (Benko 1971: 66; Plutarch 1952: 54–55); the Cynics, also in first-century Rome, a group of wandering renunciants patterned after Hindu ascetics (Benko 1984: 33–47); the Children of Iruska, a Pawnee association of young "contraries" (Murie 1916: 580–581); the Aztec priestly class (Sahagun 1932; Soustelle 1962); and Inca "virgins of the sun" (Metraux 1969; Vega [1871] 1961).

Although data are sometimes sketchy, the predicted pattern of kinship cue manipulation appears to be present in all of these cases, even where force is clearly used both to recruit and to reinforce expected behavior. For example, the Inca virgins, according to Vega ([1871] 1961: 292–301), were set apart at age eight or earlier to live in seclusion in the Temple of the Sun in Cuzco. Unlike others reserved for service to royalty, these women were to live in lifelong chastity. They wore uniform clothing and identifying markers and lived in close association only with each other and *mama-cunas* (literally, "matrons," women who must perform the duties of a mother) (p. 293).

Although a detailed discussion of historical and ethnographic data pertaining to the kinship manipulation model can be found elsewhere (Qirko 1998), three points should be emphasized here. First, the manipulation of kinship recognition mechanisms appears to occur in many religious, military, and other organizations that demand dramatic forms of nonkin altruism from their members (see, for example, literature on secret societies; e.g., Chesneaux 1971; Heckethorn 1965). Whether the organizational goal is to obtain material resources, loyalty, or group cohesion from members, induced altruism can facilitate the process.

Second, the terminal altruism engendered through vows of celibacy need not be of primary importance to the institutions that manipulate kin recognition among members. For example, military institutions are unlikely to be overly concerned with altruistic suicide in battle; group cohesion and a willingness to risk (not give) lives in attacking the enemy are much more important objectives (Henderson 1985). Yet some of the processes through which these behaviors are reinforced may also encourage terminal altruism. Such is the case as well with vows of lifelong non-reproduction. Institutionally it is likely that the avoidance of marriage (and therefore heirs) is much more important than sexual abstinence (which may explain why the Christian Church has tolerated concubines and illegitimate children at different periods in its history). Certainly general altruism, in the form of labor and commitment, is a prime institutional objective. Yet again, the means through which these behaviors are engendered can reinforce the reproductive sacrifice inherent in sexual abstinence.

Finally, even if manipulation plays a role in reinforcing certain behaviors, humans may still frequently act in ways to benefit others for purely altruistic reasons. The model of kinship manipulation advanced here only suggests that cultural practices which tap into an evolved psychology can reinforce particular behaviors, even those with significant costs. Individuals do often choose to live a life of permanent sexual abstinence, serving gods, leaders, and communities. They make this choice for many reasons, including a genuine desire to help others. It is doubtful that kinship deceit can fool any individual into adopting behaviors in which he or she does not wish to engage. Yet the continuing desire to remain celibate may frequently be reinforced through institutional socialization based on the successful manipulation of kinship recognition cues.

Notes

1. Celibacy has historically referred to sexual or marital abstinence or both (de Valk 1990). In this chapter the term is synonymous with lifelong sexual abstinence.

2. An additional possibility is that a generalized tendency to be altruistic can evolve through group selection. Because vows of celibacy often occur in contexts which appear to violate several conditions necessary for group selection to operate (Peres and Hopp 1990: 123), it will be dismissed as a potential explanation (but see Caporael 1989; and Wilson and Sober 1994).

3. Additionally, direct genetic recognition without learning is theoretically possible but unlikely, particularly for humans (Wilson 1987).

References Cited

Ainsworth, Mary D. S. 1977. Attachment Theory and Its Utility in Cross-Cultural Research. In *Culture and Infancy,* ed. P. H. Leiderman, S. R. Tulkin, and A. Rosenfeld, 49–68. New York: Academic.

Alexander, Richard D. 1979. *Darwinism and Human Affairs.* Seattle: University of Washington Press.

Alexander, Richard D. 1987. *The Biology of Moral Systems.* Hawthorne, N.Y.: Aldine de Gruyter.

Alexander, Richard D. 1990. Epigenetic Rules and Darwinian Algorithms. *Ethology and Sociobiology* 11: 241–303.

Anderson, Myrdene. 1986. Cultural Concatenation of Deceit and Secrecy. In *Deception: Perspectives on Human and Nonhuman Deceit,* ed. R. W. Mitchell and N. S. Thompson, 323–348. Albany: State University of New York Press.

Andreoni, James. 1990. Impure Altruism and Donations to Public Goods: A Theory of Warm Glow-Giving. *Economic Journal* 100: 464–477.

Archer, John. 1991. Human Sociobiology: Basic Concepts and Limitations. *Journal of Social Issues* 47(3): 11–26.

Balch, Stephen H. 1985. The Neutered Civil Servant: Eunuchs, Celibates, Abductees and the Maintenance of Organizational Loyalty. *Journal of Social and Biological Structures* 8: 313–328.

Bandura, Albert. 1980. The Social Learning Theory of Aggression. In *The War System: An Interdisciplinary Approach,* ed. R. A. Falk and S. S. Kim, 141–156. Boulder: Westview.

Barkow, Jerome H., Leda Cosmides, and John Tooby. 1992. *The Adapted Mind: Evolutionary Psychology and the Generation of Culture.* New York: Oxford University Press.

Batson, C. Daniel. 1990. How Social an Animal? The Human Capacity for Caring. *American Psychologist* 45(3): 336–346.

Benko, Stephen. 1971. The History of the Early Roman Empire. In *The Catacombs and the Colosseum,* ed. S. Benko and J. J. O'Rourke, 37–80. Valley Forge: Judson.

Benko, Stephen. 1984. *Pagan Rome and the Early Christians.* Bloomington: Indiana University Press.

Bernstein, Irwin S. 1991. The Correlation between Kinship and Behavior in Non-Human Primates. In *Kin Recognition,* ed. P. G. Hepper, 6–29. Cambridge: Cambridge University Press.

Birge, John K. 1937. *The Bektashi Order of Dervishes.* Luzac's Oriental Religions Series, vol. 7. London: Luzac.

Boyd, Robert, and Peter J. Richerson. 1985. *Culture and the Evolutionary Process.* Chicago: University of Chicago Press.

Brooke, Christopher. 1974. *The Monastic World: 1000–1300.* New York: Random House.

Brown, Donald. 1991. *Human Universals.* Philadelphia: Temple University Press.

Bunnag, Jane. 1973. *Buddhist Monk, Buddhist Layman: A Study of Urban Monastic Organization in Central Thailand.* Cambridge: Cambridge University Press.

Campbell, Donald T. 1983. The Two Distinct Routes beyond Kin Selection to Ultrasociality: Implications for the Humanities and Social Sciences. In *The Nature of Prosocial Development,* ed. D. L. Bridgeman, 11–41. New York: Academic.

Caporael, Linnda. 1989. Selfishness Examined: Cooperation in the Absence of Egoistic Incentives. *Behavioral and Brain Sciences* 12(4): 683–740.

Cela-Conde, C. J. 1990. On the Phylogeny of Human Morality (Ten Years Later). *Human Evolution* 5(2): 139–151.

Chagnon, Napoleon. 1981. Terminological Kinship, Genealogical Relatedness and Village Fissioning among the Yanomamo Indians. In *Natural Selection and Social Behavior,* ed. R. D. Alexander and D. W. Tinkle, 490–508. New York: Chiron.

Chagnon, Napoleon. 1988. Male Yanomamo Manipulations of Kinship Classifications of Female Kin for Reproductive Advantage. In *Human Reproductive Be-*

havior: A Darwinian Perspective, ed. L. Betzig, M. Borgerhoff Mulder, and P. Turke, 23–48. Cambridge: Cambridge University Press.

Chesneaux, Jean. 1971. *Secret Societies in China.* Ann Arbor: University of Michigan Press.

Cholij, Roman. 1989. *Clerical Celibacy in East and West.* Hereford: Fowler Wright.

Cole, Michael, and Sheila R. Cole. 1989. *The Development of Children.* New York: Scientific American Books.

Conner, Richard C. 1995. Altruism among Non-Relatives: Alternatives to the "Prisoner's Dilemma." *Trends in Ecology and Evolution* 10(2): 84–86.

Cronk, Lee. 1995. Is There a Role for Culture in Human Behavioral Ecology? *Ethology and Sociobiology* 16: 181–205.

Cunningham, Michael R. 1985–1986. Levites and Brother's Keepers: A Sociobiological Perspective on Prosocial Behavior. *Humboldt Journal of Social Relations* 13: 35–67.

Daly, Martin, Catherine Salmon, and Margo Wilson. 1997. Kinship: The Conceptual Hole in Psychological Studies of Social Cognition and Close Relationships. In *Evolutionary Social Psychology,* ed. J. A. Simpson and D. T. Kenrick, 265–296. Mahwah, N.J.: Erlbaum.

Dawkins, Richard. 1995. *River out of Eden.* New York: HarperCollins.

de Valk, Alphonse. 1990. *Priestly Celibacy in History.* Pamphlet #27. Toronto: Life Ethics Centre.

Dickinson, James C. 1961. *Monastic Life in Medieval England.* New York: Barnes and Noble.

Dontas, Cleo, Olga Maratos, Maria Fafoutis, and Anigone Karangelis. 1985. Early Social Development in Institutionally Reared Greek Infants: Attachment and Peer Interaction. *Monographs of the Society for Research in Child Development* 50(1–2): 136–146 (issue entitled *Growing Points of Attachment Theory and Research,* ed. I. Bretherton and E. Waters).

Draper, Patricia, and Henry Harpending. 1988. A Sociobiological Perspective on the Development of Human Reproductive Strategies. In *Sociobiological Perspectives on Human Development,* ed. K. B. MacDonald, 340–372. New York: Springer-Verlag.

Driver, G. R., and John C. Miles. 1952. *The Babylonian Laws.* Vols. 1 and 2. Oxford: Clarendon.

Durham, William H. 1991. *Coevolution: Genes, Culture, and Human Diversity.* Stanford: Stanford University Press.

Emlen, Stephen T. 1984. Cooperative Breeding in Birds and Mammals. In *Behavioural Ecology: An Evolutionary Approach,* ed. J. R. Krebs and N. B. Davies, 305–339. Sunderland, Mass.: Sinauer.

Essock-Vitale, Susan M., and Michael T. McGuire. 1980. Predictions Derived from the Theories of Kin Selection and Reciprocation Assessed by Anthropological Data. *Ethology and Sociobiology* 1: 233–243.

Essock-Vitale, Susan M., and Michael T. McGuire. 1985. Women's Lives Reviewed from an Evolutionary Perspective, part 2: Patterns of Helping. *Ethology and Sociobiology* 6: 155–173.

Evans, Joan. 1968. *Monastic Life at Cluny.* Hamden, Conn.: Archon.

Fialkowksi, K. R. 1990. An Evolutionary Mechanism for the Origin of Moral Norms: Towards the Meta-Trait of Culture. *Human Evolution* 5(2): 153–166.

Flohr, H. 1987. Biological Bases of Social Prejudices. In *The Sociobiology of Ethnocentrism,* ed. V. Reynolds, V. Falger, and I. Vine, 190–207. London: Croom Helm.

Hamilton, W. D. 1964. The Genetical Evolution of Social Behavior. Parts 1 and 2. *Journal of Theoretical Biology* 7(1): 1–52.

Heckethorn, Charles W. 1965. *The Secret Societies of All Ages and Countries.* Hyde Park, N.Y.: University Books.

Heider, Karl G. 1976. Dani Children's Development of Competency in Social Structural Concepts. *Ethnology* 15(1): 47–62.

Henderson, Wm. D. 1985. *Cohesion: The Human Element in Combat.* Washington, D.C.: National Defense University Press.

Hepper, Peter G. 1991. Recognizing Kin: Ontogeny and Classification. In *Kin Recognition,* ed. P. G. Hepper, 259–288. Cambridge: Cambridge University Press.

Hillery, George A., Jr. 1992. *The Monastery: A Study in Freedom, Love, and Community.* Westport, Conn.: Praeger.

Hoffman, Martin L. 1981. Is Altruism Part of Human Nature? *Journal of Personality and Social Psychology* 40: 121–147.

Hunt, Noreen. 1971. Cluniac Monasticism. In *Cluniac Monasticism in the Central Middle Ages,* ed. Noreen Hunt, 1–10. Hamden, Conn.: Archon.

Hurford, James R. 1991. The Evolution of the Critical Period for Language Acquisition. *Cognition* 40: 159–201.

Ike, Ben W. 1987. Man's Limited Sympathy as a Consequence of His Evolution in Small Kin Groups. In *The Sociobiology of Ethnocentrism,* ed. V. Reynolds, V. Falger, and I. Vine, 216–234. London: Croom Helm.

Johnson, Gary R. 1986. Kin Selection, Socialization, and Patriotism: An Integrating Theory. *Politics and the Life Sciences* 4: 127–154.

Johnson, Gary R. 1989. The Role of Kin Recognition Mechanisms in Patriotic Socialization: Further Reflections. *Politics and the Life Sciences* 8: 62–69.

Johnson, Gary R., Susan H. Ratwik, and Timothy J. Sawyer. 1987. The Evocative Significance of Kin Terms in Patriotic Speech. In *The Sociobiology of Ethnocentrism,* ed. V. Reynolds, V. Falger, and I. Vine, 157–174. London: Croom Helm.

Keesing, Roger M. 1975. *Kin Groups and Social Structure.* New York: Holt, Rinehart and Winston.

Kiernan, Kathleen E. 1988. Who Remains Celibate? *Journal of Biosocial Science* 20: 253–263.

Kitch, Sally L. 1989. *Chaste Liberation: Celibacy and Female Cultural Status.* Urbana: Univeristy of Illinois Press.

Knowles, Dom D. 1963. *The Monastic Order in England.* 2d ed. Cambridge: Cambridge University Press.

Lea, H. C. 1932. *History of Sacerdotal Celibacy in the Christian Church.* London: Watts.

Logan, Michael H., and Hector Qirko. 1996. An Evolutionary Perspective on Maladaptive Traits and Cultural Conformity. *American Journal of Human Biology* 8(4): 615–629.

MacDonald, Kevin. 1984. An Ethological-Social Learning Theory of the Development of Altruism: Implications for Human Sociobiology. *Ethology and Sociobiology* 5: 97–109.

MacDonald, Kevin. 1988. *Social and Personality Development: An Evolutionary Synthesis.* New York: Plenum.

McGuire, Michael T., Fawzy I. Fawzy, and James E. Spar. 1994. Altruism and Mental Disorders. *Ethology and Sociobiology* 15: 299–321.

Messenger, John C. 1971. Sex and Repression in an Irish Folk Community. In *Human Sexual Behavior,* ed. D. S. Marshall and R. C. Suggs, 3–37. New York: Basic Books.

Metraux, Alfred. 1969. *The History of the Incas.* New York: Pantheon.

Mitchell, Robert W., and Nicholas Thompson. 1986. *Deception: Perspectives on Human and Nonhuman Deceit.* Albany: State Univeristy of New York Press.

Moore, John H. 1990. The Reproductive Success of Cheyenne War Chiefs: A Contrary Case to Chagnon's Yanomamo. *Current Anthropology* 31: 322–330.

Murdock, George P., and Douglas R. White. 1969. Standard Cross-Cultural Sample. *Ethnology* 8(4): 329–369.

Murie, James R. 1916. Pawnee Indian Societies. *Anthropological Papers of the American Museum of Natural History* 11: 545–644.

Napier, Michael. 1989. Preface. In *Clerical Celibacy in East and West,* by Roman Cholij, 13–15. Hereford: Fowler Wright.

Ozment, Steven. 1972. Marriage and the Ministry in the Protestant Churches. In *Celibacy in the Church,* ed. W. Bassett and P. Huizing, 39–56. New York: Herder and Herder.

Peres, Y., and M. Hopp. 1990. Loyalty and Aggression in Human Groups. In *Sociobiology and Conflict: Evolutionary Perspectives on Competition, Cooperation, Violence and Warfare,* ed. J. van der Dennen and V. Falger, 123–130. London: Chapman and Hall.

Pfanner, David E. 1966. The Buddhist Monk in Rural Burmese Society. In *Anthropological Studies in Theravada Buddhism,* 77–96. Cultural Report Series No. 13. New Haven: Yale University Southeast Asia Studies.

Piliavin, Jane A., and Hong-Wen Charng. 1990. Altruism: A Review of Recent Theory and Research. *Annual Reviews in Sociology* 16: 27–65.

Pinker, Steven. 1994. *The Language Instinct.* New York: HarperPerennial.

Piontelli, Alessandra. 1995. Kin Recognition and Early Precursors of Attachment as Seen in the Analysis of a Young Psychotic Adopted Boy. *Journal of Child Psychotherapy* 21(1): 5–21.

Plutarch. 1952. *The Lives of the Noble Grecians and Romans —the Dryden Translation.* Great Books of the Western World, vol. 14. Chicago: Encyclopedia Britannica.

Porter, Richard H. 1991. Mutual Mother-Infant Recognition in Humans. In *Kin*

Recognition, ed. P. G. Hepper, 413–432. Cambridge: Cambridge University Press.

Qirko, Hector. 1998. Induced Altruism in the Maintenance of Institutionalized Celibacy. Ph.D. dissertation, University of Tennessee.

Rappoport, Leon, and George Kren. 1993. Amoral Rescuers: The Ambiguities of Altruism. *Creative Research Journal* 6(1–2): 129–136.

Reynolds, Vernon. 1986. Religious Rules and Reproductive Strategies. In *Essays in Human Sociobiology,* ed. J. Wind and V. Reynolds, 105–117. Vol. 26 of V.U.B. Study Series. Brussels: V.U.B.

Rosetti, Stephen J. 1994. Statistical Reflections on Priestly Celibacy. *America* 170(20): 22–24.

Sagi, Abraham, M. E. Lamb, K. S. Lewkowicz, R. Shoham, R. Dvir, and D. Estes. 1985. Security of Infant-Mother, -Father, and -Metaplet Attachments among Kibbutz-Reared Israeli Children. *Monographs of the Society for Research in Child Development* 50 (1–2): 257–275 (issue entitled *Growing Points of Attachment Theory and Research,* ed. I. Bretherton and E. Waters).

Sahagun, Fray Bernardino de. 1932. *A History of Ancient Mexico.* Nashville: Fisk University Press.

Sahlins, Marshall. 1976. *The Use and Abuse of Biology.* Ann Arbor: University of Michigan Press.

Salter, Frank K. 1995. *Emotions in Command: A Naturalistic Study of Institutional Dominance.* Oxford: Oxford University Press.

Scheidel, Walter. 1996. Brother-Sister and Parent-Child Marriage outside Royal Families in Ancient Egypt and Iran: A Challenge to the Sociobiological View of Incest Avoidance? *Ethology and Sociobiology* 17: 319–340.

Schroeder, David A., Louis A. Penner, John F. Dovidio, and Jane A. Piliavin. 1995. *The Psychology of Helping and Altruism: Problems and Puzzles.* New York: McGraw-Hill.

Sesardic, Neven. 1995. Recent Work on Human Altruism and Evolution. *Ethics* 106: 128–157.

Sherman, Paul W., and Warren G. Holmes. 1985. Kin Recognition: Issues and Evidence. In *Experimental Behavioral Ecology and Sociobiology,* ed. B. Holldobler and M. Lindauer, 437–460. New York: Gustav Fischer Verlag.

Simon, Herbert A. 1990. A Mechanism for Social Selection and Successful Altruism. *Science* 250: 1665–1668.

Skertchly, J. A. 1974. *Dahomey as It Is.* London: Chapman and Hall.

Soustelle, Jacques. 1962. *The Daily Life of the Aztecs.* New York: Macmillan.

Stickler, Alfons. 1972. Historical Note on the Celibacy of Clerics in Sacred Orders. *Osservatore Romano* (March 19): 9–10.

Talmon, Yohina. 1964. Mate Selection in Collective Settlements. *American Sociological Review* 29: 491–508.

Tooby, John, and Leda Cosmides. 1992. The Psychological Foundations of Culture. In *The Adapted Mind: Evolutionary Psychology and the Generation of Culture,* ed. J. H. Barkow, L. Cosmides, and J. Tooby, 19–136. New York: Oxford University Press.

Trivers, Robert. 1985. *Social Evolution.* Menlo Park, Calif.: Benjamin/Cummings.

Turner, Terence S. 1987. Cosmetics: The Language of Bodily Adornment. In *Conformity and Conflict,* ed. J. P. Spradley and D. W. McCurdy, 93–103. 6th ed. Boston: Little, Brown. Original publication, 1969.

van den Berghe, Pierre L. 1981. *The Ethnic Phenomenon.* New York: Elsevier.

van der Veer, Peter. 1987. Taming the Ascetic: Devotionalism in a Hindu Monastic Order. *Man,* n.s., 22: 680–695.

Vega, Garcilaso de la. [1871] 1961. *Commentarios reales.* New York: Orion.

Wei-hsun Fu, Charles, and Sandra A. Wawrytko. 1994. *Buddhist Behavioral Codes and the Modern World.* Westport, Conn.: Greenwood.

Wells, P. A. 1987. Kin Recognition in Humans. In *Kin Recognition in Animals,* ed. D. J. C. Fletcher and C. D. Michener, 395–415. New York: John Wiley.

Williams, B. J. 1981. A Critical Review of Models in Sociobiology. *Annual Reviews in Anthropology* 10: 163–192.

Wilson, David S., and Elliott Sober. 1994. Reintroducing Group Selection to the Human Behavioral Sciences. *Behavioral and Brain Sciences* 17: 585–654.

Wilson, Edward O. 1975. *Sociobiology.* Cambridge, Mass.: Belknap.

Wilson, Edward O. 1987. Kin Recognition: An Introductory Synopsis. In *Kin Recognition in Animals,* ed. D. J. C. Fletcher and C. D. Michener, 7–18. New York: John Wiley.

Wolf, Arthur. 1995. *Sexual Attraction and Childhood Association.* Stanford: Stanford University Press.

Wright, Robert. 1994. *The Moral Animal: Evolutionary Psychology and Everyday Life.* New York: Pantheon.

Wyatt, Gail E., Stephanie D. Peters, and Donald Guthrie. 1988. Kinsey Revisited, part 1: Comparisons of the Sexual Socialization and Sexual Behavior of White Women over 33 Years. *Archives of Sexual Behavior* 17(3): 201–239.

Wynne, Edward A. 1988. *Traditional Catholic Religious Orders: Living in Community.* New Brunswick: Transaction Books.

Alice Schlegel

The Chaste Adolescent

Paintings of the late Middle Ages and the early Renaissance, I have often observed, depict adolescent girls, like adult celibate saints, as slight, underdeveloped, and rather pale — creatures far removed from the lusts of the flesh. Boys are portrayed somewhat similarly, even though their models must have spent years in hard physical training for the battles that they would be fighting in early manhood. The image of the virginal youth was shattered even before Caravaggio's sensual streetboys appeared on canvas, but it was almost three centuries before the sexuality of the adolescent girl was captured by such artists as Edvard Munch and Suzanne Valadon.

Against this European backdrop of idealized adolescent chastity, Margaret Mead's (1928) description of lusty Samoan adolescents stood in sharp relief. Elwin's (1947) account of the goings-on in the adolescent houses of the Muria, a tribal group in the central highlands of India, would have attracted even more attention had it been better publicized. It became clear that tolerance of adolescent sexuality was not just one more vice of backward or depraved sectors of European society but, rather, was a norm in some places.

Just how many societies did not impose celibacy on adolescents emerged in a cross-cultural study that included questions about the value put on virginity (Schlegel and Barry 1991). This study used the Standard

Cross-Cultural Sample (Murdock and White 1969), a representative sample of 186 preindustrial societies from every continent.[1] Coders coded the ethnographies of these societies for questions regarding adolescent socialization. Data analysis included statistical tests of associations between and among the coded variables. Somewhat to our surprise, the majority of these societies showed little concern in regard to virginity. The celibacy of their adolescent children was simply not a cultural issue.

If a majority of cultures, at least those outside the sphere of influence of the old high cultures of Eurasia, were unconcerned about adolescent chastity, then explaining this concern where it existed became the problem. I took up this challenge in a study (Schlegel 1991) using data from Schlegel and Barry's study (1991) and other sources, which I will draw on for this discussion. Here, I want to explore the relations that adolescents have with their families and with one another when celibacy is or is not demanded of them.

Adolescence, as I define it, is a social stage that intervenes between childhood and adulthood. During this phase, the young person characteristically behaves and is treated somewhat differently from either a child or an adult. This stage is found in all the traditional societies of the Standard Cross-Cultural Sample. In most of these places, children enter social adolescence somewhere around puberty, sometimes through an adolescent initiation ceremony (see Schlegel and Barry 1980). The age at which adolescence ends is variable. Commonly, adolescence ends and social adulthood begins with marriage, frequently when girls are 16 or 17 and when boys are a few years older.[2]

A value on virginity presupposes adolescent celibacy, at least for girls. Although most cultures pay little attention to the virginity of boys, adolescent boys are usually celibate by default when girls are, since the sexual partner of an adolescent is almost always another adolescent. Even when prostitutes are available, adolescent boys rarely have the means to visit them. In some socially stratified societies, boys of a higher social class may seek sexual partners from a lower class, but this is successful only when attitudes toward premarital sexuality differ by class or when lower-class girls have more freedom of movement and adults are more tolerant of "slip-ups."

One might argue that celibacy that is imposed on adolescents is not true celibacy. This is drawing too great a distinction between what is desired but denied and what is freely chosen. Adolescent girls who remain chaste have been socialized to do so. There is no evidence that they find their celibacy particularly onerous. Adults who freely choose celibacy may also have been socialized to do so; at least, they are influenced by cultures that value a celibate life as higher and purer than a sexually active one. And one might question just how voluntary the celibacy of many celibates has been throughout history, when families made decisions about which child was to marry and which was to enter a monastery or a nunnery or remain at home as an unmarried helper.

Where Adolescent Virginity Is Valued

When I examined the value on virginity, I took the point of view of the girl's family, because it is her family that bears the burden of surveillance and that is dishonored if she should slip. I asked, "Why it should matter to them?"

One motive is suggested by the covariation of the value on virginity with marriage transactions (p < .0001). *Marriage transactions* involve goods and services given at marriage by the bride's side, the groom's side, or both sides (Schlegel and Eloul 1988). Most of the societies in which there is no marriage transaction do not value virginity; that is, the large majority of these societies are permissive of adolescent heterosexuality. Contrary to common belief, societies in which the groom or his family provides goods and services are not likely to value virginity either — so much for the assumption that bridewealth buys a virgin bride. This assumption, I should add, has arisen because bridewealth as the form of marriage transaction has been incorrectly assigned to a large number of societies, particularly Islamic ones, which value virginity. When those transactions were given a closer look (Schlegel and Eloul 1987), it turned out that many of them actually give indirect dowry, which does correlate with the expectation that brides will be virginal.

This confusion over marriage transaction form bespeaks a central need: to understand the value on virginity, one must be able to discriminate between the five types of transaction that exist (for more detailed descriptions than I can provide here, see Schlegel 1997; and Schlegel and Eloul 1988). *Bridewealth* refers to goods that go from the family of the groom to the family of the bride, where they or similar goods are passed on to another family to acquire a wife for one of the men of the bride's family. This form is common where animals are raised for subsistence but not for market. *Brideservice* is the labor the groom performs for a period of time for the bride's family, either before or after the wedding. *Gift exchange* involves the exchange of more or less equivalent goods between the two families. This does not benefit either side economically, for what is given is not only of the same value but also of the same type as what is received. The purpose, rather, is to ensure that both sides are of equal wealth or have access to equal sources of goods. *Dowry* is the goods given by the family of the bride to take into her conjugal home. She may have control

over all or part of these goods, or she may lose control to her husband or
to his relatives in an extended-family household. *Indirect dowry* refers
also to goods that accompany the bride, but they originate with the
groom's family. That is, the groom's family gives goods — often jewelry or
other valuables — either to the bride or to her family, who in turn pass on
all or part of them to her. The latter custom is widespread in North Africa
and the Middle East. Historically, it has arisen by adding dowry to existing
bridewealth or bridewealth to existing dowry. This seems to have been
what happened in much of the Islamic world, for the Koran prescribes
that the groom or his family gives some goods, the *mahr,* to the bride. For
example, in Egypt the pre-Islamic form of dowry, at least for those who
owned property, seems to have been turned into indirect dowry through a
small payment of bridewealth when that nation converted to Islam.

Of the societies in the Standard Cross-Cultural Sample that give
bridewealth or perform brideservice, almost twice as many are sexually
permissive as restrictive. Where goods are given by the bride's family,
however — gift exchange, dowry, and indirect dowry — these figures are
reversed. The correlations are not perfect, but the reasons for the exceptions are usually clarified by an analysis of the conditions surrounding
marriage in those cases. Paradoxically, families pay to *give* a virgin bride
rather than to *receive* one.

Although societies that prescribe celibacy for adolescent girls often explain and justify the value on virginity by the value on purity, I believe that
this celibacy has a more practical basis. Maintaining a girl's "purity" conveniently prevents her from getting pregnant. Premarital pregnancy does
not seem to be such an issue when families do not give goods along with
their daughters. It is not uncommon in Africa, for example, for a child
born out of wedlock to remain with the mother's parents when the mother
joins her husband's household after he has given bridewealth for her.
Explaining a value on virginity by a value on purity simply raises the question of why purity is valued in some places but not others.

The value on virginity originated and is maintained, in my view, as a
concern for keeping daughters from being seduced and impregnated by
young men who would not be welcome as sons-in-law. It is of no particular
social or economic advantage to a boy to seduce a girl who must be married with bridewealth; he has nothing to gain by so doing, since he would
have to pay in any event if he wants her for his wife. It is a different story
when property accompanies the girl into her marriage.[3] The seduction of
a dowered girl or an heiress can substantially improve the position of a
young man or at least his children. The trick is not only to seduce her but
also to get her parents to accept a marriage.

The irony here is that a value on virginity, which puts parental control over a daughter's sexuality into the moral realm, also devalues girls who have lost their virginity. Thus, the boy who seduces a girl has at least some chance of being tolerated as the husband of the "spoiled" girl, the best that can be gotten in these circumstances. It is in such societies that seduction of virgins becomes a test of one's social potency, the challenge being to overcome the hurdles of surveillance and the girl's own fear and shame. At the same time, the girl who has been seduced has given evidence of her and her family's fallibility, particularly in cultures that see loss of purity as a sign of moral weakness.

In societies that value virginity, sexuality is one more area of adolescents' lives that is regulated by others. The imposition of celibacy on their adolescent members is one way the family ensures that daughters are not inappropriately married. If a boy or man cannot impregnate a girl, he cannot make a paternity claim on her child and a marriage claim on her. The girl, and whatever tangible or intangible goods accompany her into the marriage, can be used strategically to a family's best interest, but only when there is no claim on her through a claim on her child. The following ethnographic sketch shows how adolescents manage their sexuality in one such highly restrictive society. Davis and Davis relate the experiences of adolescents in Zawiya, a Moroccan town, in the 1980s (Davis 1995; Davis and Davis 1989).

Adolescent Sexuality in a Highly Restrictive Society

Girls in Zawiya marry later today than in past generations, when 16 was about average. Now, when marriage is often delayed until age 20 or 21, Moroccan girls face the same dilemma as European and U.S. girls faced in earlier times: they must attract the interest of boys while preserving their virginity and, moreover, their good reputations as girls *believed* to have preserved their virginity. Their task is made more difficult than it was for U.S. or European girls by the degree of scrutiny they face, for almost any public contact with a boy starts the gossip mills grinding. Yet, if a girl avoids all contact with boys, perhaps no one will find her interesting enough to ask his parents to arrange a match. A girl's fear of losing her reputation is well founded, for it may be difficult to find a husband willing to take a girl whose reputation is questionable. At the same time, the very body who would not marry a spoiled girl will eagerly seek to persuade an attractive girl to become his lover.

Girls and boys have contact in school and in passing on the street or at public events. When girls reach about age 16, boys begin to exhibit more than a casual interest in them, making remarks when they pass and trying to attract their attention. Girls can smile or make a pert reply without loss of reputation. If two young people actually want to get together, they arrange somehow, using a friend or younger sibling as a go-between, to meet at a dark street corner. After several such furtive encounters, the boy may convince the girl to embrace or even kiss. Very few girls are prepared to go beyond this.

The next step, if it is taken at all, is to meet in some private place like a field outside the town or in a house when no one is at home. This meeting is for the purpose of serious sexual activity. At this time, the couple may engage in such virginity-preserving acts as mutual masturbation or interfemoral or anal intercourse. The ideal form, for the boy, is vaginal intercourse. After they have established a sexual relationship, the boy may ask his parents to arrange a marriage with the girl. On the other hand, he may abandon her. As Davis and Davis relate: "Some of the older males we knew mourned the loss of relationships with girls they claimed to have loved but could not consider marrying because of the dishonor brought on the girl — by the male's own seduction of her. The male simply assumes that since the girl gave in to him she will (and perhaps has) to others" (1989: 120). In other words, a girl's success or failure in abstaining from sex is considered a prediction of what she would do generally. The Davises were unable to get accurate assessments of the number of girls or women who had had sexual encounters or what these encounters entailed. Probably most girls in the town had at least kissed a boy, but the number engaging in genital contact of any kind was very small.

In such a setting, there is very little trust between the sexes. It is taken for granted that a boy will not seek a girl's company unless he wants to have sex with her. In most cases this means that his intentions are, from a local viewpoint, dishonorable. There is no code of conduct that tells boys to restrain themselves, or to protect the reputation of the girls they seduce, or that to boast about conquests is loutish. In this Moroccan town, the male–female relationship before marriage seems not to exist outside of sexual contact of some kind. The romantic fiction consumed by girls who view French or Egyptian television programs has no counterpart in their daily lives.

Not all societies that value virginity are equally restrictive. Although abstention from vaginal intercourse may be expected, there can be degrees of permissible sexual contact. Morocco is a highly restrictive culture. Other cultures may be more tolerant, leaning toward permissiveness. One such is portrayed in the following ethnographic sketch, drawn from my own experience and my discussion with age-peers.

Adolescent Sexuality in a Mildly Restrictive Society

America of the 1950s was closer to the sexual revolution of the late 1960s than many realize. At least, this was the case for adolescents growing up in middle-class midwestern suburbs. The college-bound teenagers of this portrait may differ in certain respects from adolescents of some other regions or social classes, but the situation depicted here was widespread at that time, as reported to me by friends from different parts of the United States.

Although mothers and grandmothers warned girls about the loss of honor through the loss of virginity and about the resulting difficulty in finding a husband, these warnings fell mainly on deaf ears as girls reviewed what they knew or fantasized about the lives of the movie stars they idolized. If men were only too eager to marry glamorous divorced women, what was all the fuss about loss of virginity? The real danger was pregnancy in those days when abortions were illegal and difficult to obtain. So for high-school girls, sexual intercourse was something to be put off until marriage or engagement, when one was really in love. It was believed that some of the "fast" girls were already having intercourse with their boyfriends, but such girls were not admired by their peers of either sex.

Abstention from intercourse did not mean abstention from all sexual contact. Without parents or older relatives to guide them, adolescents learned the rules from one another: no kissing until about the third date, light petting (caressing above the waist) sometime after that, and heavy petting (caressing below the waist) only when "going steady," that is, in an exclusive dating relationship. It was generally assumed that boys had trouble controlling themselves, and so it was up to the girls to stop them before they "went too far," whatever that meant in the circumstance. The degree of permitted activity increased in proportion to the exclusivity of the relationship. Adolescents who wanted more sexual contact had to be temporarily monogamous, and those who wanted to date many people had to be satisfied with less.

This stimulation without release was handled differently by boys and girls. If girls masturbated, they did not discuss it among themselves. There was something rather shameful about self-stimulation. Girls who, when younger, had "played doctor" with one another as an opportunity to explore their own and their playmates' bodies, became shy at puberty and often did not like to undress in front of one another. Part of this was modesty; part was the dissatisfaction with her own body that almost every teenage girl felt.

Boys' experience was somewhat different. A man who grew up in this setting told me that when he and his early-adolescent friends were in Boy Scout camp, these 12–14-year-olds talked and joked about masturbation and sometimes masturbated in each other's company. By high school, however, masturbation became a private activity.

High-school boys sought contact with girls, and there was a lot of interest in who did what with whom. Boasting about conquests, however, was bad form. It took a certain art to let one's fellows know or imagine that one succeeded in getting a kiss or an embrace or a feel of a breast without saying so in so many words. Boys who were clearly unsuccessful or were caught out in lies were teased mercilessly.

Heavy petting was approved for couples who were going steady, and in such cases there was very little talk about it. A girl who permitted this liberty to boys to whom she was not monogamously attached, however, was labeled a tramp and was considered fair game for anyone.

By and large, adolescents remained technically celibate (i.e., no penetration). Boys speculated about the allegedly loose girls in a nearby suburb, a working-class community of eastern European ethnicity. Girls there were reputedly willing to "go all the way," some of them engaging in anal intercourse (which the boys in question did not understand very well) in order to preserve their virginity. Since no one had any first-hand knowledge of such girls, their reputation seems to have been part of this town's adolescent mythology.

A mildly restrictive society like suburban America in the 1950s places much of the burden of controlling sexuality on the adolescent himself and, more often, herself. U.S. high-school students, particularly girls, were expected to be celibate in the sense of refraining from sexual intercourse. The management of one's reputation, however, was more important than the actual preservation of virginity.

The girls in Zawiya are in some ways similar to European and U.S. middle-class girls of the late nineteenth and early twentieth centuries. These girls interacted with boys in school and to a limited degree in public places, but they forestalled gossip that could ruin their reputations by avoiding any circumstances in which sexual advances of any kind could take place. Through the peer-group activities of their communities and neighborhoods, U.S. and European girls actually had much more direct contact with boys than Zawiya girls do, and young unmarried women had many more opportunities to meet young men. Nevertheless, the value on virginity was as strong in Europe and the United States as it has been in Morocco.

By the 1950s, the situation had drastically changed. The pin-ups of World War II accelerated the public celebration of female sexual attractiveness that was already apparent in the bathing-beauty contests of the

1930s. Middle-class adolescent life, as portrayed in the ethnographic sketch of suburban America, included a fair degree of sexual stimulation. It was not a big step to the sexual revolution of the late 1960s, which in many ways gave public acknowledgment to what had been increasingly happening in private.

This shift in the value on virginity can be placed in the historical context of changes in family relations. With massive alterations in economic structure and rapid geographic and social mobility, the long-term corporate character of the family virtually disappeared. There was no need to select a son-in-law to advance the family's economic or social well-being. Along with this, investment in daughters changed from dowry to education, and marriages were no longer accompanied by the formal transfer of goods. Adolescents' access to abortion and contraception, the latter of which had long been available to adult women, came in the wake of this social trend. Virginity became a personal issue rather than a public one. Thus, the variation that can still be seen across cultures can be traced over time in Western cultural development.

Effects of Adolescent Sexual Restrictiveness or Permissiveness

The imposition of celibacy on adolescents affects several aspects of their lives, particularly their relations with family members, who have primary control over the adolescent, but other aspects as well. As one might expect from the discussion of marriage transactions, parental control over marriage for both sexes is strongly associated with sexual restrictiveness (Schlegel and Barry 1991). While it is true that marriages are arranged in many permissive societies, it is also the case that adolescents in these places have considerable influence in the selection. They usually can veto an odious match or attempt to gain one more to their liking, even if they cannot demand the partner of their choice. Although Barry and I did not look specifically at elopement, my impression is that it is not uncommon, certainly not impossible, in many permissive societies. Barring unusual circumstances, elopement by mutual consent is much less likely in restrictive societies, where the girl is constantly watched by her family.

Girls, especially, are affected by imposed celibacy. In highly restrictive societies, girls are generally more subordinate to their mothers than they are in permissive ones (Schlegel and Barry 1991); mothers, after all, are responsible for what their daughters do. However, closely watched daughters are no less intimate with their mothers than less restricted daughters are, nor do they have more conflict with them. For boys, on the other hand, sexual restrictiveness does not seem to affect relations with parents at all. Restrictions on girls take possible heterosexual partners out of boys' reach, giving parents no particular reason to monitor the sexual behavior of their sons.

Relations with peers are also affected by sexual permissiveness or restrictiveness. Cross-cultural research, as well as the observations we make around us, tells us that attachment to a romantic or sexual partner of the opposite sex reduces the attachment to same-sex friends, because time and attention are diverted from friends and devoted to the partner. As stated elsewhere, "Lovers, not parents, are the enemies of the peer group" (Schlegel and Barry 1991: 124).

In my current research on German industrial apprentices, several of the boys remarked that they wish their girlfriends were not so demanding of their time; others regard the *Festefreundin* as a close friend and confidante and would rather be with her than anyone else. A 17-year-old American apprentice I interviewed in Wisconsin responded to my questions about girlfriends by saying, "We're attracted but we don't want to get involved with girls yet." His peer group ostracized one of its members for wanting to spend time with a girl.

There are some noteworthy exceptions to this conflict between attachment to peers and attachment to a romantic or sexual partner. Sexual permissiveness may be combined with strong same-sex peer groups, as in much of Oceania (e.g., the Trobriand Islands) and sub-Saharan Africa (e.g., the Masai). In these places, heterosexual play is a normal part of adolescent life, but firm emotional attachments are discouraged through the allowance or expectation of multiple partnerships. When girls and boys get together only for sexual relations, particularly when these are not monogamous, there is little chance of strong emotional bonding. The peer group retains its hold on the loyalty of its members.

Alternatives to Heterosexual Intercourse

Adolescents may engage in sexual acts of various types. When heterosexual relations are denied them, by custom or through lack of opportunity, young people with sexual interests turn to other forms of expression.

Perhaps the most common form is masturbation, although in the cross-cultural study (Schlegel and Barry 1991) we found almost no references to it, no doubt because masturbation is usually a private activity or is confined to groups of children or adolescents when no adult, including the ethnographer, is present. Nor was there much information on bestiality. However, we found more data on homosexual activity in adolescence than we had expected to find, given the reticence of our anthropological forebears to discuss the subject. The most comprehensive account of homosexuality in societies worldwide through time is Greenberg's *Construc-*

tion of Homosexuality (1988), and much information on adolescence can be gleaned from it and the sources he used. In our cross-cultural study, we found information on attitudes toward homosexual activity for 57 societies for boys, 47 for girls. This information can be supplemented by descriptions of cultures not in the sample.

Although we had expected to find that attitudes toward adolescent homosexual activity were associated with other cultural features we measured, as was permissiveness or restrictiveness toward heterosexual activity, that was not the case. Tolerance toward adolescent male homosexual activity was not related to strong male bonding, for example. We did find that if a culture is permissive or restrictive toward the homosexual acts of girls, it is likely to be the same toward those of boys. Likewise, attitudes toward homosexual activity among boys are similar to those pertaining to adult men, although these attitudes may be more tolerant toward adolescent than toward adult same-sex eroticism. Adolescent homosexual activity is widely viewed as a form of youthful play, which will be abandoned when the adolescents eventually marry and have free access to heterosexual intercourse.

There has been considerable discussion recently of societies that have institutionalized sexual relations between adolescent boys and some other age group of males. In some parts of Melanesia, these practices follow the belief that younger males need to ingest the semen of older males in order to grow properly. Among the Sambia (Herdt 1981), adolescent boys are fellated by younger boys, but fully adult men are not engaged in this activity. In other Melanesian cases, adolescent boys are the fellators of adult men.

More commonly, approved homosexual relations between adolescent boys and unmarried youths or men are found where marriage for men is delayed, unmarried girls are required to be celibate, and no category of sexually available women is readily at hand (e.g., female prostitutes, who may be present but beyond the means of boys and youths). These conditions have occurred together in a number of preindustrial states, including Ottoman Turkey, feudal Japan, the central African Azande Kingdom, and the ancient Greeks and Germanics (Dumézil 1967; Greenberg 1988). In all these states, unmarried warriors had sexual access to prepubescent or young adolescent boys. The encouragement of homosexual relations there, as an alternative to heterosexual ones, protected the interests of married men by deflecting sexual desire away from their wives and daughters.

Cross-generational homosexual activity, like cross-generational heterosexual activity, is rather rare worldwide. An adolescent's sexual partner is most likely to be another adolescent. The most common attitude in those societies that tolerate adolescent homosexual relations is that this is a substitute for heterosexual activity that is either prohibited or is not very accessible. Boys, and perhaps girls, may engage in sexual activity with members of the same sex until they are able to find partners of the opposite sex.

In Morocoo, according to Davis and Davis (1989: 111–113), homoerotic contacts among adolescent boys are quite common. They serve as an outlet, unaccompanied by romance or by the tensions that characterize romantic or sexual relations between the sexes. Boys are expected to drop these activities upon marriage, and Davis and Davis think that most do. Female homoerotic activity at any age is believed to be extremely rare, and some of the Davises' informants denied that it even occurred.

Celibacy and Control over Adolescents' Lives

Restrictiveness toward adolescent sexuality in the cross-cultural study is related to a double standard in adulthood; that is, where adolescents are celibate, married men, but not women, usually have freedom to engage in sexual encounters outside marriage. As stated elsewhere, "Restricting the sexual freedom of women, adolescent girls, and adolescent boys is part of a general pattern of control over subordinate persons" (Schlegel and Barry 1991: 109). Heterosexual freedom is a privilege accorded only to adult men.

The power dimension is also part of the homoerotic relationship between youths or adults men and adolescent boys (see Creed 1982). The dominance can be very mild, as where the older partner is expected to be a kind of mentor to the younger one. This was the ideal of the classical Greek pattern of homosexual activity, in which the unmarried youth was both sexual partner and mentor of his boy companion. (A similar mentor–protégé relationship characterizes the one society I know of, the Lesotho, in which there is institutionalized sexual friendship between adolescent girls and older young women, described in Gay 1986 as a "mummy–baby" relationship.) Most descriptions of institutionalized adult–adolescent male homosexual partnerships depict the older partner as dominant over the younger one, just as married men in these same societies dominate their wives and other females of the household. Such relationships serve to reinforce the general dominance of men over other categories of subordinate persons.

Although the major reason for enforcing adolescent celibacy is to prevent the pregnancy of unmarried daughters, it also reinforces the control of parents over their sons. When girls are restricted, boys have little opportunity to form serious romantic attachments, thus making it easier for parents to control their marriages. Sexual restrictiveness gives parents the power to make decisions for their children that may be more compatible with their own interests than with their children's. However, there are times when adolescents use celibacy to subvert parental control — when adolescents and youths reject marriage and thwart the plans of their parents, who had intended to use the marriage of their children for their own social or economic advantage (Schlegel 1995).

A rather large number of early Christian saints were young people who refused to obey their parents' command to marry. The virgin martyrs of the late Roman Empire were sometimes girls whose fathers killed them for their defiance. When they were not killed, they devoted their celibate lives to spiritual exercises, charity, or monastic life. These adolescent spiritual paragons tended to disappear among the later saints; after the Church became a political as well as a religious institution, it could not afford to antagonize powerful families by encouraging disobedience in their daughters. Nevertheless, the hagiography of the Middle Ages as late as the tenth to the twelfth century contains many accounts of young people, often youths, who entered the Church against the wishes of their families (Goodich 1989). By the later Middle Ages, entrance into religious celibacy for most adolescents was more likely to be with the consent, or at the insistence, of their parents, who used the celibate institutions of the Church as repositories for sons who would not inherit and daughters for whom a respectable dowry could not be provided. In the early years of the Church, however, insubordinate virgins could be publicized as exemplars of Christian chastity, encouraging others to flock to the banner of the Church and carry forward its mission.

Young Christians were not the only adolescents to reject parental marriage plans. In China, Kuan Yin, the goddess of mercy, is popularly believed to have been a princess who became a Buddhist nun over her parents' objections (Topley 1975). More recently, some female silk workers of nineteenth-century southern China led lives of defiant chastity (Topley 1975). These were girls and women who rebelled against social control by refusing to marry or, if forced to go through a wedding, by refusing to remain with their husbands. Instead, they went to work in silk factories, remitting most of their wages to their parents or their husbands' families. They lived in all-female celibate communes, with older women in authority over younger ones. Since the girls would have married in their mid- to late teens (typically at about 16), they made their decision to enter these communes during adolescence.

All societies face the problem of lusty sons and fertile daughters whose sexuality is not yet channeled into socially approved marriage. One way of handling this problem is to forbid adolescents to engage in sexual inter-course. While this prevents unwanted pregnancies, it puts the burden of surveillance on the families of girls. Where girls have free contact with boys, as in the U.S. middle-class culture of the 1950s, the responsibility for maintaining their virginity falls on the girls themselves, and they must be socialized to fear the consequences of an illegitimate pregnancy.

As we have seen, tolerance of adolescent sexual intercourse is rather widespread outside the complex societies of Eurasia and their derivative cultures. One reason for this may be that girls commonly marry young, about 16. There is a period of adolescent subfecundity, lasting about two years after menarche, during which time the likelihood of pregnancy is rather low. In the cross-cultural study (Schlegel and Barry 1991), we esti-mated that the typical age of menarche, except in places of extremely poor nutrition, is about 14. Thus, even if girls were allowed sexual free-dom during their social adolescence, during the couple of years from about menarche (or before) to marriage, most would not get pregnant. However, some of the societies in which girls marry young also impose celibacy on their adolescent daughters. This seems to be an extra precau-tion against pregnancy where a paternity claim would seriously interfere with the family's plans for the daughter's marriage. The imposition of celibacy is even more important where marriage for girls is delayed until the late teens or twenties, as it is in many dowry-giving societies (Schlegel and Eloul 1987).

Restraints on adolescent sexuality fall heaviest on daughters. When girls are *de jure* restricted, boys are *de facto* restricted. Keeping girls and boys socially separated, as in Zawiya, makes it easier for families to ar-range the marriages of children of both sexes, for no serious romantic attachments are allowed to form.

While the imposition of celibacy means that adolescents have no con-trol over this important aspect of life, celibacy can backfire on dominating parents. In cultures that value virginity, especially when virginity is a higher state, self-imposed long-term celibacy puts parents in a dilemma. They may be enraged at their children's disobedience. Virgin martyrs are a witness to the consequences this rage can have in rare cases, but defiant children who insist on celibacy by refusing marriage cannot be cast out or brutally treated without calling down severe social disapproval on the heads of the parents. Permanent celibacy was one of the few morally de-fensible measures that rebellious girls in traditional societies have been able to take to resist parental control legitimately, but it has worked only when adult celibacy is held in esteem. Christian and Buddhist girls have had this option; Muslim and Jewish girls have not (see Phillimore, this volume, on Hindu celibate women).

Chastity may seen to be an unwelcome state to many adolescents, and it certainly reduces their freedom. However, it is questionable that celibate adolescents are unhappier than those who have sexual freedom. The only measure of relations with family or peers in the cross-cultural study that showed any association with sexual restrictiveness was subordination of girls to their mothers, and even greater subordination did not appear to affect their intimacy. We had hypothesized that aggressiveness of boys might be associated with restrictiveness as a result of sexual frustration, but that did not prove to be the case; either sexual frustration is not a dominating theme in the lives of celibate adolescent boys, or boys seek other outlets like masturbation or homoerotic activity. Neither was there any association between general competitiveness and permissiveness, although one might expect boys to be more competitive when they are each other's rivals for girls' favors.

It is probably a myth of our day that sexual fulfillment is necessary for happiness, at least for adolescents. The most glowing descriptions of adolescent sexual freedom come from the pens of Mead (1928) and Elwin (1947), writing about Samoans and the Muria of the central highlands of India. In both cases, if one reads the actual accounts, one sees that the authors' rhapsodies must be taken with a grain of salt. There are indeed snakes in these adolescent paradises (see Schlegel 1995).

In all but a few of the most permissive societies, sex is frequently not available to adolescents. Girls do not usually initiate encounters or give themselves readily. They must be courted and presented with gifts and favors before acceding to their boyfriends' pleas. For example, Nyakyusa boys of East Africa, who in theory have sexual access to girls their age, in fact do not find it easy to get partners. They may make do with other unsuccessful boys by practicing interfemoral intercourse, which they would also practice with girls if they were lucky enough to find a girlfriend (Wilson 1963: 86–87, 196–197).

The extremely permissive societies, those like the Muria, have adolescent houses where young people congregate after the evening meal to frolic and sleep, usually in couples. Here it is peers, rather than adults, who regulate sexual activity, pressuring the group's members to rotate partners. Thus, while one's sexual impulses may not be frustrated, one's romantic sensibilities may well be. Moroseness and anger from jealousy are not unknown, and true despondency can arise when one's favorite partner is taken away to be married to someone else. Furthermore, the lack of privacy in the dormitory inhibits the free play of lovemaking. The Muria themselves acknowledge that married sex is better.

Adolescent sexual freedom or its reverse, socialization for celibacy, is not related to gender ideology in any straightforward way. Some societies that are permissive toward adolescents are highly restrictive of the sexuality of adult married women, whereas others that restrict adolescents tolerate the discreet affairs of wives. The expectation of celibacy of teenage girls is not in itself a measure of male dominance over adult women, for a low value on virginity can characterize male-dominant cultures. Sexual restrictiveness has more to do with the management of the lives of children in the best interests of the family. Sexual permissiveness in modern industrial societies has grown along with the decline of the family as a property-owning corporate group that is concerned with the perpetuation of its line and its estate.

There is no ideal solution to the problem of adolescent sexuality. Fortunately, adolescence does not last very long. For most people worldwide, it ends fairly early, when they marry at a young age. But marriage introduces another set of problems all its own.

Notes

1. The study employed the cross-cultural method, which uses samples of cultures widely separated by space or time in order to ensure that each is an independent case. The purpose is to test hypotheses concerning culture and human behavior by looking for associations between and among variables in spite of differing cultural contexts, to find whether similar cultural and behavioral features have similar determinants or consequences. For a more detailed discussion of the method as it was used in the study on which this chapter draws, see Schlegel and Barry (1991: 16–17 and appendices 1 and 2).

2. In some societies there is an intervening "youth" stage for boys only or, more rarely, for both sexes. This is generally true for developed nations and some sectors of developing ones, but it was also the case for the Spartans and Athenians of the ancient world and militaristic African states like Swazi and Zulu. These are the people we refer to as young adults, from about 19 or 20 to whenever they "settle down." The end of youth and the assumption of full adulthood varies across cultures and historical periods from the early 20s to much later (Schlegel 1999).

3. Dowry is just one form of property that women bring into marriage. Inheritance by daughters was once widespread in the populations that gave dowry or indirect dowry, primarily the propertied classes of Europe, Asia, and the Near East; daughters still inherit in many of these populations whether or not they retain the custom of dowry. Intangible goods might also be brought by brides, as used to be the case in Samoa and other Polynesian societies in which the titles of high-ranking women passed on to their children.

References Cited

Creed, Gerald W. 1982. Sexual Subordination: Institutionalized Homosexuality and Social Control in Melanesia. *Ethnology* 21: 151–176.

Davis, Douglas A. 1995. Modernizing the Sexes: Changing Gender Relations in a Moroccan Town. *Ethos* 23: 69–78.

Davis, Susan S., and Douglas A. Davis. 1989. *Adolescence in a Moroccan Town.* New Brunswick: Rutgers University Press.

Dumézil, Georges. 1967. *The Resting of the Warrior.* Chicago: University of Chicago Press.

Elwin, Verrier. 1947. *The Muria and Their Ghotul.* Bombay: Oxford University Press.

Gay, Judith. 1986. "Mummies" and "Babies" and Friends and Lovers in Lesotho. In *Anthropology and Homosexual Behavior,* ed. Evelyn Blackwood, 97–116. New York: Haworth.

Goodich, Michael E. 1989. *From Birth to Old Age: The Human Life Cycle in Medieval Thought, 1250–1350.* Lanham, Md.: Univeristy Presses of America.

Greenberg, David F. 1988. *The Construction of Homosexuality.* Chicago: University of Chicago Press.

Herdt, Gilbert H. 1981. *Guardians of the Sacred Flutes: Idioms of Masculinity.* New York: McGraw-Hill.

Mead, Margaret. 1928. *Coming of Age in Samoa.* Ann Arbor: Morrow.

Murdock, George P., and Douglas R. White. 1969. The Standard Cross-Cultural Sample and Its Codes. *Ethnology* 8: 329–369.

Schlegel, Alice. 1991. Status, Property, and the Value of Virginity. *American Ethnologist* 18: 719–734.

Schlegel, Alice. 1995. The Cultural Management of Adolescent Sexuality. In *Sexual Nature Sexual Culture,* ed. Paul R. Abramson and Steven D. Pinkerton, 177–194. Chicago: University of Chicago Press.

Schlegel, Alice. 1997. Dowry and Indirect Dowry. In *The Blackwell Dictionary of Anthropology,* ed. Thomas Barfield, 129–130. Oxford: Blackwell.

Schlegel, Alice. 1999. The Social Criteria of Adulthood. *Human Development* 41: 323–325.

Schlegel, Alice, and Herbert Barry III. 1980. The Evolutionary Significance of Adolescent Initiation Ceremonies. *American Ethnologist* 7: 696–715.

Schlegel, Alice, and Herbert Barry III. 1991. *Adolescence: An Anthropological Inquiry.* New York: Free Press.

Schlegel, Alice, and Rohn Eloul. 1987. Marriage Transactions: A Cross-Cultural Code. *Behavior Science Research* 21: 118–140.

Schlegel, Alice, and Rohn Eloul. 1988. Marriage Transactions: Labor, Property, and Status. *American Anthropologist* 90: 291–309.

Topley, Marjorie. 1975. Marriage Resistance in Rural Kwangtung. In *Women in Chinese Society,* ed. Margery Wolf and Roxane Witke, 67–88. Stanford: Stanford University Press.

Wilson, Monica. 1963. *Good Company: A Study of Nyakyusa Age Villages.* Boston: Beacon.

5 *Peter Collins*

Virgins in the Spirit
The Celibacy of Shakers

The United Society of Believers in Christ's Second Appearing, more commonly known as the Shakers, has been called "the most successful communal society in history" (Garrett 1987: viii).[1] Because of the rule of celibacy, recruitment from within has been impossible, and new members, apart from adopted orphans (only a few of whom came into full membership), have tended to be drawn in during periods of religious revival (Brewer 1986: 30–42). The United Society gained in numbers until around 1840, when it had approximately 4,000 members distributed across 8 states in America and 21 semiautonomous communities. These communities, which held all property in common, traded energetically, and Shakers gained a reputation for excellent quality and honest dealing (Stein 1992: 133–148).

The 1840s were a time of widespread mystical experience in the society. "Mother Ann's Work" (or "Holy Wisdom's Work") involved young women who experienced visions of an intensely spiritual nature — angels and figures from the Bible, as well as past Shaker saints. Crosthwaite (1989: 192) points out that, as a result, the artistic works, or "spirit drawings," produced during this period " articulate a broad and imaginative commitment to celibacy." A variety of messages were communicated and the "gifts," or drawings, were often copied by others in the Shaker village and sometimes by the United Society at large.

This period of spiritual revival was short-lived; within a decade the rate of recruitment slowed dramatically, and departures, either through death or apostasy, outnumbered new recruits. By 1900 Shaker numbers were down to around 1,000, and by 1937 there were six communities remaining. By 1990 there were a dozen or so members in the single remaining village at Sabbathday Lake, Maine.[2]

Mother Ann Lee, Celibacy, and the Genesis of Shakerism

In the mid-eighteenth century, Lancashire, in the northwest of England, was in the vanguard of the Industrial Revolution. It was during intense social and political turmoil, rapid urbanization, and nonconformist religious revival that a young factory worker, Ann Lee, joined a small though active dissenting Christian group known as the Shaking Quakers. Ann Lee was born in 1736 into a poor family in Manchester. Her father is reported to have been a strict disciplinarian. She had a number of brothers and sisters, including William, who later immigrated with her to the United States. Like her father, her husband, Abraham Standerin, was a blacksmith. Ann Lee gave birth to four children, all of whom died young. It is therefore somewhat ironic that after taking control of the group, she was generally known as Mother Ann. The appropriation of the parental and heavenly metaphor excited suspicion among outsiders concerning the claims made regarding her status by her followers.

The Shaking Quakers, led at first by Jane and James Wardley, were millenarian charismatics who believed in the in-dwelling spirit, present in all men and women.[3] Their avowed pacifism did not stop them from being ardent proselytizers in and around Manchester between 1748 and 1774. Members of the group, including Ann Lee, were imprisoned on a number of occasions for offenses akin to disturbing the peace (Axon 1875). During one particularly difficult spell in prison, it is said that Ann underwent a profound mystical experience. Visions of an intensely spiritual and prophetic nature led her to believe that she had discovered the single reason for the degeneracy of the human race, sexuality: "Their lust is their torment" (*Testimonies* 1816: 238–239).[4] Mother Ann persuaded the small group of Shaking Quakers that they must accept the rule of celibacy. Despite their commitment to continuing revelation, they chose, as other contemporaneous sects did, to turn to the Bible for confirmation of prophetic insight.[5] Mother Ann held up the biblical account of the Fall (Gen. 3:1–24) as proof of the legitimacy of her claim.[6] She soon became the leader of the nascent sect.

The vigor of her evangelizing was matched by an equal and opposite force from the civil and religious authorities, and in 1774 she and eight

followers left for New England, where they hoped to find a greater tolerance. They eventually established a community at Niskeyuna (later called
Watervliet), near Albany in New York State.[7] Within 10 years they had
established the first Shaker community, and by 1820 there were 17 members. Shakerism emerged, therefore, during a period of intermittent, but
growing, religious fervor and millenarianism, between the American War
of Independence and the Civil War.[8]

By 1790, under the joint leadership of Joseph Meacham and Lucy
Wright, the sect's foundation had shifted, in Weberian terms, from charisma to routine. The Shakers became the United Society of Believers in
Christ's Second Appearing, with a complex organizational structure and a
developing theology. During the period 1790–1820 the sayings of Mother
Ann and other early Shakers were collected, thereby justifying and legitimating current practices. Ann lee's theology was radically egalitarian in
relation to gender. She held that the identity of God was dual — male and
female. She explained, in answer to a question put to her by Joseph
Meacham, that since the Father, Jesus Christ, was no longer on earth, his
responsibilities must fall to the Mother — Ann Lee.[9] This facet of Shaker
belief might be seen as the ultimate theological justification for gender
quality, and in the sphere of worship at least it probably did have this
outcome: men and women took an equal part in religious devotions. It
might be argued that women, unencumbered with the traditional roles of
wife and mother, were more readily able to play an equal role in the spiritual and social life of the community. This may be true up to a point, but
there is no reason that gender equality might not have been espoused and
achieved without proscribing sexual relations. Clearly, celibacy had a
more profound meaning for early Shakers.

Throughout her life, Mother Ann seems to have spoken regularly on
this issue and repeated the insights she experienced as a poor young
woman in prison. But now her words were recollected and written down;
an oral tradition became fixed on paper. For example:

If you take up your cross against the lust of the flesh, while you have power to
please yourselves, you offer to God the first fruits; and there is a glorious crown
for all who take up their cross against the flesh in this world; such souls will have a
privilege of this gospel; either in this world, or in the world of spirits but those who
have the offer of the gospel in this world, if they reject it, they will never have
another day. (*Testimonies* 1816: 27)

Because of their theology of continuing revelation, however, Shakers
were loathe to publish anything that might seem creedal. In this sense,
routinization of church organization was offset by a continuing charismatic theology. The official line on marriage, even during the first de-

cades, was therefore ambivalent. Ann Lee clearly believed that true Believers must be celibate and refrain from both sex and marriage, but she also accepted that for some, sex within marriage might be the next best thing:

She also said to Daniel Mosely and others, "Do not go away and report that we forbid to marry; for unless you are able to take up a full cross, and part with every gratification of the flesh, for the Kingdom of God, I would counsel you, and all such, to take wives in a lawful manner, and cleave to them only; and raise up a lawful posterity, and be perpetual servants to your families: for of all lustful gratifications that is the least sin." (*Testimonies* 1816: 296)[10]

Notwithstanding, the Shakers believed that their justifications of the celibate life — theological, moral and rational — were necessary and sufficient to sustain their practice. The celibate life has remained a pillar of Shakerism, coloring all aspects of their culture, symbolically and also practically.[11]

The majority of accounts of Shaker celibacy offered by Believers and non-Believers alike concentrate on getting the historical record straight; few attempt to theorize the issue.[12] However, explanations of the genesis of religious sects often turn on the personality and social context of the founding members. Although little is known for certain of Ann Lee's life, a number of anecdotes of her life in England were collected from the first Believers, and such accounts have been significant in subsequent Shaker writing. For instance:

From her childhood she was the subject of religious impressions and divine manifestations. She had great light and conviction concerning the sinfulness and depravity of human nature, and especially concerning the lusts of the flesh which she often made known to her parents entreating them for that counsel and protection by which she might be kept from sin. . . . It is remarkable that, in early youth, she had a great abhorrence of the fleshly cohabitation of the sexes; and so great was her sense of its impurity, that she often admonished her mother against it; which coming to her father's ears, he threatened and actually attempted to whip her. (*Testimonies* 1816: 2–3)

Shaker writers often suggest that Ann Lee's championing of celibacy was at least partly a result of her upbringing. It is possible that the young Ann Lee was abused by a man and grew up despising all men. It is further possible that her marriage to a man whose occupation was the same as her father's may have served to deepen an existing dread or trauma. However, there is no record of her ever accusing anyone of such abuse. Rather, her belief in celibacy may have stemmed from the simple facts of life in eighteenth-century England and from the influence of the Wardleys, leaders of the charismatic group she joined in her 20s. This is suggested not only in canonic Shaker texts but also in later academic accounts.[13] The Wardleys claimed they no longer had a sexual relationship. Ann, who greatly respected the Wardleys, was therefore presented, at an impressionable age, with a possible alternative to the customary conjugal relationship. In eighteenth-century England, such a relationship often involved a wife giving birth more or less annually for the first 15 years of marriage, with the real possibility of death on each occasion.[14]

Ann Lee, we know, gave birth to four children in typically rapid succession and probably in the grimmest of circumstances. While in prison she had a vision which confirmed what might already have occurred to her in more mundane moments — that sexual relations were the cause of evil and suffering in the world and should be avoided by everyone, always. She stopped sleeping with her husband and began preaching this simple message, though convinced very few. The nine Shaking Quakers who arrived in New York in the summer of 1774 taught by example, eschewing sexual relations, and eventually harvested the first American converts.

That Ann Lee's upbringing and experiences as a young adult, in the harsh social milieu of working-class Manchester, may well have contributed to her espousal of a celibate way of life is simple explanation. For one thing, Ann Lee's upbringing was little different from the majority of working-class girls. It would be unhelpful reductionism to explain Shaker celibacy wholly in terms of the tortured self of Ann Lee. Because of this, and while accepting that this charismatic woman provided the impetus for a new and eventually influential religious movement, we must look elsewhere for sufficient reasons why that impetus was sustained. Many other communitarian sects, both religious and secular, took root in eighteenth- and nineteenth-century America, but very few have survived for as long as the Shakers (Desroche 1971: 66). Furthermore, the words attributed to Ann Lee were recorded more than 30 years after her death, when the United Society was developing rapidly as a religious organization. The accounts might be said to have been shaped to support extant faith and practice.[15] However, such texts have undoubtedly had enormous influence on subsequent generations of Shakers, and we would do well at this point to recall a dictum famous in sociology: "If men define situations as real, they are real in their consequences" (Thomas and Thomas 1928: 572). I query the point of academic anxiety concerning the "truth" of such accounts.[16]

The Organization of Shaker Celibacy: From Orthopraxy to Orthodoxy

Before accounts of the teaching of the first Believers appeared in print, there must have been considerable confusion concerning the delineation of Shaker belief, or at least a marked variation in its interpretation. By 1800 a number of texts had appeared which recorded the doctrines preached by Ann Lee; William, her brother; James Whittaker, her protégé; and Joseph Meacham.[17] It is likely that accounts of the *ad hoc* comments and modes of behavior of Mother Ann were shaped by these men, all of whom are characterized by contemporary commentators and later by chroniclers as persuasive and competent preachers.

One distinctive feature of early Shaker texts is that orthopraxy overshadows orthodoxy: statements of belief reflect the practice rather than the theology of the founders. Mother Ann continually instructed her followers on how to behave. Shakers were, from the outset, pacifist, sharing the Quaker belief that if God could be found within everyone, then to violate any human being would be to violate God.[18] Shakers were expected to live morally pure and physically clean lives. Accounts include many examples of Ann chiding Believers for their lack of cleanliness and tidiness: "There is no dirt in heaven" (*Testimonies* 1816: 265). She believed that she and those who accepted her gospel (which was for her identical with Christ's gospel) were perfect. Impurity, in any form, confirmed that such perfection had not yet been attained.

The practice of celibacy is a case in point. Ann Lee persuaded her group that celibacy (as abstinence from all sexual activity) should be practiced even within marriage. Her followers accepted that it was right for them to abstain from what they had come to understand as the fundamentally impure sexual act. In the first instance it was Ann Lee's gospel that provided all the authority necessary to adhere to this severe practice. Quite simply, she told her followers that God had shown her that sexual activity was the root of all evil: to attend to one's carnal nature was to deny God. In order to experience Christ's Second Appearing or regeneration (spiritual transformation) it was necessary to renounce generation (coition). She pointed, for further justification, to the life of Jesus Christ, a man she proclaimed to have attained perfection through continence. Finally, she held that universal love was the purest form of love and was only diluted by the lesser, more particularistic love of friends or family members. In this connection it is worth noting that Ann Lee's message questioned the legitimacy of the institution of marriage and family, during that period when the American family was undergoing a major transformation. According to Degler (1980: chap. 1) it was during this period (1760–1830) that the "modern" American family emerged. Marriage was becoming a matter of choice between two independent individuals, increasingly particularistic and based on romantic love and mutual affection. The development of the nuclear family ensured that the roles of wife and husband became more clearly differentiated — the wife tending home and family, the husband working, increasingly for a wage, outside the home. This arrangement was central to America's accelerating capitalist development. Some contemporaries viewed with deep concern the Shaker model, which sought to turn the world upside down. The point is that the stakes were high in so stridently rejecting a kind of conjugal relationship and family structure increasingly legitimated in moral and economic terms (O'Day 1994: esp. chap. 2; Stone 1979: esp. 149–253).

The path from generation to regeneration began with the confession of one's sins to an elder of the church. Confession was public and complete, particularly in relation to sins of the flesh. To renounce the carnal life was to renounce the devil and to set out on the road to perfection. Having confessed one's sins, one should sin no more. The proof of the change wrought by confession was demonstrated in the everyday lives of Believers, in their personal habits and in their behavior toward other Believers.[19]

Salvation was open to anyone willing to submit to public confession, regardless of his or her previous sins. In order to convert to Shakerism it was not necessary to have lived a pure life, only to renounce one's sinful past life. In the following passage, the influential Shaker elder Calvin Green deals with the prospects of those who had already indulged in sexual relations:

If they have been married, how then can they be virgins, or are such to be excluded. . . . suppose they have been "in the flesh"; this no more prevents them from becoming virgins in the spirit than it does the wicked from becoming righteous. . . . therefore I say, as they come into Christ, and are one with him, so they are virgins, according to his nature. It matters not what they have been; for old things are done away, and all things become new in that element. . . . when souls are gathered into Christ, they partake of his nature. (Green 1830; excerpted in Whitson 1983: 164)

Among Shakers, the transformation of celibacy from orthodoxy to orthopraxy had a number of repercussions. Until the 1780s Shakers continued to live with their families, and those who were married attempted to abstain from having sexual intercourse, as the Wardleys had in Manchester and the Lees following Ann's vision. After their immigration to the United States, however, the Shakers continued to be harassed by those suspicious of their beliefs and practices. Shaker leaders saw that life would be safer and their movement more likely to expand if they gathered themselves into villages, separate from the people of the world.

The establishment of Shaker villages was an important development in terms of the practice of celibacy. The separation of male and female became both a symbolic and a practical achievement. Complex and stringent regulations were implemented to ensure that men and women did not come into physical contact.[20] Now men and women, even those who had been married in the world, were separated into different sleeping quarters and kept apart as far as was necessary to avoid opportunities for carnal temptation.[21] Men's and women's accommodations were either partitioned or, increasingly, separated in different buildings. Where men and women were likely to come together, for meals and worship, for example, arrangements were made which ensured that they need not come into physical contact. Buildings were built with two doors, so that men and women need not dally with one another while entering or leaving; dual staircases served the same purpose. The symbolism of separation had maximum impact during public and relatively formal occasions such as mealtime and worship.

Worship itself became increasingly formalized after the events known collectively as Mother's Work. Ritual dance or movement continued to be organized so that men and women remained apart. By and by, regulations became increasingly minute and specific; for example, women were expected to refrain from sewing buttons on shirts while being worn by men. Touching a non-Shaker member of the opposite sex, however accidental, required immediate confession before an elder.[22] Furthermore, the sexual division of labor meant that certain tasks would be carried out almost entirely by either men or women, leading to a more thorough segregation of the sexes. This is not to say, however, that men and women never met. Accounts by Believers throughout the nineteenth century, along with photographs from midcentury on, indicate that men and women did work and spend leisure time together (Stein 1992).

During the second half of the nineteenth century, Shaker writers began to offer further arguments legitimating the practice of sexual abstinence. Following the moral, though secular, Malthusian thesis, Shakers began to emphasize the practical benefits to society at large of reducing the size of the population. Such a point of view is not apparent in accounts of the first Believers, but by 1850 the Industrial Revolution was fully underway in the United States, and the notion of a population explosion was gaining credence.

Shaker writers maintained that celibacy (specifically as freedom from marriage) was an important inducement to women to enter membership, first, because marriage sometimes licensed the physical and sexual abuse of women; second, because abstention from marriage facilitated communal, and therefore egalitarian, property ownership. They argued that when women are given the opportunity to eschew economic dependence on men, they become men's equals in all spheres of life (White and Taylor [1904] 1971: 256).[23]

Further, subsidiary, arguments were occasionally presented. Sexual abstinence would lead to a longer and healthier life, and the longevity of many Believers was taken as proof.[24] Shakers came to appreciate the benefits of healthy living, not only in sexual restraint, but also in relation to diet, proper sleeping positions, and so forth.[25] Such rational argument became more commonplace after the advent of the first Shaker periodical, the *Manifesto*. This shift in emphasis from mystery to rationality indicates the degree to which Shakers were now accommodating the ideas, mostly secular, of the outside world. Believers were no longer content to explain their behavior to themselves in terms relevant to a religious sect, but increasingly targeted their explanations toward non-Believers, in appropriately rationalistic or scientific terms.

As we have seen, Ann Lee, while always starting with the advice that an aspiring Believer ought immediately to abstain from sex, often added that if this was impossible then Christian marriage was the next best thing. She was clear, however, that only those abstaining from sexual activity could be saved. The membership decided that married couples would dissolve their marriage upon joining the society and agree to live separately (any children would be communally cared for). For Shakers, then, celibacy increasingly meant not only sexual abstinence but also the denial of marriage as such. Their argument, put simply, is that marriage is to sex as war is to murder; that is, marriage is the state's legitimation of a sin, the greatest sin. They widened their critique of the established churches, especially Catholicism, by pointing out the evil of saving a few souls by hiving them off into monastic orders while giving the laity leave to sin as they pleased, spuriously protected by the sacrament of marriage (Desroche 1971: 178).

That the rejection of marriage was central to Shaker faith and practice is beyond doubt. During the mid-nineteenth century the Shaker position regarding marriage led them to view sympathetically groups with whom they had very little else in common, such as the Mormons and the Perfectionists of Noyes's Oneida community.[26] The customs of such groups regarding sex and marriage were perceived by some Shakers to constitute a legitimate and alternative, if not laudable, critique of conventional Christian practice.

The rational justification of celibacy was rehearsed repeatedly in early editions of the *Manifesto*. The editor clearly expected the journal to be read by outsiders interested in the society, who might be persuaded, by rational argument, to inquire further. In answer to letters from members of the public, the editor, or some competent substitute, would attempt to offer a succinct statement of Shaker belief and practice, always including an explanation and justification of celibacy. For example:

Do you ask: "What you must do to be a Shaker?" . . . Be as a virgin henceforth; abstain from fleshly lusts and from lascivious thoughts. Had you a wife? Now use her as a sister. Is she unwilling? The Spirit never concedes to the flesh — stand firm. (*Manifesto* 2 [1872]: 63)

In another, the editor explained:

Every marriage, however proper for the *world and its children,* crucifies Christ afresh; every sexual congress of the twain, however necessary for the peopling of the earth, pollutes the *Christian* temple. (*Manifesto* 8 [1878]: 43; emphasis in original)

The latter excerpt is of particular interest for two reasons: First, it reminds us that Shaker doctrine was quite clear that generation, that is, sexual reproduction, is un-Christian — the implication being that Shakerism, founded as it is upon chastity, is coterminus with Christianity. The churches that permit sexual activity are therefore considered not Christian. Second, it suggests that Shakerism might be practiced not only within a Shaker village but also in the world. Communal life and the shared ownership of property were a vital yet secondary tenet (but see Desroche 1971).

Despite the evolution of other aspects of Shaker theology, it is remarkable that the practice of celibacy has remained unchallenged throughout the life of the movement. I can find no account of any Shaker man and woman engaging, clandestinely, in a sexual relationship while remaining in membership. Members seem always to have been aware that to remain a Shaker is to remain celibate. Even relatively innocent encounters, if discovered by the elders, would lead to one party, normally the woman, being moved to another Shaker village.[27] In many cases, individuals who felt increasingly drawn to one another chose to leave the society altogether.

For Shakers themselves, then, celibacy has consisted both of the abstinence from sexual activity and the denial of the moral, social, and religious legitimacy of Christian marriage. This is clearly the ideology, the orthodoxy, but it is more than that insofar as records suggest that it has been and remains the orthopraxy. These two facets of celibacy — one prescribing continence, the other proscribing marriage — form the keystone of what Shakers think they ought to do and also what they define themselves to be; the facets are central to the delineation of Shaker identity.

The Celibacy of Shakers

Having discussed the question of Ann Lee's celibacy, we will now consider the different and more general question of Shaker celibacy. There have been few concerted efforts to treat Shaker celibacy as a sociological problem. Sociological interpretations tend to focus either on Shaker communitarianism or on the position of women within the group, though these discussions do sometimes have a bearing on our understanding of Shaker celibacy (but see Desroche 1971; Garrett 1987; Whitworth 1975). Although individuals might become Shakers while still living at home, particularly in the early years, an important tenet of Shaker orthodoxy is the communal life in which all property is held in common ownership. Communal living and celibacy are understood as two sides of the same coin. Greed, murder, and other sins have their cause in the existence of private property. Private property is based on the family and on inheritance along one line of descent or another, according to custom. In order to abolish the cause of greed and violence one needs to abolish private property, and in order to abolish private property one needs to abolish the traditional family. The most obvious alternative is the communal society in which individuals own nothing and therefore have nothing to lust after. The keystone of the family is the procreating couple, and only after the legitimacy of this relationship has been denied can the basis of private property be suspended. Of course, marriage might also be replaced by the "free love" of Noyes's Oneidans, but Shakers have been further constrained by an entrenched and overarching theology that deems all sexual relations profoundly sinful. From the Shaker point of view, then, celibacy and communalism go hand in hand.

The consequence of celibacy for the status of women has been the subject of much debate. Could it be that celibacy was a conscious strategy by early Believers, supported by later converts, of gender equalization? Newby (1990) has argued that Shakerism was in the vanguard of antebellum feminism; Campbell (1978: 24) believes Shakerism to be "the best example of utopian designs reflecting sexual equality."[28] Although a division of labor based on gender existed within nineteenth-century Shaker villages, women have, to a large extent, had the same opportunities as men in both the religious and the secular spheres of Shaker communal life. The practice of celibacy meant, for instance, that women did not have the time-consuming responsibility of bringing up their own children. Everyone helped raise any children who entered the society with their parents or who were admitted as orphans. Shaker children were provided with a relatively high standard of elementary education, as well as being given the opportunity to learn a range of practical skills, from bread making to house building.

In comparison with other women, nineteenth-century Shaker women had considerable autonomy, holding positions of power and responsibility in both secular and spiritual arenas. Shaker women made these claims explicit in many publications. The reality, as opposed to the ideology, of gender equality was strengthened as the number of male members diminished.[29] The important role of trustee was opened up to women at that point.[30] Even so, the trustees were always subordinate to the ministers, and the ministry was composed of two men and two women in each community (Brewer 1986: 215; Stein 1992: 256).

Celibacy and Shaker Identity

In recent years anthropologists have become interested in the ways in which groups establish and maintain their identity (Boon 1981; Cohen 1985). Celibacy has had, from the first years of the movement, a powerful symbolic resonance for Shakers. Celibacy has marked Shakers off not only from established churches but also from other millenarian and communitarian sects. The sufferings that the first Believers underwent were largely on account of their preaching in relation to sex and marriage. Celibacy, more than any other aspect of their faith and practice, has helped to define the Shaker corporate identity. It has been a boundary-defining device of extraordinary potency, helping to sustain the distinctiveness of the group.[31] Within the society three divisions have marked the various levels of commitment that Believers subscribe to; even the least committed have been expected to remain sexually continent. Celibacy, more than any other practice, serves to mark off the purity of Believers from an impure world (see Douglas 1984: 29–40 on secular defilement).

In this way the social order has been held to reflect the cosmic, or heavenly, order. The Shaker community has strived to attain the perfection of paradise, represented most powerfully by chastity wherein reproduction is explicitly asexual. And while it is impossible to know for certain the extent to which Believers have practiced sexual restraint (let alone the extent to which they have kept unchaste thoughts at bay), in subscribing to the simple act of denial they become Shaker, they belong to the United Society. It would be a fundamental mistake, however, to present Shaker celibacy as primarily a symbol or metaphor; it has first of all been a practice, an act of self-denial: the actual and experienced embodiment of the perfect life.

Envoi

Shaker celibacy is a complex social construction. I have put off discussion of one important aspect of this complexity and intend merely to touch upon it here. Shakers have been concerned to discipline themselves in relation to both sex and marriage. They have shunned the institution of marriage, primarily because it serves to legitimize sexual relations on the one hand and private property on the other. There is a tendency to conflate these two issues, both within Shaker writing and in academic glosses on it (but see Desroche 1971: 139). In any analysis of celibacy, two prominent and partly connected themes might be traced: first, celibacy as sexual abstinence, and second, celibacy as denunciation of marriage. These themes may, but do not necessarily, stand in a metaphoric or metonymic relation. There are here, then, two celibacies and not one.

There is a further specifically Shaker complexity. Shaker sexual abstinence was presented by early Shakers as primarily a spiritual act, and marriage was presented as a social institution which serves to legitimate and perpetuate a rank abomination. Later, the arguments for celibacy became increasingly temporal and rational, relating to gender equality, health, longevity, and population control. There is a perceptible shift toward the secular in the celibate self as presented in Shaker texts. The reason for this lies primarily in the diminution of millennial fervor among members as the movement progressed from charisma to routine. Shaker villages grew less isolated, more open, partly because of the burgeoning interest of outsiders and partly because of the increasing dependence of Shakers on the world for goods and services. As the boundary between Shakerism and the wider U.S. society became increasingly blurred, justifications of celibacy multiplied and became increasingly elaborate (see Cohen 1985: 44, 50).

Etic interpretations such as these do not necessarily add anything to the ideology constructed by Shakers and are themselves the product of one ideology or another. Therefore, they speak as much of their own context as that of the world of the Shakers. Although such interpretations may provoke further interest and stimulate worthwhile discussion, they should not be taken to imply an analytic or interpretive closure. While it is true that not every interpretation is of equal value, I would argue that each of those offered above leads us to a more finely tuned understanding of Shaker celibacy. The personal circumstances of Ann Lee led her to a certain world view that she encouraged others to share. She was the charismatic catalyst who sowed the seeds of a new religious movement. Early Believers were influenced, in their faith and practice, by other religious groups. Both the Quakers and French Prophets, though neither of these groups espoused celibacy, practiced endogamy and eschewed marriage to all but their own, in order to maintain their own purity; each allowed women a considerable amount of authority, particularly in spiritual matters (Jones 1921: 117; Schwartz 1980: 134–146). Later, other models of the communitarian life became available, along with alternative visions of what it might mean to live the good life (Holloway 1951; Nordhoff 1875).

The wider society has violently rejected Shaker celibacy and Shakers' denial of traditional marriage and the type of family life it gives rise to. More than any other aspect of faith and practice, it has been celibacy that has separated the world from the United Society, leaving it to develop, creatively but not procreatively, behind a densely meaningful symbolic boundary.

Notes

1. The United Society was also held in high esteem for various reasons by Tolstoy, Engels, and Robert Owen (see Desroche 1971: 257–297).

2. Shaker demographics remain an approximate science, however, and different estimates are found, for example, in Andrews 1963: 290–292, and Brewer 1986: apps. A, B, and C. The general trend is not in doubt, however.

3. The sect was influenced, most likely, by the Quakers and the French Prophets, or Cevenoles, though actual contact with either group has not been proven. The Quakers had established a worshipping group in Bolton, where the Wardleys worked as tailors. For further discussion see Andrews 1963: 3–13; Campion 1990; Garrett 1987: 140–159; Schwartz 1980; and Stein 1992: 3–10.

4. James Whittaker, Ann Lee's immediate successor, was to adopt this tone immediately after her death. In 1785 he wrote in a letter that he had discovered "redemption from the bondage of corruption; which is that sordid propensity, or ardent desire of copulation with women" (quoted in Brewer 1986: 15).

5. Continuing revelation is the experience of the divine presence in everyday life, over and above that which is found in the Scriptures.

6. Later, Shaker writers would seek to justify the rule of celibacy by citing other passages from the Bible, particularly Matt. 22:30; Mark 12:25; Luke 20: 34–35; 1 Cor. 7:33 and 38.

7. By this time Ann had separated from her husband.

8. For further details see Desroche 1971; Foster 1984; Marini 1985; Muncy 1973; Nordhoff 1875; and Whitworth 1975.

9. Later Shaker interpretations waver on the exact nature of Ann Lee's Christhood. On this thorny issue see Procter-Smith 1985, 1990. Humez (1992) discusses the way in which Ann Lee is presented in early Shaker texts (see also Campion 1990).

10. These sentiments mirror those of Paul in 1 Cor. 7:1–40.

11. Geertz (1973) cautions against treating culture purely as a symbolic system.

12. Among the best general historical accounts by non-Believers are Andrews 1963; Brewer 1986; Garrett 1987; and Stein 1992. The following focus on Shaker sexuality: Foster 1984; Kern 1981; and Muncy 1973.

13. For example, Gooden argues, "Jane Wardley helped Ann Lee resolve her deeply rooted conflict over sexuality, a conflict which had become more acute after marriage and the loss of four children" (1990: 1). Schroeder (1921) offers an account of Ann Lee's antipathy toward sexual intercourse from a psychoanalytic perspective.

14. Lawrence Stone (1979: 54) writes of eighteenth-century England: "The most striking feature which distinguished the Early Modern family from that of today does not concern either marriage or birth; it was the constant presence of death. Death was at the centre of life, as the cemetery was at the centre of the village."

15. See Aguilar (this volume) for further discussion of "the invention of tradition."

16. The psychology of individual members' decisions for joining the Shakers can only be guessed at. See Desroche 1971: 139–143 for an interesting classification of psychosociological interpretations offered by (women) Believers themselves.

17. The most significant of these were *Testimonies* (1816; revised by Seth Wells and Calvin Green and reprinted 1827) and *A Summary View of the Millennial Church* (Green and Wells 1823).

18. Shakers successfully avoided conscription during both the War of Independence and the Civil War (see Stein 1992: 12–13, 52–53, 315–317).

19. That is not to say there were no apostates. There are many instances of apostasy cited in Stein 1992 and in Brewer 1986. It is clear that some left the United Society because they could not or did not want to uphold the rule of chastity. Children and adolescents posed particular problems.

20. The Millennial Laws, first recorded in 1821, touch on most aspects of life in the community (see them, revised, in The Millennial Laws [1845] 1963). Very specific advice is given on the relations between the sexes, and section 5, alone, includes 29 regulations relating to this subject.

21. Although men shared rooms and women shared rooms, proscriptions relating to homosexuality appear wholly absent from Shaker texts. It is likely that Shakers shared the ambient belief, then current in U.S. society, that homosexuality was wrong and should be avoided. I know of no account of the prevalence of homosexuality among Shakers (but see Elkins [1853] 1973 regarding same-sex friendships).

22. Regarding everyday life in Shaker villages see Stein 1992: 148–165; and Elkins [1853] 1973.

23. Several examples of this argument appear in the *Manifesto* (a Shaker monthly published between 1871 and 1899). For example, a piece entitled "The Shaker Woman's Rights," by Asenath C. Stickney, states, "Here let us state that it is by virtue of our loyalty to our God and to the covenant which we maintain, that we come into possession of all that truly enobles, elevates and enfranchises women" (4 [1874]: 53).

24. See, for example, "Celibacy," by Daniel Frazer (*Manifesto* 3 [1873]: 4), which begins: " 'What are the effects of abstinence from exercising the generative functions?' Freedom from all diseases of those functions."

25. Editions of the *Manifesto* are full of articles relating to such matters. See also Brewer 1986: 106–113 on diet and the influence of Grahamism.

26. See Foster 1984; Muncy 1973; and Whitworth 1975 for further discussion of these groups.

27. For an account of such a development see Elkins [1853] 1973: 105–125. Elkins also says that same-sex friendships were frowned upon because of the negation of universal love implicit in such particular and local relationships.

28. For further debate on this issue, see also Bednarowski 1980; Brewer 1992; Crosthwaite 1989; Humez 1992; and Kern 1981: 114–134.

29. By 1860, women accounted for nearly 60 percent of total membership, and in 1900, for over 72 percent (Bainbridge 1982: 360). See Stein (1992: 256–272) for an account of the feminization of the United Society.

30. Desroche (1971: 215–216) calls the trustees "bursars," which makes explicit their preeminent role in the economic organization of each community.

31. As Cohen says, "The most striking feature of the symbolic construction of the community and its boundaries is its oppositional character. The boundaries are *relational* rather than absolute; that is they mark the community in relation to other communities" (1985: 58; emphasis in original).

References Cited

Andrews, Edward D. 1963. *The People Called Shakers: A Search for the Perfect Society.* Rev. ed. New York: Dover.

Axon, William E. A. 1875. A Manchester Prophetess. *Transactions of the Historic Society of Lancashire and Cheshire, 27th Session,* 3d ser. 3: 51–70.

Bainbridge, William S. 1982. Shaker Demographics, 1840–1900: An Example of the Use of U.S. Census Enumeration Schedules. *Journal for the Scientific Study of Religion* 21(4): 352–365.

Bednarowski, Mary F. 1980. Outside the Mainstream: Women's Religious Leaders in Nineteenth Century America. *Journal of the American Academy of Religion* 48(2): 207–231.

Boon, James A. 1981. *Other Tribes, Other Scribes.* Cambridge: Cambridge University Press.

Brewer, Priscilla J. 1986. *Shaker Communities, Shaker Lives.* Hanover: University Press of New England.

Brewer, Priscilla J. 1992. "Tho' of the Weaker Sex": A Reassessment of Gender Equality among the Shakers. *Signs: Journal of Women, Culture and Society* 17: 609–635.

Campbell, D'Ann. 1978. Women's Life in Utopia: The Shaker Experiment in Sexual Equality Reappraised, 1810–1860. *New England Quarterly* 51: 23–38.

Campion, Nardi R. 1990. *Mother Ann Lee: Morning Star of the Shakers.* Reprinted. Hanover: University Press of New England. Original publication, 1976.

Cohen, Anthony P. 1985. *The Symbolic Construction of Community.* London: Routledge.

Crosthwaite, Jane F. 1989. A White and Seamless Robe: Celibacy and Equality in Shaker Art and Theology. *Colby Library Quarterly* 25(3): 188–198.

Degler, Carl N. 1980. *At Odds: Women and the Family in America for the Revolution to the Present.* New York: Oxford University Press.

Desroche, Henri. 1971. *The American Shakers: From Neo-Christianity to Pre-socialism*. Trans. J. K. Savacool. Amherst: Univeristy of Massachusetts Press.

Douglas, Mary. 1984. *Purity and Danger*. Reprint ed. London: Ark. Original publication: Harmondsworth: Penguin Books, 1966.

Elkins, Hervey. [1853] 1973. *Fifteen Years in the Senior Order of Shakers*. New York: AMS.

Foster, Lawrence. 1984. *Religion and Sexuality: The Shakers, the Mormons, and the Oneida Community*. Urbana: University of Illinois Press.

Garrett, Clarke. 1987. *Spirit Possession and Popular Religion: From the Camisards to the Shakers*. Baltimore: John Hopkins University Press.

Geertz, Clifford. 1973. *The Interpretation of Cultures*. New York: Basic Books.

Gooden, Rosemary D. 1990. The Shakers: A Brief Historical Sketch. In *Locating the Shakers: Cultural Origins and Legacies of an American Religious Movement*, ed. Mick Gidley and Kate Bowles, 1–10. Exeter: Exeter University Press.

Green, Calvin. 1830. Atheism, Deism &c. Manuscript. Sabbathday Lake Society Library.

Green, Calvin, and Seth Y. Wells. 1823. *A Summary View of the Millennial Church or United Society of Believers (Commonly Called Shakers)*. Albany: Packard and Van Benthuysen. Reprinted, 1848.

Holloway, M. 1951. *Heavens on Earth: Utopian Communities in America, 1680–1880*. London: Turnstile Press.

Humez, Jean M. 1992. "Ye Are My Epistles": The Construction of Ann Lee Imagery in Early Shaker Sacred Literature. *Journal of Feminist Studies in Religion* 8(1): 83–104.

Jones, Rufus. 1921. *The Later Periods of Quakerism*. 2 vols. London: Macmillan.

Kern, Louis J. 1981. *An Ordered Love: Sex Roles and Sexuality in Victorian Utopias—the Shakers, the Mormons, and the Oneida Community*. Chapel Hill: University of North Carolina Press.

Manifesto. Vols. 1–29, January 1, 1871 — December 1899. [Title variations: *The Shaker* (1871–1872, 1876–1877); *Shaker and Shakeress Monthly* (1873–1875); *The Shaker Manifesto* (1878–1882); *The Manifesto* (1883–1899)]. The United Society.

Marini, Stephen A. 1985. *Radical Sects in Revolutionary New England*. Cambridge, Mass.: Harvard University Press.

The Millennial Laws. [1845] 1963. Reprinted as an appendix in *The People Called Shakers*, by Edward D. Andrews, 249–289. New York: Dover.

Muncy, Raymond L. 1973. *Sex and Marriage in Utopian Communities: 19th Century America*. Bloomington: Indiana University Press.

Newby, Alison M. 1990. Shakers as Feminists? Shakerism as a Vanguard in the Antebellum American Search for Female Autonomy and Independence. In *Locating the Shakers: Cultural Origins and Legacies of an American Religious Movement*, ed. Mick Gidley and Kate Bowles, 96–105. Exeter: Exeter University Press.

Nordhoff, Charles. 1876. *Communistic Societies of the United States*. New York: Harper and Brothers.

O'Day, Rosemary. 1994. *The Family and Family Relationships, 1500–1900: England, France and the United States of America.* London: Macmillan.

Proctor-Smith, Marjorie. 1985. *Women in Shaker Community and Worship: A Feminist Analysis of the Uses of Religious Symbolism.* Lewiston, N.Y.: Edwin Mellen.

Proctor-Smith, Marjorie. 1990. "Who Do You Say That I Am?" Mother Ann as Christ. In *Locating the Shakers: Cultural Origins and Legacies of an American Religious Movement,* ed. Mick Gidley and Kate Bowles, 83–95. Exeter: Exeter University Press.

Schroeder, Theo. 1921. Shaker Celibacy and Salacity Psychologically Interpreted. *New York Medical Review* (June 1): 800–805.

Schwartz, Hillel. 1980. *The French Prophets: The History of a Millenarian Group in Eighteenth-Century England.* Berkeley: University of California Press.

Stein, Stephen J. 1992. *The Shaker Experience in America.* New Haven: Yale University Press.

Stone, Lawrence. 1979. *The Family, Sex and Marriage in England 1500–1800.* Harmondsworth: Penguin Books.

Testimonies of the Life, Character, Revelations, and Doctrines of Our Ever Blessed Mother Ann Lee and the Elders with Her. 1816. Handcock, Mass.: J. Tallcot and J. Deeming, Junrs.

Thomas, W. I., and D. Thomas. 1928. *The Child in America.* New York: Knopf.

Wells, Seth Y., and Calvin Green, eds. 1827. *Testimonies Concerning the Character and Ministry of Mother Ann Lee and the First Witnesses of the Gospel of Christ's Second Appearing . . . &c.* Albany: Packard and Van Benthuysen.

White, Anna, and Leila S. Taylor. [1904] 1971. *Shakerism: Its Meaning and Message.* Reprint ed. New York: AMS Press.

Whitson, Robley E., ed. 1983. *The Shakers: Two Centuries of Spiritual Reflection.* London: SPCK (Society for Promoting Christian Knowledge).

Whitworth, John M. 1975. *God's Blueprints: A Sociological Study of Three Utopian Sects.* London: Routledge and Kegan Paul.

Youngs, Benjamin S. 1808. *The Testimony of Christ's Second Appearing, Exemplified by the Principles and Practice of the True Church of Christ.* Lebanon, Ohio: John MacLean (The United Society).

PART II
CELIBACY IN CULTURAL SYSTEMS

6 *Michael Duke*

Staying Clean
Notes on Mazatec Ritual Celibacy and Sexual Orientation

It was while on a hunting trip that I first learned of celibacy's importance for the Mazatecs. Sharing a single shotgun, my five companions and I spent many hours beneath the soft blue glow of a hunter's moon, fruitlessly stalking rabbits. Although the woods and cornfields around Cerro de Conejos were thick with rabbits, and we could see the faint glow of their eyes watching us from a distance, we were simply having no luck hitting our prey. After missing what he considered to be yet another easy shot, Chayo, who came from a family of experienced hunters, turned to us and asked in frustration, "Is everyone clean here?" Because we had all been in good spirits despite our bad luck, I was taken aback by the solemnity with which everyone responded in the affirmative. Chayo reminded us that it was critical to remain "clean," or celibate, for four days before going hunting.

He told us a cautionary tale about don Ignacio, a family friend who was an experienced deer hunter. While out hunting one day, he accidentally shot himself in the foot when he tripped over a rock. Although the wound was relatively minor, Ignacio's friends and relatives were surprised by his uncharacteristic clumsiness. Eventually the mystery was solved when Ignacio sheepishly admitted that he had not remained celibate for the required period of time.

Among the Mazatec Indians of southern Mexico,[1] acts of ritual celibacy are carried out in association with hunting, agricultural production, metaphysical activities, and curing rituals. As with other Mesoamerican groups, Mazatecs practice celibacy in order to ensure that a dangerous or critically important activity has a positive outcome.[2] At a minimum, celibacy is used to ensure that such activities do not yield disastrous results, as they did for don Ignacio.[3]

This chapter examines the ways in which Mazatec sexual abstinence as both a practice and a cultural construct is informed by beliefs about gender roles, reciprocity, sexual orientation, and the body. In particular, I argue that Mazatecs use ritual celibacy and other abstaining activities to affect the outcome of produtive activities positively by temporarily absenting themselves from reproductive behaviors and social relations.

Everyday Forms of Ritual Celibacy

In addition to hunting, ritual celibacy — euphemistically referred to as being clean (*tsjé*) or as watching your diet (*guardando el dieta*) — is also carried out by agriculturists during certain stages in the production cycle (turning the soil, planting, harvesting, processing, etc.). The practice ensures an abundant harvest and good health for those who consume the products of their fields and orchards.[4] Because of the restrictions on sexual behavior, it can be hard to hire workers who are clean: "When shucking corn, you need to watch your diet. That's why my father preferred to look for women who were widows (to work for him). . . . If you take this casually, if you treat it as a joke, you will never get anywhere in this life. We had that tradition for initiating a task, and for turning the soil" (Incháustegui 1984: 61).

Although it is likely that ritual celibacy was practiced in pre-Columbian times, beliefs about abstinence have been undeniably influenced by the Catholic Church. The vast majority of Mazatecs consider themselves to be devout Catholics. Priests and nuns are thought to be imbued with considerable moral and spiritual authority. As presumably celibate men and women with a socially recognized connection with God, the saints, and the Church hierarchy, their eschewing of sexual relations is undoubtedly seen as a contributing factor to their metaphysical power.

Mazatecs thus also practice abstinence before engaging in certain religious activities; the rituals and objects associated with the metaphysical world are considered *shcón,* powerful, something to be approached with great caution. For example, because one must guard one's diet before receiving Communion, it is a common sight to see men standing at the back of the church during Mass, sheepishly refusing to participate in the Sacra-

ment. Men's lack of participation during Communion became such an issue that, during one particular Mass, the priest made the unusual move of
declaring a blanket absolution and proclaiming that everyone present was
now clean and thus free to receive the Sacrament with impunity.

A period of abstinence is also required before reading the Bible or
other religious texts, which Mazatecs consider to be *shcón* in the extreme.
The Mazatecs' firmly held conviction that one must be clean in order to
read the Bible proved to be a particular challenge to the work of Protestant missionaries. Because the evangelists stressed the importance of reading the Scriptures every day, they met with little enthusiasm from local
Mazatecs, who did not feel that conversion to Protestantism would be
worth subjecting themselves to a lifetime of celibacy (Pike 1960).

While these and many other important activities require a period of
abstinence (e.g., making offerings to mountain spirits, mourning), ritual
celibacy is perhaps most scrupulously maintained by participants in curing
rituals, particularly those that involve the consumption of morning glory
seeds (in the eastern lowlands) or hallucinogenic mushrooms (in the western highlands). These nocturnal rituals, referred to simply as *vi yo choan*
(stay awake), are carried out by a curing specialist, usually in darkness
and always involving the consumption of hallucinogens by those who happen to be present: the curer, friends and relatives of the sick person, and
occasionally the patients themselves.[5]

Apart from sexual abstinence, participants will often literally watch
their diet by avoiding certain foods, typically pork and chile peppers, for a
few days prior to the ritual. Furthermore, on the day in which they are to
stay awake, Mazatecs will invariably fast after midday in order to intensify
the somatic effects of the mushrooms or the morning glory seeds.

However, making oneself sexually clean prior to these rituals is of far
greater importance, since to do otherwise leads to madness, to becoming
so disoriented within the awful labyrinthine contours of another world
that it can sometimes take months to find your way back to your senses. I
was told of one man who consumed some mushrooms without watching
his diet and subsequently spent the better part of a year wandering
through the streets, talking to himself and raving at passersby, until his
senses gradually returned to the quotidian world.

The dangers of breaking the period of abstinence before consuming the
mushrooms have been an ongoing problem among tourists who opt to
"stay awake" when they visit Huautla de Jiménez, the largest community
in the region. A frequently told story concerns a Japanese tourist who
took the mushrooms without watching his diet and awoke the next morning in a state of terror when he came to the awful realization that he had

lost the ability to speak in any language. His every attempt to speak either in Japanese or in the few words of Spanish he had learned came across as gibberish.

However, the spiritual pollution which results from intercourse does not always remain localized within the body of those who do not watch their diet. Rather, under certain circumstances the uncleanliness is contagious, spread (often inadvertently) through acts of reciprocity. For example, if a man who is watching his diet in preparation for staying awake lends his machete to a neighbor who has recently had sexual relations, the mushrooms will not have the desired medical or divinatory results. As one of Incháustegui's consultants points out: "It's that in terms of diet, you shouldn't give or take anything. If someone comes along who has had, for example, sexual contact, that person is stained and the offering will not be received" (Incháustegui 1984: 64). Conversely, the person who borrowed the machete may himself fall ill with the same malady as the patient being treated through the ritual. In order to avert these dangers, those wishing to stay awake must remain *encerrado,* staying within their home for four days in order to remove themselves from possibly contagious social interactions.

Ritual Specialists

Although the practice is distributed unevenly and with considerable variation, most Mazatecs will practice some form of ritual celibacy throughout the course of their lives. However, the burdens of such practices weigh particularly heavy for the region's many ritual or medical specialists. Despite the fact that midwives, bone setters, specialists who "stay awake," *chuperos* (practitioners who suck ailments out of the bodies of their patients), and *rezadores* (prayer specialists) typically carry out their craft on a part-time basis, they must nonetheless "watch their diet" at all times. While members of the general population who break these taboos risk bringing harm to themselves and to their families, specialists risk visiting harm on their clients as well. For example, if a bone setter is not clean when setting a leg, the set may not hold or the leg may not heal properly. Likewise, a midwife who is careless about watching her diet puts the health of both the mother and her unborn child at risk.

The need to be clean is perhaps even more essential among the *rezadores,* given their critical importance in petitioning God and the saints to allow the souls of the departed to enter into heaven. Following the death of an individual, a series of wakes are held: before the internment and then 3, 7, 10, 20, and 40 days later. At each of these wakes, a *rezador* leads a hypnotically performed series of prayers for the soul of the deceased. Prior to each of the wakes, it is imperative for the *rezador* to remain clean for four days. To do otherwise risks putting the deceased in jeopardy, denying her the divine intervention necessary to free her soul from the purgatorial confines of her interred body at the conclusion of the 40-day wake.

Widows as Ritual and Medical Specialists

Because clients often fall ill or expire at short notice, ritual specialists of all types must be prepared to perform their duties at a moment's notice. Unlike members of the general population, who have the luxury of knowing in advance when they need to watch their diet, specialists must take extraordinary precautions to ensure that, like priests, they are always in the proper condition to perform their craft. Occasionally, a specialist will be faced with a situation in which he must turn clients away because he is not ritually clean, requesting that they return when he has achieved the required period of abstinence. Specialists go to considerable lengths to avoid this dilemma, however, not only because it denies them a source of supplemental income,[6] but also because it puts their professional reputation at risk.

Since the professional demands of staying clean are so arduous, female ritual and medical specialists tend to be widows. Of course, it would be erroneous to assume that widows never engage in sexual activity. Indeed, it is not uncommon for widows to provide young men with their first sexual experience (Boege 1988: 68). On the other hand, the preponderance of widows in these vocations is related to their being culturally marked as celibate as a social category, as evidenced by the tendency of parents of deceased adult males to severely restrict the movements and activities of their daughters-in-law.

More important for this discussion, widows tend to gravitate toward these professions for reasons of status and control. As frequently powerless members of a patriarchal society, Mazatec women, particularly those in the highlands, enjoy few freedoms outside the household, their movements and activities restricted by the fear of being the target of gossip (often by other women) or of verbal or physical rebukes by their husbands. On the other hand, ritual specialists do enjoy some measure of status within their communities because of the high degree of knowledge, talent, and stamina that these professionals require. Consequently, women who become specialists tend to enjoy a greater degree of personal autonomy than those engaged in strictly domestic, mercantile, or agricultural activities.

To some extent, this sense of autonomy also carries over to sexual activity. While in no way immune from the pervasiveness of community gossip and innuendo nor always completely free from the oppressive bonds of their in-laws, widows are able to exercise a degree of control over their sexual activity, which would otherwise leave them open to gossip and censure. This sense of personal control, however, is far greater in terms of voluntarily remaining abstinent than for engaging in sexual activity. In other words, without the responsibility of satisfying a spouse, a widow can be free to meet the sexual preconditions necessary to pursue a vocation as a ritual specialist. This was indeed the case with María Sabina, the most famous shamanic healer in the region, who entered into her profession only after she became a widow: "One month after [my husband] died, I began to take the little things [mushrooms].[7] As I've already said, it isn't good to use the children [mushrooms] when one has a husband.[8] When one goes to bed with a man their cleanliness is spoiled. If a man takes them and two or three days afterward he uses a woman, his testicles rot. If a woman does the same, she goes crazy" (Estrada 1981:67).

Male Ritual Celibacy and Sexual Orientation

While some male ritual specialists are married or widowers, most are either single or separated from their spouses.[9] Partly because of this Mazatecs often assume that male specialists are homosexual.[10] As one Mazatec commented about the shamans in the neighboring community of Huautla, "All of them are queers" (Incháustegui 1977:170).

As in much of Mexico, Mazatec attitudes toward male homosexuality are extremely complex, encompassing revulsion, indifference, and admiration, depending on the circumstances and the social actors involved (Carrier 1995; Murray 1995; Paz 1985; Taylor 1995). In the Mazateca region, homosexuals (*shondá*) face oppression and ridicule, despite the relatively common occurrence of homosexuality there (Boege 1988: 72; Duke 1996: 175).[11] The term *shondá* is often used derisively, particularly by young men who taunt each other mercilessly with this epithet. Furthermore, some Mazatecs strenuously resist the presence of *shondá* in certain professions. For example, during a civic parade in Huautla de Jiménez, teachers from the María Sabina Cultural Center who were homosexuals marched alongside their students. From the sidelines I overheard a number of spectators complaining that *shondá* should be forbidden to provide instruction to their children.

On the other hand, within certain domains, homosexuals can enjoy considerable prestige. Many, for example, play an active role in the administrative and theological affairs of the Catholic Church.[12] Paradoxically, some are also highly regarded catechism teachers, and parents are not at all reticent about allowing them to teach doctrinal matters to their children. Likewise, as ritual specialists, they can enjoy a relatively high status as well, if only to the extent that their particular expertise is recognized by the community.

The association of homosexuals with ritual and theological activities is evidenced by their obvious popularity within these professions, their prevalence due at least in part to their clients' confidence that they will be clean. In contrast, a Mazatec who is ill or whose relative is in need of a *rezador* for a wake would be extremely wary of approaching a specialist whom she suspects of being slack about watching his diet.

Although it is possible that *shondá* ritual specialists also practice abstinence, their highly visible presence and social recognition within these professions lead to the distinct possibility that sexual relations between men are not of consequence in terms of disrupting the act of celibacy because, as some heterosexual consultants have observed, homosexual intercourse is barren, unable as it is to fulfill one of the primary functions of sexual relations: biological reproduction. Thus, the notion that same-sex unions do not disrupt periods of celibacy makes *shondá* uniquely suited to the rigors of ritual and medical activities, for, whatever their sexual behavior, they are always clean, free from the spiritual residue of procreational activities.

It would be erroneous to define *shondá* solely in terms of sexual practice. As indicated above, the social category of *shondá* is far too complex to be wholly defined by particular sexual activities. Nonetheless, it is worth noting in the present context that the sexual behavior that marks a man as *shondá* is the act of being penetrated during anal intercourse. A male playing the insertive role, in contrast, would not necessarily be considered homosexual, depending upon whether the community perceives him to be sexually interested in women, among other factors. The penetration of *shondá* does not appear to detract from their being clean, however. As mentioned above, heterosexual women, who are also penetrated during intercourse, typically become ritual or medical specialists only when they assume a sexually celibate social role, such as that of a widow. Like widows, *shondá* are ideal ritual practitioners, not just because they are often highly skilled in their craft, but also because they are thought to be completely removed from the polluting aspects of reproductive sex.

Reproduction and the Production of Effects

While sexual abstinence allows Mazatecs to exercise a measure of control over particularly risky situations—hunting, agricultural production and processing, participation in certain ritual or medical activities — the relationship between abstinence and possible outcomes in these contexts is nonetheless opaque. Mary Douglas has noted that in many societies, sexual relations are symbolically polluting, reflecting the belief that "each sex is a danger to the other through contact with sexual fluids" (1988: 3). This model makes a certain degree of sense in the Mazatec case, since the belief that abstinence makes one clean implies that there is a polluting aspect to sexual activity. Furthermore, there is a certain correspondence between the different values placed on heterosexual and homosexual relations vis-à-vis ritual celibacy and the danger of male–female interactions more generally. Nonetheless, this model falls short in its ability to explain Mazatec ritual abstinence, because celibacy as both an activity and a manifestation of particular, sometimes contradictory and contested, cultural beliefs is fundamentally about removing oneself from the epistemic and interactional messiness of the social world.

An understanding of Mazatec celibacy thus requires focusing not so much on sexual abstinence per se as on the ensemble of practices of which it is a part, specifically in terms of the way in which they suggest a metaphoric separation of the self from the social world. These prescriptions are most elaborated as a preparation for "staying awake" because of the potential of hallucinogens to bring forth danger of the profoundest sort if not handled by people who are ritually clean: madness, illness, and the possibility of having one's native language erased from consciousness. Recall that, apart from sexual abstinence and the eating of certain foods, a person who stays awake must remain in seclusion, or *encerrado,* for a given period of time. Accordingly, one must absent oneself from social networks, including those of reciprocity.

Like sexual relations, social relations among the Mazatecs are shot through with tenderness, friction, joy, and uneasiness. As in most rural communities and small towns, the intimacy and familiarity of social interaction is instrumental in creating and maintaining networks of friendship, solidarity, and mutual help. On the other hand, social intercourse carries significant risk. Mazatecs must remain vigilant about what they say and do, since the eyes and ears of the community act as a panopticon, ever attentive to possible indiscretions, to inexplicable — and thus, suspicious — behavior. A lingering glance, an offhand comment made in a cantina when cane liquor has loosened the tongue, a solitary walk to an unknown destination, all are fodder for baroque conspiracy theories determined to link their targets to scandal. Indeed, social relations are not just risky but dangerous. The possibility of being struck ill by envy or witchcraft, of having your child fall prey to the evil eye, must always be calculated into any social encounter. More concretely, a confrontational situation can sometimes spiral out of control, as evidenced by the region's high homicide rate

Thus, to cloister oneself temporarily from the world of mutual obligations and social intercourse allows the messiness and contingencies of everyday life to dissipate from the body. Likewise, the ecstatic dissonance of (hetero)sexual relations, with their momentary fragmentation of the self, their direct engagement with gender and class hierarchies, and, most important, their joyful and uneasy entrance into the contingencies of human reproduction, creates a sociosexual messiness that can be scrubbed clean only through a period of abstinence.

The relationship among pollution, cleanliness, and the body can perhaps best be illustrated through the ritual use of San Pedro within the context of staying awake. A paste made from tobacco, garlic, and quick lime, San Pedro is a substance of extraordinary power for the Mazatecs. For example, some parents tie a small bundle of the material around their children's necks in order to avert the evil eye or other dangers. The poultice is also rubbed onto the forearm in the shape of a cross during a number of ritual practices. Most important for this discussion, it is often taken in conjunction with the mushrooms as a purgative. This has to do in part with the alleged benefits of violently expelling illnesses from the body. However, San Pedro is widely thought to heighten the effects of the mushrooms, providing a profound and bitter cleansing that allows ritual participants greater access to the curative and metaphysical powers of the mushrooms. Like celibacy and other abstaining acts, which metaphorically entail removing social pollutants from the body, San Pedro brings a literal cleanliness through the vomiting forth of illnesses whose origins are for the most part products of the social world.

In sum, ritual celibacy among the Mazatecs is part of an ensemble of abstaining gestures that seek to influence positively the outcome of particular productive acts such as hunting, agriculture, curing, and prayer. This is accomplished, paradoxically, by symbolically removing oneself from certain essentially *reproductive* processes: the reproduction of labor power (through the consumption of food); social reproduction (through interaction and exchange); and, most important, biological reproduction (through heterosexual intercourse). Thus, far from being merely an absence, a nonactivity, ritual abstinence is itself a productive act, given its critical roles in the production of effects and in the protection against danger.

The analysis outlined above should not be seen as a totalizing narrative which definitively "explains" ritual celibacy. Indeed, much important work needs to be done on this topic in Mesoamerica in general and among the Mazatecs in particular. More important, because of celibacy's enormously varied and contradictory uses in Mazatec society, analysts must resist all attempts to reduce it to a set of prescribed rules and meanings, because much of the power of abstinence as a cultural form stems not from its logic and internal consistencies but from its contradictions and silences, which make it resistant to totalizing explanations.

Notes

1. The Mazatec region has a population of approximately 119,000 residents (according to the 1990 census [INEGI 1991]), occupying an area of approximately 2,400 square kilometers that transverses portions of the states of Oaxaca, Puebla, and Veracruz.

2. I learned this from Brian Stross (personal communication, October 31, 1996).

3. Some examples of ritual celibacy in Mesoamerica can be found in Colby and Colby 1981; Lipp 1991; Madsen 1955; Sandstrom 1991.

4. Neiberg (1988: 78) has noted that in Tenango, ritual behavior associated with farming, presumably including celibacy, occurs only in relation to the production of foodstuffs for local consumption and not in relation to cash crops such as coffee. However, in the area around Huautla de Jiménez, local consumption of coffee is so important to social relations (Duke 1996: 62–65) that it is likely that a farmer who engages in ritual behavior in his field will also do so when tending his coffee trees. On the other hand, ritual behavior seems to be of little or no importance in economic spheres that are wholly dependent on exchange values, such as wage labor or mercantile activity.

5. Among participants in these rituals, there is considerable ambiguity as to the causal relationship between staying awake and healing. Some Mazatecs suggest that the purpose of the ritual is to affect a cure more or less directly (with the mushrooms having medicinal properties). Others insist that staying awake has a more divinatory character: to ascertain the cause of the illness, through both visions and direct consultations with the mushrooms themselves.

6. With the notable exception of specialists who perform the mushroom ritual for tourists, payment for services is modest even by local standards. It is thus uncommon for specialists to rely on clients' fees as a primary source of income.

7. Literally, *'ndi xi tjo,* "the little ones that spring forth," which refers either to the mushrooms' sudden appearance after a rainfall or else to their highly disorienting somatic effects.

8. "The children" comes from a fuller Spanish euphemism, *los niños santos* (the saint children), which the Mazatecs use to refer to these mushrooms.

9. Married male specialists, some of whom are highly regarded, tend to practice their craft on a very irregular basis.

10. Because of the highly circumspect nature by which Mazatecs discuss sexual matters, coupled with the predilection of rumor and innuendo in local communities, it would be impossible to determine the extent to which this is objectively the case. However, what is important for this discussion is not their sexual orienta-

tion per se but the sexual categories by which they are defined in the Mazatec society.

11. In the discussion that follows, I am referring only to male homosexuality. While lesbianism undoubtedly exists among the Mazatecs, it does not appear to be a highly marked social category.

12. In particular communities and at particular historical moments, on the other hand, *shondá* have also been persecuted by the Catholic Church. Boege (1988: 172) reports that in San José Tenango, the town's priest had expelled a group of homosexual *rezadores,* who in turn converted to Protestantism, ironically with the stipulation that they no longer engage in homosexual acts.

References Cited

Boege, Eckart. 1988. *Los Mazatecos ante la nación: Contradicciones de la identidad étnica en el México actual.* Mexico: Siglo Veintiuno Editores.

Carrier, Joseph. 1995. *De los otros: Intimacy and Homosexuality among Mexican Men.* New York: Columbia University Press.

Colby, Benjamin N., and Lore M. Colby. 1981. *The Daykeeper: The Life and Discourse of an Ixil Diviner.* Cambridge, Mass.: Harvard University Press.

Douglas, Mary. 1988. *Purity and Danger: An Analysis of the Concepts of Pollution and Taboo.* London: Ark Paperbacks.

Duke, Michael. 1996. Gordon Wasson's Disembodied Eye: Genre, Representation and the Dialectics of Subjectivity in Huautla de Jiménez, Mexico. Ph.D. dissertation, Anthropology, University of Texas at Austin.

Estrada, Alvaro. 1981. *María Sabina: Her Life and Chants.* Trans. Henry Munn. Santa Barbara: Ross-Erikson.

Incháustegui, Carlos. 1977. *Relatos del mundo mágico Mazateco.* Mexico: Secretaria de Educación Pública, Instituto Nacional de Antropología e Historia.

Incháustegui, Carlos. 1984. *Figuras en la niebla: Relatos y creencias de los Mazatecos.* Mexico: La Red de Jonas.

Instituto Nacional de Estadistica, Geografía, e Informática (INEGI). 1991. *Oaxaca: Resultados definitivas: Datos por localidad (integración territorial).* Vol. II: *Censo general de población y vivienda, 1990.* Aguascalientes, Ags. Mexico City: published by the institution.

Lipp, Frank J. 1990. *The Mixe of Oaxaca: Religion, Ritual, and Healing.* Norman: University of Oklahoma Press.

Madsen, William. 1955. Shamanism in Mexico. *Southwestern Journal of Anthropology* 11: 48–55.

Murray, Stephen O., ed. 1995. *Latin American Male Homosexualities.* Albuquerque: University of New Mexico Press.

Neiberg, Federico G. 1988. *Identidad y conflicto en la Sierra Mazateca: El caso del consejo de ancianos de San José Tenango. Mexico City: Instituto Nacional de Antropología e Historia.*

Paz, Octavio. 1985. *The Labyrinth of Solitude.* Revised ed. New York: Grove. Original publication, 1961.

Pike, Eunice V. 1960. Mazatec Sexual Impurity and Bible Reading. *Practical Anthropology* 7(2): 49–53.
Sandstrom, Alan R. 1991. *Corn Is Our Blood: Culture and Ethnic Identity in a Contemporary Aztec Indian Village.* Norman: University of Oklahoma Press.
Taylor, Clark L. 1995. Legends, Syncretism, and Continuing Echoes of Homosexuality from Pre-Columbian and Colonial México. In *Latin American Male Homosexualities,* ed. Stephen O. Murray, 80–99. Albuquerque: University of New Mexico Press.

7 *Hiroko Kawanami*

Can Women Be Celibate?
Sexuality and Abstinence in Theravada Buddhism

> While the avowed Buddhist goal is to transcend gender and sexuality . . . it is female sexuality that becomes a major impediment, while "maleness" is the prerequisite for enlightenment.
> —Rajyashree Pandey, "Women, Sexuality, and Enlightenment"

This chapter sets out to explore the issues of sexuality and abstinence in Theravada Buddhism and examines whether the notions of female sexuality that have been constructed in the Buddhist tradition are compatible with the notion of spirituality in the monastic tradition. I am particularly interested in the celibate practice of female renunciants and will argue that the function of female celibate practice cannot be understood if we impose on it the assumptions that govern male celibate practice. Celibacy may be seen as an effective tool to achieve the collective goals of the members of the Buddhist monastic community, but it has also been an important practice for its male members to realize their masculine identity. By adhering to the vow of sexual abstinence, a monk becomes truly male. For a nun, the same practice does not imply the realization of her womanhood. On the contrary, celibate practice implies the shedding of femininity, which consequently allows the nun to transcend both the notion of female sexuality permeating the Buddhist texts and the limitations prescribed to her by her reproductive faculties. By renouncing womanhood altogether, a nun is finally free to pursue her inner spirituality.

I start my inquiry into this contradiction by looking at the notions of female sexuality through images of the feminine in popular Buddhist texts and in social stereotypes in a Buddhist society. These representations are generally unfavorable to women because they project certain types of

137

female characteristics and womanhood that have been constructed primarily by the male religious authority. Notwithstanding, there is a wide
discrepancy between the official representations and social stereotypes
that are perpetuated, on the one hand, and the everyday experiences of
Myanmar women, on the other. I demonstrate this by presenting information I have collected in the field. I draw on information obtained mainly
from observations and personal interviews conducted over the course of
four visits to Upper Myanmar.[1]

For the initial period of fieldwork, which lasted 18 months (1986–87), I
lived with Buddhist nuns in one of the largest monastic communities of
the Sagaing Hills, 12 miles west of the ancient capital, Mandalay. The
community included approximately 10,000 monks, novice monks, and
nuns, who lived side by side. A small lay community nearby catered to the
religious population. I took part in communal events and religious activities and observed the vows of the Eight Buddhist Precepts. I committed
myself to a life of stoic discipline, which implied celibacy, fasting in the
afternoons, abstaining from alcohol, and staying away from so-called
worldly pleasures such as watching television, listening to music, going
out with friends, and so on. While living with the nuns and talking to the
monks and lay devotees who frequented the nunneries, I collected information about the actual religious life and spiritual practice of the people.[2]
After having learned the vernacular language, engaged in participatory
observation for a relatively long period of time, and established a level of
communication without the use of intermediaries, I also attempted in
many interviews to explore how women perceive their sexuality in contemporary Myanmar society. The majority of my informants actively participated in these interviews and provided me with their personal life stories.

Images and Stereotypes of Women in Theravada Buddhism

When we examine female representation and images of women in Buddhist literature, we notice a tension "between the usually positive assessment of women and the feminine on the one hand, and the blatantly negative, on the other" (Sponberg 1992: 3). The positive image is that of a
married woman who is obedient and faithful to her husband, and the
negative is that of a greedy and undisciplined seductress. We notice strong
social expectations for women to surrender their own ambitions, get married and bear children, and stay within the confinement of marriage. This
theme permeates many passages. The pattern is also evident in *Lokanīti*,[3]
one of the most popular religious treatises in Myanmar, which has traditionally served as an effective medium for the moral instruction of the
people. It was taught in almost every monastic school until education was

secularized in the mid-nineteenth century by the British administration. The moral parables, compiled by the monks and taught by them to Myanmar children, serve as cautionary tales and provide a set of behavioral guidelines for Myanmar women.

In *Lokanīti,* as in most Buddhist literature, we are introduced to two opposing typologies of women. One image is exemplified in a section that says, "A buffalo delights in mud, a duck in a pond, a woman delights in a husband, a priest in the law" (*Lokanīti* 1886: 22). A "good" woman is valued by "her devotedness to her husband" (p. 22); she should be one "who, during meals and in her adornments, delights like a mother, who in things that should be concealed is bashful like a sister, who during business and when approaching her husband is respectful like a slave" (pp. 23–24). These positive images (i.e., of "good" women) are accompanied by another well-known theme from the Laws of Manu: that a woman's "worth" (sexuality) has to be closely guarded, supervised, and kept under the authority of her male kin.

There is an opposing image, however: that of a "dangerous" woman, who is difficult to control from a male point of view. Spiro (1997: 23) distinguishes the typology of dangerous female as two sets of characteristics, one moral and the other sexual. In fact, Buddhist literature is full of negative depictions of women, who are seen as lustful and greedy, jealous and deceitful, fickle and unreliable, vain and sexually undisciplined, and warns its readers to approach them with great care. Paul also states that Buddhist literature has depicted women as "biologically determined to be sexually uncontrollable" (1979: 7). *Dhammanīti,* another treatise of maxims and didactic stories, depicts women as greedy not only for sex but for all aspects of life. One passage states that their "appetite is twice that of men, their intelligence four times, their assiduity six times, and their [sexual] desires eight times" (see second part of *Lokanīti* 1886: 71–72). The last section of this passage and the section that says, "If each woman had eight husbands . . . she is indeed not satisfied" (p. 72), are often quoted or taken out of context in order to make exaggerated claims regarding the strength of the female sexual libido.

However, it seems to me misleading to place the focus only on a woman's sexual appetite. We can interpret the former passage to be a statement about her energetic attitude toward life, and the latter to be about a general tendency of a wife who is dissatisfied with whatever her husband does. These passages reflect a strong Brahmanic influence that is emphatically patriarchal, reinforcing the social imperative for lay women as well as serving as a warning about the grave danger of female sexuality. So while the myth of female eroticism and sexual prowess is highlighted on the one hand, acceptable values such as chastity, honor, and virtue are

promoted on the other hand to set moral standards for women in everyday life.

Now we turn to the concept of motherhood, regarded in the literature
as a female role of primary importance. But even mother images do not
seem to be free from innate tension. While a mother in the Brahmanic
tradition is sanctified and accorded an almost divine status, Buddhist literature seems to treat her in a rather ambiguous manner. She is depicted
as wise and compassionate in some contexts, but she is also seen as the
episymbol of attachment and suffering. There seems to be some expectation for a mother to remain exceptional. The Buddha's mother, Māyā, the
paragon of virtue and chastity, is said to have conceived him without sex.
Even so, she had to die seven nights after giving birth to him lest she
should become polluted and lose her sacred status (*Mahāvastu* 1952: 3).
Besides, no living woman can possibly emulate her.

Generally speaking, motherhood in Theravada Buddhist societies is
viewed as secular. For a Burmese person, motherhood represents love
and deep emotional attachment. Her loving care is much appreciated,
and the majority of my informants, both male and female, admitted that
they were deeply attached to their mothers. Some said that a mother
could endure excruciating pain in childbirth because of her love, and her
suffering was such that "even her blood turned into milk for the suckling
infant" (for the self-sacrifice made by a mother and the depth of a
mother's love, see Horner 1930: 11–14).

A mother is seen as highly virtuous because she is giving to the point of
self-sacrifice. In this respect, she becomes almost sanctified in her role as
martyr. However, a mother in her reproductive role is seen to have become caught up in her attachment to her family, and this is identified with
samsara, the endless cycle of rebirths. It is a vicious cycle for a woman if
she eventually wants to pursue the spiritual path and become liberated.
On the other hand, it seems to me that the ideological scheme has become
complete. In this, "women's prevailing involvement with reproduction
and motherhood as dictated by society does not allow them the freedom
to renounce family responsibilities in the name of religion" (Paul 1979:
60), so the mother's very existence presupposes a religious ideal that is
opposed to the ultimate ideal of spiritual detachment. While a man leaves
home to seek his spiritual liberation, like the Buddha, who left his wife
and young son for his solitary spiritual quest, a woman stays at home and
looks after the family for the rest of her life. Thus, despite all the gratitude
and respect she reaps, her spiritual position remains severely limited.[4]

The imagery of woman in general, as one who is a stranger, is almost
always presented in a negative light. That is, a woman who is not in a
desexualized kin category (one's mother, wife, or daughter) becomes

objectified as dangerous and threatening. The common conception of a woman is embodied in the three daughters of the Buddha's evil rival, Māra, whose names are Rāga (sexual attraction), Arati (aversion), and Trsna (craving). They appear before the Buddha, who is deep in meditation, to seduce him away from his mindful efforts to achieve enlightenment. Images of a wicked woman who tempts and distracts the male practitioner as he struggles to concentrate his mind are widespread. Furthermore, woman is traditionally perceived by monks as a major hindrance to their spiritual welfare and thus has been made into a symbol of something that has to be renounced. Although the root of this image may have been in the mind of the male ascetic afraid "to lose his celibate purity" (Kloppenborg 1995: 152), blame for monks' moral lapses has always been placed on women. Schuster-Barnes (1987: 112) says that a monk's unresolved desire turned resentful, which consequently generated hatred of the woman he lusted after, and then images of the devil woman, the temptress, were conjured.

The images of woman in the Buddhist literature swing between virtuous and sensual, tamed and wild, obedient and willful, but they all seem to be ultimately complementary. The reproductive and chaste woman, the mother and wife, is naturally given a more affirmative recognition than the sensual woman, who is lusted after but looked down upon with contempt. The juxtaposition involves a passive vessel for procreation and an object of desire for men. In either case, a woman is described as having no control over her own destiny and sexuality. She is either an attached mother sucked into the endless cycle of reproduction or a jealous temptress caught up in the vicious cycle of obsession and sexual desire. In these images of the feminine, women are objectified, their attributes are exaggerated and appropriated in order to serve the androcentric Buddhist ideology.

Celibate Ideal and Female Ascetics

In early Buddhism, the purity of sexual abstinence seems to have appealed to the religious scheme of the Buddha as he consolidated his monastic community. His followers were those who had left their secular existence and entered the stoic lifestyle defined by celibacy (brahmacharya), which became the prerequisite for the monk's vocation. Sexual abstinence, fasting, and the control of one's passions all served as important strategies to strengthen the fraternal solidarity for its collective goal of spreading the teachings of the Buddha. The monk was called a bhikku, meaning "the one who begs," for he lived off the goodwill and material support of his lay devotees, who received spiritual merit in return. His religious life centered on textual learning, meditation, moral discipline, and ascetic austerities. Only the ordained monks in the Theravadin tradition, who had left the secular world for self-realization, could proceed further on the path to ultimate spiritual liberation. Consequently, celibate monkhood became elevated as a superior way of life in comparison to a layman's marital life, which was seen as less conducive to his spiritual progress.[5] In addition, sex, even for the purpose of procreation, was viewed as an activity of a base nature and regarded as a source of suffering, which again perpetuated the endless cycle of rebirths.

In Buddhist literature, it is the male renunciants who are treated with high respect and regarded as spiritually superior to the laity. In contrast, the images of female renunciants or Buddhist nuns are in most passages treated rather negatively.[6] Falk states that their representations are treated less favorably than those of laywomen (1980: 219–220). *Lokanīti* also takes a spiteful tone toward this category of religious women, saying "All rivers are crooked; all forests are made of wood; all women, going into solitude, would do what is evil" (as quoted in Falk 1980: 23). If pursuing a religious vocation was the only way for a woman to "go into solitude" during its time, becoming a nun implicitly signified that she was up to something wicked that was shunned by society.

There is a similar trend in the images of the feminine put forth in the literature and popular stereotypes that circulate in Theravada Buddhist societies. A well-known Myanmar proverb says, "Buddhist nuns are women whose sons are dead, who are widowed, bankrupt, in debt, and broken-hearted," conveying a prevailing stereotype of nuns in Myanmar society. Some of my lay informants told me that ugly girls from poor families and infertile women become nuns, and others said nuns are women who have brought bad luck to others. People have frequently commented that a healthy young woman should not be celibate. A male informant asked, "Why would a young woman shave off her long hair and enter a religious life unless she has some kind of a problem?" Buddhism preaches that all humans are subject to suffering and mortality, and there is no permanent essence that one can point to and say is definitely oneself. Social attributes such as gender, social status, and nationality are taught to be irrelevant for one's spiritual quest. So this ultimate ideal should allow everyone to work at inner progress by advocating a move toward overcoming ideological prejudice and all forms of discrimination. However, the cultural beliefs commonly held in Theravadin societies are fundamentally dualistic; here, one is not free from the ideological opposition between man, associated with the religious and spiritual, and woman, associated with the worldly and sensual, the body and reproduction. So it is not uncommon for nuns, who have digressed from the designated cultural norm of wife and mother, to be treated with suspicion and mockery. They are at times even cast as women who have failed in their secular womanhood. Such negative stereotypes that denigrate the nuns are strong and prevalent. Despite the fact that most nuns have voluntarily chosen their religious career, they are not entirely immune from what people say, and at times their self-confidence is undermined.[7]

Many of the nuns I interviewed left home against their parents' wishes, so defying social expectations and discarding their gender attributes. As one nun commented, "I am freer now that I have no hair. I don't have to worry about what I wear, for I have my religious uniform. I don't have to put on makeup and behave like a woman anymore." The nuns seem to have made a conscious attempt to move away from what Nash has described as a "vanity culture," in which Myanmar girls are trained and brought up to be "ladylike" (1965: 249). Comparing their married sisters' "hot and troubled" lives with their own, nuns referred to their celibate lifestyle as "cool and peaceful," and most of them stated that they were happier and better off than they were before. Thus, contrary to our assumptions, a celibate life for women may be "a preference rather than an ordeal, more blessing than self-transforming discipline" (Phillimore, this volume).

However, because of her biological womanhood, a nun still has to shoulder the burden of the constructed ideological opposition between the spiritual male and the carnal female, the ascetic monk and the sensual nun. Even her commitment to the religious career displayed by her shaven head is seen as an act of defiance rather than as a proof of her devotion and spiritual quality. In real life, a female ascetic has to strive much harder than her male counterpart in order to overcome various obstacles imposed by the general implication of her sexuality. She also suffers from the double standards that uphold a male celibate's religious vocation as spiritually superior while penalizing the female renunciant, who has opted out of the social norm, by relegating her to a secondary religious position. In short, her presence on the ascetic path is in itself problematic because she encroaches upon the sacred territory of men and threatens their valued place in the spiritual hierarchy.

On the other hand, Myanmar women have had certain religious roles traditionally reserved for them: those of witches and spirit mediums. Here again, however, their role and significance are played down because of the immodest nature of associated ritual performance, excessive consumption of alcohol, and the release of repressed passions. One of my informants said that it is because of their shortcomings, not their special skills, that women have been active as spirit mediums. Another added, "Women are physically weak, so it's easier for the spirits to take over and possess them." A similar trend was observed by Nissan in Sri Lanka: "Women became possessed while men renounced" (1984: 32).

Social Practice and Cultural Ideology

In the secular realm of bilateral and matrilocal societies such as Thailand and Myanmar in Southeast Asia, women have traditionally enjoyed a high degree of freedom and strong standing in every aspect of social, economic, legal, and domestic life. Their social independence seems to have impressed many colonial officers and missionaries. Brown (1926: 88) noted from his observations at the turn of the last century that Myanmar women, whether married or unmarried, were by far more economically independent from men than their counterparts in England. Indeed, there is no purdah, and women are active members in the public domain. They are the sole agents in market transactions, and most of them work as breadwinners for their families while bringing up their children. Marriage or divorce does not change a woman's position, since she keeps her name, and her premarital property stays as her own in these instances. Husbands and wives treat each other as almost equal partners and share tasks and chores at home: "In theory and in public the husband is supposedly dominant, but this dominance is so tenuous, so indefinite and ambiguous that its social visibility is virtually nil" (Nash 1965: 253–254). Thus there seems to be no clear pattern of authority between spouses. But this does not extend into the religious domain. Furthermore, when pressed, Myanmar of both sexes say that men are nobler in essence and inherently superior to women (Khaing 1984: 89).

The ultimate source of Myanmar masculinity lies in the *hpoun,* "an ineffable essence, investing its possessor with superior moral, spiritual and intellectual quality" (Spiro 1977: 236, 259). Being equipped with *hpoun,* men are generally believed to be superior to women. The belief in this superior male essence is countered by the belief in the dangerous sexual powers of a woman, which are deeply threatening to the very source of male virility. This manifests itself in the male's ambiguous attitude toward female genitals, for example, which are viewed as repulsive and polluting on the one hand and dangerous and powerful on the other. There are also specific cultural taboos that surround material objects associated with female sexuality; the head and right part of the male body must be protected from various forms of contact with women. This is symbolized in a fearful attitude toward the lower garment traditionally worn by Burmese women.[8]

Brahmanic values and ideology have remained influential in social norms and ethics that are unfavorable to women. For example, people believe that Myanmar women are prone to more suffering than men. The "five forms of female suffering," often referred to by Myanmar Buddhists, are menstruation, pregnancy, childbirth, separation from parents, and having to serve a husband sexually and otherwise (see also Kloppenborg 1995: 163–164). These sufferings relate mostly to procreation, and because a woman's primary role is seen to be in reproduction, they act as a reminder that the very fact of being a woman is the result of her bad karma or past bad deeds. Belittled by popular beliefs like this, beliefs that devalue womanhood, many women welcome an alternative life in the religious community. During my research in Myanmar, I found that more than 80 percent of the nuns had entered the monastic community because of some kind of anxiety about a situation which had caused them "suffering" in either an abstract or a concrete manner. The majority of them had become nuns as young virgins in their early teens, mostly between the ages of 12 and 16. Most seemed to have had little experience of sex, the fear of which was one of the primary reasons they left home.[9]

Married women are usually discouraged from becoming nuns at the point of entry. The nuns consider them to be still attached to worldly pleasures, thus they are seen to be easily tempted back to the secular world. Moreover, they are looked upon as suspect; having had sexual experience, they might even tempt innocent members to leave their religious vocation. I came across several women who had entered the nunnery after having problems in their marital home. Their problems included domestic violence, alcohol abuse, unfaithful husbands, and financial difficulties. Nevertheless, in most cases they stayed only for a temporary period, departing as soon as they saw some kind of solution to their problem, thereby confirming the view of the senior nuns. In one case, 10 years ago, a young mother had stabbed her husband's mistress after being severely distressed. She was brought to the nunnery by her father, for she had nowhere to go after being ostracized in the village. The nuns accepted her, albeit reluctantly, because her father had been one of their regular donors. But they assumed that the woman would not stay for more than a few months. In their eyes, she lacked discipline and could not have endured the simple life in the nunnery. In her case, however, the nuns were proved wrong. The woman managed to endure the stoic and eventless life and came to realize her religious faith. She still lives as a Buddhist nun.

Now let me add another dimension to the picture of female celibate practice. There are many laywomen in Myanmar who remain as spinsters and retain control of their sexuality without becoming nuns. They are not uncommon; every joint family seems to have at least one unmarried member. In fact, more than 2 out of 10 women over the age of 35 were single in Sagaing town, a half hour away from the monastic community (women usually do not get married after their mid-30s because this is considered to be past the reproductive age).

Spinsters are referred to as *apyo-gyi*, meaning "big virgins" in Myanmar.[10] Most seem to pursue a professional career; some are well known as important entrepreneurs. They look after their sisters' children, care for infirm parents, and are often in charge of the household finances. They are indeed what the Myanmar term implies, for sex in Myanmar is still equated with marriage, especially for women. They are not disrespected, because virginity, for both men and women, is highly valued as a symbol of purity. Indeed, they are generally admired for their willpower and economic independence. They are also feared for having the mental strength to resist sensual pleasures, which is regarded as an almost impossible feat for an ordinary Myanmar person. Married women in particular commented that their spinster sisters were higher on the spiritual ladder than they themselves were. They added that these women could resist sexual temptation because, in their previous existence, they were celestial nymphs. In other words, coming from a higher (superior) spiritual abode than the human's, spinsters are equipped with better karma than their married sisters. They are seen as disciplined and strong-willed, independent and religious. In practice, spinsters are generous donors, and with more free time and independent resources at their disposal, many of them devote themselves almost full time to the welfare of the monastic community.

Accounts of Women's Actual Experiences

I now turn to the actual sexual experiences of Myanmar women. Their stories seem to present a rather different picture from the images conveyed in scriptural passages, social stereotypes, and sexual allusions. I have collected many data on sexual matters over the last decade in intimate conversation with Myanmar village women. The information I gathered seems to reverse the picture presented by male anthropologists, whose information generally appears to reflect cultural ideology and popular conceptions rather than the actual sexual experiences of women. For example, Spiro asserts that many male informants in Yeigi village viewed women as "almost insatiable" (1977: 239), explaining that "once she tastes sex, she wants more and more" (p. 214). He argues that their belief about the strong female sexual libido comes not only from personal experience but also from common observation (p. 239).

What is remarkable is that in spite of such claims it would be almost impossible to locate a wild and uncontrollably oversexed female in a society where people consider it shameful to be seen naked even by their own spouse. An unmarried Myanmar woman never goes out alone, and in my experience it was young teenage girls who expressed their anxiety at being coerced into a sexual situation by insatiate males, not the other way round. In one case, family members had to chaperon their teenage daughter wherever she went because she had been pestered and followed by an earnest admirer. Her family told me how uncontrollable young men were and how difficult it was to protect their beautiful daughter from their persistent advances. Khaing goes further to state that the Myanmar "do not hold the Hindu view of women as the irrational sex, easily swayed by emotions" (1984: 17). She argues that the Myanmar male is regarded as the energetic and volatile sex, whereas a woman is seen as the sensible guide. She also mentions a Myanmar saying: "Man is flowing water and woman the restraining influence which husbands his energies towards fruition" (p. 18). So in this context, the Myanmar woman is regarded as the restraining agent. In fact, the thought of a woman enticing a man into having sex with her was received with disbelief and embarrassment by my informants. Moreover, there seems to be a wide discrepancy between the low incidence of extramarital sex or infidelity among women and their assumed voracious sexual appetite.

In rural villages, most of the married women I spoke to said they endured sex because it was one of their marital duties, and many of them listed having to satisfy sexual needs as one of the major forms of female suffering and a source of misery and unhappiness. Many of those I spoke to were unable to regard sex as pleasure. None had any instruction or sex education from their parents or other family members. One woman said that she never thought of sex as pleasure because no one had told her how to do it properly. She was already in her late 50s with four children. What I gathered was that sex was always initiated by the husband with little foreplay and rapid ejaculation, and since a woman's needs were dependent on her husband, who in most cases did not understand hers, many women I spoke to did not seem to regard it as pleasure. Sexual dysfunction was further exascerbated by the often crowded sleeping conditions in villages, where family members slept together, making privacy impossible for married couples. Most women said they found it embarrassing or painful, and none of them removed their clothes for the act. Some of them even questioned me whether women had sexual desire at all, and others claimed to have little knowledge of female orgasm. In addition to all this, a proper Myanmar wife is not supposed to show her sexual passion at home. Thus she might become, to use a Freudian term, delibidinized.

In sexual matters, all the village women I spoke to said that they did not take any initiative with their husbands simply because a man makes decisions in that sort of thing. One woman told me about "a friend" whose husband mocked her and called her a whore when she asked for sex. The women also suggested that a wife rarely resisted her husband even if she was tired or not in the mood. One nun who was married previously with two young children said, "If I hadn't left home then, I would still be bearing children. Probably by now I would have had a dozen or more." When I asked her why she did not use contraceptives, she replied with embarrassment, "Men don't like them and they do what they want with you." Birth control was rarely practiced in villages, and although urban dwellers were generally more informed, contraceptives were obtainable only on the black market. In general, it seemed to be a common practice for a wife simply to comply with whatever her husband desired until they had a certain number of children, and women seemed generally resigned in their submissive reproductive role.

Although literary sources and popular sayings seem to exaggerate and distort female sexuality, everyday customs and social norms for Myanmar women are restrictive and puritanical. Sexual modesty is of paramount value for Myanmar women, and they are keen to maintain their virtuous reputation. Premarital or extramarital sex is very difficult for women to manage, and since the social stigma and shame would be intolerable, the incidence of infidelity is much lower among females. A girl normally marries the man she has her first sexual experience with; otherwise her future chances of finding a husband are said to become severely jeopardized. Married women are no exception to these restrictive norms. A decent married woman would never allow a male into the house when her husband is absent. Nor would she like to be seen publicly with any other grown man, unless he is a member of her family or a close relative. While prevalent images of adulterous and sexually loose women do not seem to be empirically grounded, they seem to be firmly internalized and held with deep conviction, especially by anxious Myanmar men.

A Buddhist Monk as a Masculine Role Model

In contrast with women, man is viewed as the active agent who dictates and takes initiative in sexual relations, the act of which is perceived as very much part of his masculine identity. Among all Myanmar males, the one who is regarded to be equipped with the highest level of male essence (*hpoun*) is a Buddhist monk, addressed as *hpoun-gyì,* meaning "big *hpoun*" or "full glory." He is much revered, not only because he exemplifies the canonical teachings of the Buddha, but more so because he is willing to suffer from the ultimate sexual deprivation. For a healthy young Myanmar male, sexual abstinence is considered a severe deprivation. And although lay devotees frequently observe the religious code of abstinence on special religious days, few of them seem to be young, active men. People expect young men to be sexually voracious and say that those who can withstand sexual deprivation must be endowed with a special quality, called *pāramī,* bestowed as a result of saving up a lot of spiritual merit in their previous lives. One Myanmar man in his early 30s said that he could not remain as a monk simply because he did not have the persistent "strength" to abstain from sex. Another young man who had left the monkhood told me that he could not stay for more than a month because he was so exhausted from trying to stay celibate. He sad, "It is physically tiring to abstain from sex. Those who can remain a monk have a lot of stamina," implying that he was not physically fit for such a difficult religious ordeal.[11]

It is generally believed that to remain a monk the candidate must be physically and mentally fit enough to withstand sexual deprivation. Therefore, before becoming fully fledged members of the monastic community, men go through a rigorous ordination ritual that questions their qualifications for monkhood. Among the conditions described in the Theravadin tradition (the fourth volume of *Mahāvagga*), a male candidate has to be over 20 years of age and free from social shackles such as debt, military service, and employment in the government. He also has to be given permission to become a monk by his parents or wife. The candidate is checked for symptoms of chronic conditions such as epilepsy and eczema, and must be free of contagious diseases such as boils, leprosy, and consumption. He cannot be too ugly, too old, handicapped, malformed, or missing parts of his body, all of which are seen as the result of bad karma (Wijayaratna 1990: 120). Moreover, he must be sexually competent and heterosexual, which implies that the candidate is equipped with all the physical faculties that are later required to be renounced. The bigger this sacrifice is for him, the higher the reward on the spiritual ladder.

In contrast, a female candidate is not tested on her sexual faculties. She is asked whether she is a free woman, free from pregnancy, debts, and royal service. She has to be fit to lead a homeless life and not subject to the types of diseases listed for the male candidate, but her sexual qualifications are not contested in the ordination ritual.

Early Buddhism and the Theravada school shared with Hinduism the perception of sexual abstinence as an important part of ascetic practice that offered the male practitioner access to a substantial degree of power. Steed (1955: 135) narrates a popular story told by an informant, regarding how the monkey deity, Hanumān, in his fight to rescue Sītā from the demon king Rāvana, gained the strength to overcome insuperable obstacles by retaining his semen. This story is one example that shows how the male practitioner focuses on the retention of semen to achieve power

(Alter 1997: 285; Jackson 1992: 93). The rechanneling of sexual energy (semen) into spiritual virility has been a significant theme for male ascetics in yogic and Tantric practices hoping to access inordinate strength and success. However, in keeping with the notion that semen retention provided this access, the ascetic lifestyle was regarded as a distinctly male path, appealing to men for the construction of masculine identity.

In the secular Myanmar context also, the theme of sexual abstinence and the acquisition of psychic powers are prevalent among males, who believe that "semen is the source of a male's strength" (Spiro 1977: 238). There are many male practitioners called *weikza* in Myanmar folktales; *weikza* have mastered the "occult arts" of alchemy, astrology, charms, spells, medicines, and meditation (Ferguson and Mendelson 1981: 63). They are equipped with superhuman strength and supernatural powers, displaying miraculous abilities such as bilocation, levitation, traveling through the earth, or living under water. They can even command and outdo witches and dangerous spirits. *Weikza* exercise sexual abstinence,[12] and so are believed to have stronger physical and mental abilities than ordinary people: they can prolong their lives until the arrival of the Future Buddha. However, even they have to guard themselves from any form of female sexuality because they could lose their powers if they were to come into contact with anything that symbolizes this. In one story, I was told that a *weikza* lost all his psychic powers when he mistakenly walked under a washing line that had female underwear on it.

Ordained Buddhist monks have been strictly forbidden by the monastic codes from indulging, as the *weikza* do, in any form of such occult practices. But there continue to be monks in Myanmar known for their secular expertise in palmistry, fortune-telling, astrology, alchemy, divination medicine, and other psychic powers.[13] For these monks (sometimes referred to as *weikza*), ascetic practices such as sexual abstinence, fasting, special diet, and *samatha* meditation (one-pointed concentration) are all crucial in order to access insight, knowledge, and special abilities. Two monks I interviewed confirmed this, saying that sexual abstinence is extremely important and the success of their practice depends solely on their ability to contain male energy. As Spiro notes, "Monks have power because, being celibate, their semen remains in the body" (1977: 238). There seems to be a general realization that sexual abstinence combined with other types of ascetic practices increases power and energy for the male practitioners. The religious authorities and political power groups have feared this empowering of the individual monks. In recent history, they generated monastic rules and government edicts to control ascetic practices that might lead to subversive acts and result in the disruption of the monastic community. Of course, female practitioners were excluded at the outset from seeking empowerment in the ascetic tradition.

Carnal Men and Spiritual Women

We have seen that, especially for a Myanmar male, sexual abstinence is regarded as hard work and extreme sacrifice, which simultaneously provide him with a strong sense of masculine identity. But a Myanmar woman abstaining from sex is seen to be doing no work at all. One of my male informants commented, "A woman can't be celibate like a man because she has nothing to give up." After all, a woman's genitals are seen to be an absence of male attributes. On one hand, this means that she has no semen to contain — a definite disadvantage in pursuing an ascetic path. On the other hand, there is a traditional belief that the absence of semen in the female is the basis for her relative (physical) weakness (O'Flaherty 1973: 261–279). Women are generally described as the weaker sex, and because they are thought to be physically weak, people have commented that they lack discipline and the physical stamina to work as hard as men in remaining celibate (also see Kabilsingh 1991: 13). This was often the reason informants gave when telling me that women cannot meditate and practice the same ascetic austerities as men. A nun teacher also said that the reason nuns cannot study one of the most essential texts in the Theravada canon is not that they are intellectually incapable but that "the text is too physically punishing for women. If a woman attempts to learn it, she might even die from exhaustion." Here the rhetoric of ascribing woman's weakness to her body was used to describe her inability to achieve the same intellectual and spiritual heights as man. Physically disadvantaged, she cannot make the ultimate bodily sacrifice of celibacy. The only sacrifice left for her in pursuing the spiritual path is to give up her hair, the ultimate symbol of femininity.

Despite these beliefs, woman has also been regarded as sexually uncontrollable and undisciplined, and some have mentioned that she is unable to give up sex. There is thus a paradoxic attitude toward female sexuality in Buddhist societies: woman is treated as either an undisciplined sex maniac or a passive and weak vessel having no will of its own and no genitals to control. In other words, a woman who has no control over her body, as well as no sexual organs to control, cannot be celibate in the same manner as a man. We have seen how emphasis is laid on how hard one must strive in order to achieve control of mind over body. So the weaker one's sexual desire is, the higher one's spiritual position must be on the ladder of karmic progress. However, it does not seem to strike the general public that a man who has to strive harder because of his strong sex drive could be lower on the spiritual ladder, and a woman who has less problem in controlling her sexual desires may have achieved higher spirituality. Having said that, I never came across a nun who left the monastic order because she could not endure the rigid practice of sexual abstinence, whereas this was the primary reason for the majority of the monks who had given in to sensual impulses and returned to secular life. Thus, in contrast with the ideological model that has been internalized, which is that of men as spiritual and women as carnal, the real picture may be just the reverse: men are carnal, and women, spiritual.

I have attempted to show that the representation of the female in Theravada Buddhist tradition traverses the bifurcation of virtuous wife/ mother and sensuous whore/mistress. Woman is represented either as a passive vessel whose primary role is to reproduce, since motherhood is part of her "natural instinct," or as an object of male sexual desire and fantasy. In either role, she cannot be autonomous because she has no control over her own mind and body. These images and stereotypes have been culturally internalized. They convey the social imperative for women, as well as a warning about the danger of female sexuality, which presents a fundamental threat to the notion of male efficacy.

Female renunciants, such as nuns who opt for a celibate lifestyle, are presented with a profound dilemma because they do not fit into the Buddhist scheme of brahmacharya. Buddhist teaching advocates that the path to spiritual liberation is open to all, regardless of age, caste, and gender. But when a woman decides to leave her socially designated role to assume a religious career, she is penalized for defying the social norm of womanhood and stepping into a spiritual lifestyle that has traditionally been a male prerogative. In this respect, women are ultimately expected to be chaste but not celibate (Khandelwal, this volume). Thus the notion of celibate practice is fundamentally different for man and for woman in the Theravada Buddhist tradition.

Sexual abstinence for an ordained monk provides him with a religious opportunity to reveal his inner strength by sublimating sexual desires to achieve spiritual power, exemplifying his masculine identity to the fullest. This practice is perfected in the ascetic tradition to the extent that female sexuality serves as the antithesis of the male ascetic pursuit. Female celibate practice, which signifies the transcendence of female sexuality, has come to be considered theoretically impossible in the Buddhist ascetic tradition.

Because they are anomalies, the nuns are mocked and relegated to a secondary religious position on the one hand; on the other, they are regarded as defiant and difficult. However, celibate practice is significant for a woman, whether a virgin nun or a lay spinster, as a means to become autonomous, defy the social construction of womanhood, and subvert the patriarchal social order. Thus sexual abstinence allows the Buddhist woman an ultimate opportunity for empowerment and liberation.

Notes

1. Since 1989, Myanmar has been the official name of the country formerly called Burma. This country is in Southeast Asia situated on the Bay of Bengal between Thailand and Bangladesh. Eighty-five percent of the country's population are Theravada Buddhists, who adhere to the Doctrine of the Elders. Their tradition is conservative, and the monastic community of monks, called the Saṅgha, is the focus of their religious practices. In addition to my initial fieldwork, I undertook three subsequent three-month visits in 1989, 1991, and 1993.

2. The number of Myanmar Buddhist nuns I interviewed totaled about 300. I am confident that the information gathered is reliable in quality. Most of the nuns I lived with and spoke to were professional nuns, but I also interviewed about 25 temporary nuns. There were frequent lay visitors to the monastic community, and I had the opportunity to interview more than 30 of them, many of them spinsters. I also interviewed seven Buddhist monks, but because I am a woman, their attitudes toward me and their replies were generally formal.

3. *Loka* means "worldly" or "secular"; *nīti* is a general term for a treatise or an anthological collection. *Lokanīti,* adapted from Sanskrit works, is a compilation of maxims and sayings of a moral nature, which serve to guide lay people in matters of everyday life.

4. See Keyes 1984, in which he narrates a popular story from Thailand about a mother whose emotional attachment to her son was such that she could not let him renounce the world. Since she was not able to cut the umbilical cord on her own account and make any inner progress, her son had to take the initiative and become a monk. By this meritorious act, it was he who consequently saved his mother from falling into hell.

5. In contrast with the laity, who observe the Five Buddhist Precepts, and the nuns, who observe the Eight Buddhist Precepts, the monks abide by 227 monastic rules, forbidding them from cash transactions, indulging in sex, and engaging in activities that might endanger living creatures. The most serious infringement of the monastic code is related to sexual activities.

6. For example, even in the Therīgāthā, a Buddhist text that comprises 73 poems believed to have been sung by female renunciants during the Buddha's time, the image of a female body is used to visualize decay and impermanence.

7. This is true even though Myanmar nuns are generally well educated in the Buddhist scriptures, and some have achieved a respectable position as Buddhist scholars. Indeed, their socioreligious position is relatively high compared with nuns in other parts of Southeast Asia.

8. The *hpoun* is believed to reside in the head and the right arm and shoulder of the male body. So a Myanmar wife is careful not to sleep on the husband's right side lest he should lose his male efficacy. Woman's lower garment, considered to be the symbol of female sexuality, is never washed with men's laundry or with other clothes worn on the upper body. It is dried on a different clothesline. Direct contact between the lower garment and the head of either the man or the woman is avoided, because the head is the most revered part of the body.

9. Some did not want to get married after watching a painful labor or witnessing abuse and violence at home. Some vaguely worried about sexual intercourse; others thought it was more trouble to remain laywomen, since women are perceived to be caught up in the never-ending vicious cycle. However, the most common reason given for having chosen to become a nun was the hope of gaining spiritual merit.

10. Of the 50 women between the ages of 30 and 60 whom I surveyed in Mandalay City, 8 were spinsters. I knew three families whose daughters all remained spinsters. In one of these families, with five daughters and two sons, only one son had married. All the unmarried daughters worked as teachers. They were very religious and actively involved in supporting the local monastery. In another case, four out of five sisters remained unmarried, and two became nuns. Committed spinsters and bachelors generally seem to come from devout Buddhist families.

11. Secretly having sex is out of the question for a monk in Myanmar. Monks and nuns who are allowed to leave the order at any time said that there is no point in cheating, and it is bad for one's karma. I heard of few cases of its alleged violation in Myanmar (also see Bunnag 1973: 30). Spiro (1977: 367) interviewed 20 monks on sexual matters and reports that 17 said the vows of celibacy were difficult or very difficult to comply with; only 3 were not bothered by the lack of sex.

12. Ferguson and Mendelson report, "What is compulsory abstinence for the monk is voluntary for the *weikza*. A weikza can have a wife but renounce sex, or he can keep as many Buddhist precepts as fit his lifestyle" (1981: 65). However, he is celibate when he is in training or concentrating on the occult arts.

13. As a result of his research in the former Burma in the 1960s, Spiro estimates that as much as 10 percent of the monastic population in Mandalay is made up of monks who indulge in these practices. The number seems to have dwindled dramatically because of the "purification" of the Saṅgha conducted by the Burmese government in the 1980s. These monks seem to have gone underground, but the appeal of such knowledge is still strong among Myanmar lay devotees. There are almost no women or nuns who have access to occult arts. I tried very hard to locate some and found two Buddhist nuns who were involved in astrology and fortune-telling. They were, however, of Chinese origin, and the local Myanmar told me that Shans and Chinese were engaged in a kind of power access that the Myanmar were not aware of. These nuns were not only celibate but also practiced a variety of austerities and *śamatha* meditation. They were also strict vegetarians and slept no more than a few hours.

References Cited

Alter, Joseph S. 1997. Seminal Truth: A Modern Science of Male Celibacy in North India. *Medical Anthropology Quarterly* 11: 275–298.

Brown, R. G. 1926. *Burma as I Saw It 1889–1917.* London: Methuen.

Bunnag, Jane. 1973. *Buddhist Monk, Buddhist Layman: A Study of Urban Monastic Organization in Central Thailand.* Cambridge: Cambridge University Press.

Falk, Nancy A. 1980. The Case of the Vanishing Nuns: The Fruits of Ambivalence in Ancient Indian Buddhism. In *Unspoken Worlds: Women's Religious Lives in Non-Western Cultures,* ed. N. A. Falk and R. Gross, 207–224. New York: Harper and Row.

Ferguson, John P., and E. Michael Mendelson. 1981. Masters of the Buddhist Occult: The Burmese Weikzas. *Contributions to Asian Studies* 16: 62–80.

Horner, I. B. 1930. *Women in Primitive Buddhism: Laywomen and Almswomen.* London: George Routledge and Sons.

Jackson, Roger R. 1992. Ambiguous Sexuality: Imagery and Interpretation in Tantric Buddhism. *Religion* 22: 85–100.

Kabilsingh, Chatsumarn. 1991. *Thai Women in Buddhism.* Berkeley: Parallax.

Keyes, Charles. 1984. Mother or Mistress but Never a Monk: Buddhist Notions of Female Gender in Rural Thailand. *American Ethnologist* 11: 223–241.

Khaing, Mi Mi. 1984. *The World of Burmese Women.* London: Zed Books.

Kloppenborg, Ria. 1995. Female Stereotypes in Early Buddhism: The Women of the Therīgāthā. In *Female Stereotypes in Religious Traditions,* ed. Ria Kloppenborg and Wouter Hanegraaff, 151–169. Leiden: E. J. Brill.

Lokanīti: *Ancient Proverbs and Maxims from Burmese Sources, or the Nīti Literature of Burma.* 1886. Trans. J. Gray. London: Trubner.

The Mahāvastu. 1952. Vol. 2 of 3. Trans. J. J. Jones London: Luzac.

Nash, Manning. 1965. *The Golden Road to Modernity: Village Life in Contemporary Burma.* New York: John Wiley and Sons.

Nissan, Elizabeth. 1984. Recovering Practice: Buddhist Nuns in Sri Lanka. *South Asia Research* 4: 32–49.

O'Flaherty, Wendy Doniger. 1973. *Asceticism and Eroticism in the Mythology of Āiva.* London: Oxford University Press.

Pandey, Rajyashree. 1995. Women, Sexuality, and Enlightenment. *Monumenta Niponica* 50: 325–356.

Paul, Diana Y. 1979. *Women in Buddhism: Images of the Feminine in Mahāyāna Tradition.* Berkeley: University of California Press.

Schuster-Barnes, Nancy. 1987. Buddhism. In *Women in World Religions,* ed. A. Sharma, 105–133. Albany: State University of New York Press.

Spiro, Melford E. 1977. *Kinship and Marriage in Burma: A Cultural and Psychodynamic Analysis.* Berkeley: University of California Press.

Spiro, Melford E. 1997. *Gender Ideology and Psychological Reality: An Essay on Cultural Reproduction.* New Haven: Yale University Press.

Sponberg, Alan. 1992. Attitudes toward Women and the Feminine in Early Buddhism. In *Buddhism, Sexuality, and Gender,* ed. José Ignacio Cabezón, 3–36. Albany: State University of New York Press.

Steed, G. P. 1955. Notes on an Approach to a Study of Personality Formation in a Hindu Village in Gujarat. In *Village India: Studies in the Little Community,* ed. M. Marriott, 102–144. Chicago: University of Chicago Press.

Wijayaratna, Mohan. 1990. *Buddhist Monastic Life.* Trans. Claude Grangier and Steven Collins. Cambridge: Cambridge University Press.

8 *Meena Khandelwal*

Sexual Fluids, Emotions, Morality
Notes on the Gendering of Brahmacharya

Although the Sanskrit term *brahmacharya* is most often translated as "celibacy," the English gloss does not come close to conveying the complex meanings of its practice. First, brahmacharya means much more than abstaining from sex; it has a primary meaning of "lifestyle to obtain Brahma" and is thus understood, at least when practiced by ascetics, as a means to spiritual liberation rather than an end in itself. Sexual abstinence is one essential aspect of an overall lifestyle that usually includes a strict vegetarian diet, the avoidance of most stimulants and intoxicants, and the practice of meditation or some other variety of spiritual discipline.

Phillimore (this volume) describes women in the Kangra region of North India who practice celibacy but do not follow the total lifestyle associated with brahmacharya. They have renounced marriage and sexuality but not kinship relations, home, or property, and, for this reason, most people do not consider them to be ascetics. At the same time, those who do consider these women to be holy persons are more likely to emphasize their intention and spiritual achievement. The ambiguity regarding the ascetic status of these women (they themselves seem uncomfortable with it) leads Phillimore to suggest that this local practice may represent a more or less secular form of celibacy. In any case, the ambiguity seems to revolve exactly around the issue of purposeful, ascetic celibacy as a total lifestyle. First, practitioners of brahmacharya (male: brahmachari; and female: brahmacharini) are expected to behave with complete control not only of sexual desire but also of anger, appetite for food, and all other passions.

Second, even though both temporary and intermittent periods of sexual abstinence and celibacy may be described as brahmacharya, the former are distinguishable from the latter, which I define here as a permanent and purposeful state of complete sexual abstinence that is part of ascetic discipline. The distinction between permanent brahmacharya and temporary or intermittent brahmacharya is what separates ascetic and householder lifestyles; it is not simply that one practices brahmacharya and the other does not. This distinction is crucial for understanding how the practice of abstinence and celibacy is gendered in Hindu India.

Third, translating *brahmacharya* as "celibacy" leads us to associate its practice with ascetics and with maleness. An opposition is implied between male celibacy and a female domestic world focused on sexuality and fertility. Indeed, there is justification for scholars of Hindu culture to associate lifelong celibacy with men and chastity with women; however, brahmacharya is not limited to lifelong celibacy. Temporary and intermittent periods of brahmacharya are entirely compatible with chastity and auspicious household life. Equally important is the fact that women also take vows of lifelong celibacy, and, as I have shown elsewhere (Khandelwal 1997), women who renounce worldly life do not "become men" in order to gain legitimacy as renouncers. How, then, is brahmacharya rendered meaningful to them? Recognizing that *brahmacharya* may refer to a wide range of activities and to various degrees of sexual abstinence makes it problematic to associate its practice primarily with male asceticism, opposed to both household life and femininity.

Lifelong Celibacy as Male: Dominant Ideologies

Because textual sources describe sex as both polluting to men and women and depleting of a man's essential seminal fluids, Hindu celibacy (a lifelong vow of total abstinence) has often been attributed with the purpose of obtaining ritual purity or magical power rather than moral goodness or virtue. Clearly celibacy is understood, at least sometimes, in physiological terms that represent it as a male pursuit intended to accumulate semen (Alter 1997; van der Veer 1989). Female bodies, according to this model, are thought to benefit more from absorbing a man's semen through legitimate sexual activity than from celibacy; women are also said to be incapable of celibacy. Yet they constitute a significant minority of the ascetic population in India.[1] I conducted ethnographic research (1989–1991) with female renouncers (sannyasinis) in Haridwar and, despite warnings from a few elite men that such women were nonexistent, locating them in this pilgrimage town was not difficult. Sannyasinis are women who have been initiated into sannyasa, an ascetic tradition that was institutionalized as the Daśanāmī orders in the ninth century by Śaṅkarācārya and that defines itself as a giving-up of ordinary family life (marriage, children, vocation, home, household rituals, social status) for the pursuit of spiritual liberation. Absolute celibacy is one of the few positive defining features of renunciation. The accumulation of wealth and a sedentary (as opposed to peripatetic) lifestyle certainly deviate from the classical ideal of sannyasa, but both may be legitimated in renunciant terms, depending on sectarian affiliation and personal philosophy. Sexual activity, however, is generally incompatible with renunciant status.

Women's responses to the question of why sannyasa, historically speaking, has been a largely male pursuit included references to women not *needing* to renounce family in order to obtain liberation as well as sociological explanations about men deliberately discouraging female renunciation because of the threat that it poses to patriarchal interests. For example, Anand Mata, an unorthodox (non-Daśanāmī) contemplative sannyasini in her 50s at the time of my research, insisted that women do not need to retreat to mountaintops to find God because they are somehow "complete" in themselves, which enables them to find God in themselves, their children, their husbands. "Like all religions," she said, "the renunciant orders were started by men. There has always been a sense of rivalry between the sexes, but it is felt more by men than by women. So, you see, men feared that women would surpass them." A young, female celibate (brahmacharini)[2] remarked, "The good and learned gurus say it is not written in any scripture for women to be initiated into sannyasa, and the scriptures never lie." However, in the same conversation, she mused, "If women had written the scriptures, then they would have said that sannyasa should not be given to men."

Whether we prefer physiological explanations regarding the exchange of semen or sociological explanations about patriarchal interests in excluding women, Brahmanic Hinduism has considered lifelong celibacy to be a male pursuit and chastity to be its proper female counterpart. Yet none of the women I interviewed suggested that women do not benefit from celibacy or that they are incapable of it. On the contrary, one of the few points of consensus among the sannyasinis I interviewed in Haridwar is that women, rather than being temptresses, are more often the victims of male desire, even sannyasinis, if they are not careful, may become the sexual prey of male peers and gurus (Khandelwal 1996). Gutschow (this volume) makes similar observations about Buddhist nuns in Zangskar, concluding from this that women celibates are unable to retreat from sexuality in the same way that men are able to.

In an attempt to understand the gendered meanings of brahmacharya, I consider temporary and intermittent forms of sexual abstinence that are crucial to conventional constructions of femininity, male theories of sexual physiology that render lifelong female celibacy illogical if not impossible, and, finally, alternative understandings that make celibacy meaningful for women. Because lifelong brahmacharya and the ritual purity it produces has been a largely upper-caste male pursuit, I take textually based ideologies of semen conservation, which do present an elite male view, as my starting point and then address alternative understandings.

Even if lifelong celibacy is not considered desirable by all Hindus,[3] evidence suggests that fear of the debilitating effects of semen loss is widespread among both ascetic and married men (Alter 1992: 129–130; Alter 1997; Carstairs 1957: 83–85; Edwards 1983; van der Veer 1989). Not only do married women, especially those from the upper castes, include temporary periods of brahmacharya in their domestic religiosity, but also many women reject marriage completely by taking vows of permanent celibacy. One purpose of this chapter, then, is to address the question of how women's perspective on celibacy may differ from that of elite men. I suggest that brahmacharya is understood by many of its female (and perhaps many male) proponents as withdrawing into oneself, but with an emphasis on psychosocial rather than physiological withdrawal. More important, because bodily fluids are both metaphors and metonyms for emotions, psychosocial models expand on, rather than contradict, semen-based hydraulic models of celibacy.

Temporary, Intermittent, and Partial Abstinence: Brahmacharya for Householders

Conceptions of brahmacharya imply a distinction between temporary and lifelong sexual abstinence. One variety of temporary, premarital sexual abstinence is the first stage, or ashrama, in the ideal life cycle of a high-caste male. Brahmacharya ashrama is an adolescent period of abstinence, ritual purity, concentration on study of the Vedic texts, restricted diet, and service to a guru. The model assumes that some young men will choose to become ascetics by taking a lifelong vow of celibacy but that most will marry and devote themselves to such worldly goals as material prosperity, procreation, and sensual enjoyment. According to this scheme, Vedic study is to be followed by married life (grihastha), a forest-dwelling transition stage (vanaprastha), and complete renunciation of worldly life (sannyasa).[4] Thus, the ashrama system outlines four distinct models of

life, three of which require abstinence. Women have been largely excluded from these three stages and associated only with the stage of married householder, though, as Olivelle (1993: 188) has noted, this does not
mean that women did not participate in the system's institutions.[5] Although Hindu thinkers have debated the relative importance of celibate
and householder lifestyles for centuries,[6] the general appropriateness and
wisdom of this life-cycle model was assumed by most female ascetics and
married women whom I interviewed. Sannyasinis, or female renouncers,
see themselves as exceptions rather than exemplars and assume that the
vast majority of men and women should experience married life before
renouncing.

The life cycle of a Hindu woman is not as ideologically elaborated and
codified as for a man. But textual statements assume that a woman's life is
divided into three periods defined by the male kin member who "protects" her: the father during childhood, the husband during marriage, and
the son during widowhood. Premarital childhood is a highly idealized
stage of life for many Hindu women. The status, freedom, and affection
that a girl enjoys in her father's home, where she is symbolically
desexualized, may end abruptly when she marries and moves to the home
of her in-laws. A *kanyā* may be premenstrual or menstrual, depending on
perspective and era, but is by definition unmarried (Khare 1982: 149–
153). Unmarried girls are powerful and are worshiped in ritual. They are
sacred to their consanguineal kin because of their categoric purity and
chastity, and they have the power to bless their brothers with a long life
(Bennett 1983: 251). Eventually, however, a *kanyā* must marry and be
transformed from "one worthy of worship" to "one who worships."

The distinction between presexual and postsexual chastity is crucial for
women.[7] The Brahmanic model prohibits a widow from remarrying and
expects her to be chaste for the remainder of her life (even if she is a child
widow who has never consummated her marriage). Even so, her sexual
abstinence is not accorded the purposefulness and power usually attributed to vows of celibacy undertaken by ascetics. Women are expected to
be chaste, meaning forever faithful to a husband (whether he is living or
not), rather than celibate. Moreover, while a *kanyā* gains immense power
from her chastity, a widow's chastity is imbued with misfortune and inaus-
piciousness. My informal conversations with people in Haridwar indicate
a pervasive belief that most female ascetics are actually widows seeking to
replace the contemptible status of widow with the positive status of saint,
though this assumption is unfounded.[8] In contrast with celibacy, widowhood is neither chosen nor valued. The social stigma is less severe if the
widow is postsexual and has sons to look after her. A young, childless
widow, whose sexuality has yet to be fulfilled, is an extremely inauspicious

figure; her chastity is suspect, and her sexuality is a threat to the reputation of her family.

In addition to sexual abstinence related to stage of life, another variety of temporary sexual abstinence is that practiced intermittently and for short periods by married (i.e., sexually active) persons of either gender to ensure purity for the performance of a ritual or vow. For example, householder disciples of Baiji, a Dásanāmī sannyasini with her own ashram, would sometimes sponsor a fire sacrifice to purify a new home or a reading of the *Rāmāyana* to mark the anniversary of a loved one's death; all participants were expected to fast and avoid polluting activities like sexual intercourse for the duration. *Vratas*, optional religious observances and fasts, are primarily observed by women, who usually undertake them for the health and well-being of their husbands and children (McGee 1991; Wadley 1983). Sexual abstinence may also be required in preparation for and during the course of a pilgrimage (Daniel 1984: 246–247).

Sexual activity may also be temporarily prohibited during periods of ritual pollution. An eighteenth-century guide to women's religious duties, written by a South Indian male priest, warns that if a woman makes love to her husband during the first three days of her menstrual bleeding, her child will be an untouchable or cursed (Leslie 1989: 285). Nichter and Nichter have observed that menstrual blood is not only impure but also "heating"; in fact, their informants in Karnataka emphasized the heating nature of menstrual blood rather than its impurity: "An image commonly offered was that contact with menstrual blood was so 'heating' as to dry a man's semen" (1989a: 8). Although these examples indicate a male desire to avoid dangerous sexual contact with women during specified periods, the point is that both men and women are expected to avoid sexual activity during certain times and that these are temporary periods of brahmacharya.[9]

Occasionally, *brahmacharya* may even refer to sexuality that is strictly procreative. In the Indian wrestling tradition studied by Alter (1992), celibacy is crucial to wrestlers' identity. Hanumān, whose physical strength and spiritual power arise from unbroken celibacy, is their patron deity. Wrestlers, however, marry and have children. The saying "ek narī, brahmacāri" asserts that one can be married to just one woman and still be a brahmachari (Alter 1992: 228). By this definition, anyone can practice brahmacharya because it is compatible with family life. Babb (1986) writes about a religious order of women celibates called the Brahma Kumārīs, which was founded by a man but has a membership composed primarily of women. Like the wrestlers, they also emphasize brahmacharya within marriage; sexuality should be procreative only. However, for the Brahma Kumārīs, there is clearly some discomfort with even this, since they envision a golden age when men and women were so pure that they could procreate without sexual intercourse (Babb 1986: 115). The examples of the wrestlers and the Brahma Kumārīs suggest that the category of brahmacharya may even expand to include sexual activity, as long as it is utilitarian and passionless.

Chastity Versus Celibacy: The Difference for Women

Temporary and intermittent periods of sexual abstinence for women are compatible with, even supportive of, wifely ideals. The ideal woman is chaste rather than celibate; she is sexually active with, and only with, her husband for the dual purpose of procreation and providing pleasure. Tryambakayajvan's eighteenth-century guide advises that after observing sexual abstinence for the first three days of menstruation, a wife should bathe, anoint and ornament her body, and then make sexual advances to her husband (Leslie 1989: 286). Ideals for women specify both when sex should be performed and when it should be avoided (Edwards 1983; Nichter and Nichter 1989a). The value on female chastity involves control of women's sexuality, to be legitimately expressed in the context of marriage and subdued outside; it requires both sexual activity and abstinence.

Hancock (1995: 84) has described ways in which women, as religious virtuosi living with their husbands, might use their relationship with a deity to create sexual distance at home. Recognizing perhaps that religious vows and fasting, precisely because of their association with the duties of a good wife, have the potential to become sites of female resistance to the demands of conjugal sexuality, Brahmanic authorities insist that a woman should not perform any religious act, even fasting, without her husband's approval. Baiji, the Daśanāmī sannyasini with whom I lived in Haridwar, is a guru with many married women as lay disciples. Although, as a young woman she herself rejected marriage for an ascetic life, Baiji refused to initiate any woman, even as a lay disciple, or allow any of her married female disciples to come and stay at her ashram without the husband's permission. Female chastity, as the properly regulated expression of sexuality, allows — even requires — temporary and intermittent periods of sexual abstinence, but the ideology of gender relations leaves it far removed from the historically male pursuit of celibacy.

Vows of lifelong abstinence may be undertaken as part of one or another ascetic tradition; they are typically associated with an unmarried state though some contemporary gurus advocate celibacy within marriage. I suggest that it is specifically celibacy, rather than ascetic discipline or abstinence per se, that has been denied to women. As alternatives to Brahmanic Hinduism, the bhaktic and Tantric religious traditions have always been open to women, but they have also tended to ascribe a less central role to celibacy. In contrast, sannyasa (renunciation) is the Brahmanic ascetic tradition par excellence and holds celibacy to be absolutely crucial to spiritual progress; it has also, historically speaking, restricted initiation to high-caste men. Exceptional men, like Śaṅkarācārya himself, may be initiated at a young age and forgo marriage completely. More appropriately, though, they are initiated in their later years after having fulfilled their debts to the gods, sages, and ancestors and ensured that their children are married and economically secure.

It is thus acceptable for a man to renounce even his wife, assuming there is a son to look after her. The only nonsexual states Brahmanic theology recognizes for women are prepubertal childhood and widowhood, which assume fidelity to a future or deceased husband. Moreover, though total abstinence for a widowed or renounced woman is expected, it seems that this state is not thought to result in spiritual power or liberation. For these reasons, I feel it is misleading to describe this state as celibate. Female celibacy is indeed "repugnant to brahmanical orthodoxy" (Olivelle 1993: 188), even though particular female ascetics in legend and myth as well as in contemporary society have been venerated as saints.[10] The question that concerns me below, following a discussion of the physiological model of semen retention, is what sort of interpretations of celibacy *are* meaningful to female practitioners.

"Retentive" Men and "Leaky" Women: Sexual Fluids in Classical Models

Hindu conceptions that are text-based (which does not mean they necessarily have no popular existence) assume that the divergent meanings of male and female celibacy are a natural consequence of a sexually dimorphic human physiology.[11] Because semen contains a man's physical and spiritual strength, both are lost through sexual intercourse. Accordingly, the quintessential man is an ascetic who retains his powers by accumulating semen. Through yogic practices a male ascetic transforms his semen into spiritual energy, drawing it away from his phallus and upward toward his head, where it is stored. Swami Sivananda, the well-known contemporary guru, has warned that spiritual progress is impossible without absolute, unbroken brahmacharya. However, even though he has initiated many women into sannyasa, his comments on the topic not only assume a male audience but also use the hydraulic metaphors described above: "The semen is a dynamic force. It should be converted into *ojas* or spiritual energy by pure thoughts, *japa,* and meditation. . . . Wastage of semen brings nervous weakness, exhaustion and premature death. The sexual act destroys vigor of mind, body and senses, and annihilates memory, understanding and intellect" (Sivananda 1987: 212–213). Even more dire consequences of semen loss are predicted by Rajayogacharya, who warns, "One should not waste semen until at least 25 years of age in a dream, otherwise it is like committing suicide" (1977: 42).

If semen is the unambiguous focus of a general male physiology, there is no single perspective on the existence of a comparable female substance. O'Flaherty (1980) has shown that the early Vedic texts understand breast milk to be the most important sexual fluid in women and extend it metaphorically to describe semen. The analogy between milk (*payas*) and semen (*retas*) rests on several criteria. Both are creative and powerful substances. In popular theories of procreation, a father passes important social traits to his child through semen, and a mother passes emotional and intellectual qualities through milk. In mythology, both fluids are capable of independent creation. Both are essences distilled from blood. Both are whitish fluids expressed from a swollen protrusion of the body. And both imply a process or "outpouring" more than a substance (O'Flaherty 1980: 20–22). Ethnographic accounts suggest that these ideas have meaning for ordinary villagers. For example, Carstairs reports that male villagers described an ascetic's seed, which is presumed to be of good quality, as "rich and viscous, like the cream of unadulterated milk" (1957: 83–84).

In spite of these similarities, female milk and male semen are to be handled very differently. While the retentive phallus is powerful and good, the breast that refuses to give is anomalous and evil. This is, as O'Flaherty notes, a statement about gender relations: women should give endlessly to their children, whereas men should keep their power for themselves. It is also a statement about conventional morality: maternal flow is good, whereas sexual flow is bad (O'Flaherty 1980: 44). Though both substances are assumed to have creative power, semen is much more powerful in the sense that it produces many more mythological instances of solo creation, especially during the Upanishadic period,[12] when much is said about seed but very little about milk (O'Flaherty 1980: 32).

The late Vedas, says O'Flaherty, try to account for all female sexual fluids by suggesting that a woman has seed, just as the man does, and that this is her contribution to the process of procreation. Tantric practice, also based on the assumption that women have seed, involves a symmetric inversion of Brahmanic traditions by allowing the ritual ingestion of polluting substances and ritualized sexuality. Even though the Tantric tradition exalts the abstract feminine principle and admits female practitioners, its texts nonetheless represent a male perspective; the man is instructed to take back from the woman not only his own lost seed but hers as well, and specific techniques are described for this process (O'Flaherty 1980: 38).[13]

The theory of corresponding male and female seed was later challenged by another theory, which posits menstrual (*rajas*) or uterine (*puṣpa*) blood as the female counterpart of semen (O'Flaherty 1980: 33). Still, in models that point to blood as the female contribution to conception, male semen is seen as more powerful; it determines the identity of the child. Although the primary post-Vedic model posits male seed and female blood, there appears to be a basic ambiguity in both Sanskrit texts and popular imagination as to whether the procreative fluid in the womb is female semen or menstrual blood (Marglin 1985: 58; O'Flaherty 1980: 35; Trawick 1990: 159).

Regardless of whether milk, seed, or blood is theorized to be the primary creative fluid in a woman, male seed is seen as more consistently powerful and positive. The qualities and proper treatment of male semen are much more ideologically elaborated, and anxiety about its loss appears to be widespread. Although only further research would allow us to conclude with certainty, available ethnographic evidence does not suggest a corresponding concern for the loss of sexual fluids among women.[14] One sannyasini, when I asked her directly whether women also accumulate any substance through brahmacharya, spoke of *ūrja* (energy, vigor, vitality) as something that both women and men possess, but she did not describe this as something that is accumulated through brahmacharya. Clearly, only tentative conclusions can be made about the existence of female fluids that must be accumulated in the same way that semen must be saved.

Classical and popular conceptions assume that both men and women have power (*shakti*) to begin with but that women have more. Brahmanic perspectives say that this inequality is intensified through sex, since men lose their power to women, who, by absorbing semen, further increase their own power. It follows that while men increase their power by being celibate, women increase theirs by remaining chaste or sexually active in the socially sanctioned way (O'Flaherty 1980: 45). Even when householder men value patrilineal continuity over spiritual power, the giving of seed for the sake of producing progeny is widely viewed as a *sacrifice,* as some sort of loss.[15] Women are thought to be constantly losing bodily fluids but able to replenish their supply. They bleed every month. Where women are assumed to have seed, they are said to be losing it all the time through vaginal discharge, which has powerful (usually negative) effects on whatever it touches (Trawick 1990: 278). And they give milk, usually upon demand, to their children. As Paul Toomey says of the god Krishna's mother, "However angry Yashoda might be with her foster son, Krishna, she cannot stop her breasts from overflowing with milk at the sight of him" (1990: 163).[16] While a *kanyā*'s purity may have to do with her not (ideally) having entered the realm of menstruation, sexuality, or lactation, mature women are, to use Khare's phrase, "leaky buckets," unable to control their fluids (personal communication, 1996).

Brahmacharya and Self-Control: Sexual Fluids as Metaphors and Metonyms for Emotion

If the hydraulic model of semen retention were the only model available, then one might expect the practice of celibacy to have little relevance for women. But absolute celibacy is popularly assumed to create a concentration of power in both men and women. I suggest that more expansive understandings of celibacy as self-control and emotional detachment, beyond simply involving sexual fluids, are also prevalent and that these may hold more appeal for women (though I am not claiming they are exclusive to women). Although more research is needed in this area, I have seen no evidence that physiological models are central to the way women think of celibacy. Instead, women ascetics seem to view celibacy in emotional and sociological terms. I argue that, because bodily fluids are seen as vehicles for moral and emotional qualities, this more general meaning of celibacy is implied in the physiological model rather than being contradictory to it. This may explain why brahmacharya is not experienced as a conflict for the women renouncers I know, except to the extent that family or society has been hostile to their chosen path. There is no sense that their bodies are somehow unfit for celibacy or that it may be harmful to them in somatic terms.

Paul Toomey (1990) has argued that, for devotees of the god Krishna, food is both a metaphor and a metonym for emotion. Thus, devotional love is often described metaphorically in terms of food and feeding, and the outpouring of love between Krishna and his devotees is often symbolized by milk. Also, when pilgrims consume the consecrated food offerings, they feel that the food *is* in a metonymic sense Krishna's loving body, and by sharing the food they are sharing his love (Toomey 1990: 163–165). Similarly, Alter (1992b: 240) says that many wrestlers criticize the consumption of "public food" because of the possibility of "catching" bad emotions.

Like food, bodily fluids are both metaphors for and embodiments of emotional passion. Peter van der Veer (1989: 465) writes that the Ramanandi renouncers (*tyāgīs*) use the word *ras* to refer to stored semen, and it is the refusal to let semen flow that gives *tyāgīs* their spiritual powers. *Ras* may refer to a bodily fluid (both male and female seed in the

Vedas, according to O'Flaherty) as well as to a particular mood. That other fluids from the male body, especially tears and sweat, may serve as substitutes for semen is further evidence of a connection between sexual fluids and emotion (O'Flaherty 1980: 39–40). Tears are both products and signifiers of intense emotion. Consistent with this symbolism is the portrait of a genuine renouncer, who, in his state of detached poise, neither loses seed nor sheds sweat or tears; he stops all emotional flow.

Just as women have more fluids flowing out of their bodies, so too are they believed to be more emotionally involved in worldly life and relations. Milk from a mother's breasts contains love, whereas fluids from a woman's womb contain sexual passion. Moreover, since the emotion of maternal love is highly valued (even renouncers exalt their own mothers) and the emotion of sexual love devalued, it is bad for a woman to withhold milk and good for a man to withhold seed. A woman's genitals are passionate and greedy, but her breasts are endlessly giving (O'Flaherty 1980: 36). The problem with women is their inability to control their fluids, especially menstrual blood, and, by implication, their passions. Once again, the "leaky bucket" syndrome describes women's "compulsive emotionalism and passion" (Tapper 1979, cited in Caplan 1987: 282).

O'Flaherty has commented that in the Puranas there is very little interaction between male and female sexual fluids, even those of husband and wife during procreation.

. . . even when a man and his wife both participate in producing a child, they may do so in physical isolation from each other; the male seed reaches the female (if at all) through a series of miraculous interventions, which tend to keep the man and woman as far apart as possible; they mate like fishes, one passing gracefully over the place where the other has been before, or like stock animals impregnated with frozen sperm; there is no opportunity for sustained emotional contact. (1980: 56)

Anthropological research has shown that emotional intimacy in marital relationships is also discouraged by patrilineal, virilocal kinship structures that promote patrilineal over conjugal solidarity.[17] Myth offers the possibility of exchanging fluids, and thus of procreating, without emotional involvement. The bodily secretions of both women and men are passionate, but men (at least upper-caste men) see themselves as more capable of holding their seed and, thus, of remaining detached. Since male seed is lost through emotional arousal, its loss signals a fall into passion, even if there is no actual contact with a woman. Herein lies the ascetic fear that women are by their very nature temptresses in that their mere presence may cause a man to lose his seed.[18] In the context of controlling passions, it becomes clear why control of the palate is so important to the practice of brahmacharya: not only is gustatory pleasure a metaphor for sexual pleasure, but also certain ("hot") foods, like onions, garlic, strong spices, meat, and alcohol, are felt to increase passions metonymically.[19] Particular foods transfer not only their own intrinsic qualities to the consumer but also those of the preparer. I paraphrase here one woman's description of a female saint (Behnji) who was married before becoming an ascetic: Even when married, she was holy, but her husband was not. He already had two wives and then married a thirteen-year-old girl. Behnji cleaned each grain of wheat with a prayer that her husband's mind should change, that he would convert to holiness. And it happened. When he unknowingly consumed the food prepared with her own hands, he became changed.

In sannyasinis' understandings of brahmacharya, celibacy refers not to a strictly physiological control of seed but to the control of passions, attachments, and appetite, which are metaphorically and metonymically related to bodily fluids. The female renouncers I met never spoke explicitly about sexual fluids, though they did describe ascetic practice as a rejection of passion and emotional involvement. Anand Mata told me that when relatives brought the ashes of her dead mother to Haridwar so that they could perform the immersion ceremony in her presence, she had already achieved a state of detachment (*vairāgya*) toward her family. "Whenever my relatives came to meet me, I was polite but felt no special affection for them. They are perceptive people; eventually they realized that their visits disturbed my spiritual practice, and they reduced the visits to a bare minimum." For her, being emotionally unaffected by such things as social attachments, sexual desire, wealth, even insults, was at the heart of her spiritual practice.

Beyond Hydraulics

Although female celibacy was abhorrent to classical orthodoxy, many contemporary Hindu religious leaders have advocated celibacy for men and women and have even said that women are *more* capable of celibacy than men, which is difficult to justify if one believes that brahmacharya is strictly a somatic matter. Not only is celibacy psychosocial with the goal of self-control and emotional detachment, but it is moral and ethical as well.

Mahatma Gandhi encouraged the practice of celibacy in the interest of self-realization as well as social service. He saw brahmacharya as a matter of emotional self-control and the conservation of one's energies (energy to accomplish tasks rather than energy used for magical powers). In his autobiography, Gandhi (1957: 206) indicates that sexual activity is symbolic of household life more generally in that it diverts one's energy from community service to procreation and the care of children, and this is equally true for men and women.

The Brahma Kumārī order advocates celibacy in the interest of purity. In its view of human history, the fall of the world and the subjugation of women are both attributed to the development of body consciousness and sexual intercourse (Babb 1986: 116). Thus, brahmacharya is the virtue that defines humanity's golden age, and it is the basis for all other virtues. Moreover, because brahmacharya is a means to achieve equality for women, it is clearly moral and ethical. Some of the wrestlers described by Alter (1992: 248) propose celibacy as a solution to such national problems as poverty, population growth, and pollution.

Although Alter's explicit emphasis is on the somatic aspects of brahmacharya, it is clear from his list of methods for maintaining brahmacharya, which includes "fellowship with good men," that it is also a matter of moral and ethical behavior (1992: 130). Alter acknowledges this when, for example, he states, "Using Gandhi as an example, K. P. Singh argues for the incorporation of ascetic values into the practices of everyday life. When so translated, the practice of brahmacharya clearly becomes an ethical practice with sociomoral implications" (p. 229). Alter views this sense of responsibility to set a standard of ethical behavior as something peculiar to wrestlers, something that specifically sets them apart from renouncers, who turn their back on the ethical problems of social life (p. 229). Although it has often been argued that sannyasa has as its goals power and purity rather than ethical behavior, I believe that sannyasinis, and probably renouncers in general, do view their celibacy and their general lifestyle of self-control as an example that inspires householders to behave more ethically, even if they do not expect all householders to renounce worldly life or even wish they would.

During the time when I lived in Baiji's ashram, her lay disciples, many of whom were related to each other, gathered for a weekend of religious functions. An elderly woman (Masiji) had planned a *havan* (fire sacrifice) to consecrate the new room she had had built at the ashram; her brother (Mamaji) was coming and was bringing a sannyasini with him. There was some debate, in hushed tones, about whether or not I should meet Mamaji (who was a little "off" and "hard to get along with"). Finally, Mamaji's ex-wife informed me of the verdict: "I asked Baiji, and she said that you should stay away from him. He's not good. He doesn't have good intentions. And that sannyasini he is bringing with him — she's not good either. She takes whiskey in everything. What sadhana can you do with *tamasic* (ignorant, dark) habits? I am only telling you this about her, and then it is for you to decide." Later in the day, Baiji said to me, "You know the man who arrived this afternoon? You are not to get close to him, understand? He'll start getting loose with you. And that sannyasini he's brought with him — she stayed alone with a man for a whole month!" I had once interviewed this sannyasini, a European expatriate who had lived in India some 30 years. While sitting at the *havan*, I noted that Mamaji was extremely familiar with the sannyasini; his speech and behavior seemed to violate every cultural code about how to interact with an ascetic. He sat very close to her, spoke loudly on topics inappropriate to the ritual context (for example, asking to spend the night in her cave), and used exaggerated gestures. She, in contrast, was poised and respectful of the ritual and of Baiji.

After the duo departed, Baiji spoke of the sannyasini again. Rumor had it that she went to stay at Mamaji's house in Delhi, where she drank liquor and ate meat. A servant there told her that sannyasinis should not consume such things, and she apparently responded by saying that after reaching a high state one could consume anything. Baiji remarked that it is people like her who give sannyasinis a bad name, though she reserved some blame for Mamaji as well. Their disrepute had to do with perceived sexual impropriety, which had clear ethical and moral implications. Baiji's final comment suggested that Mamaji's uncontrolled sexuality was a matter of both somatic and ethical degradation: "He's got sex running through his blood!" she said with a look of utter disgust. "But now why does he have to corrupt (*brasht karna*) foreigners?"

Female Celibates as Exceptional Rather Than Exemplary Figures

For a *kanyā* (unmarried girl) or a married woman to take a vow of lifelong celibacy poses perhaps the most serious possible threat to the Brahmanic social order. A married woman whom I met in Haridwar vehemently warned me to stay away from a particular trio of sannyasinis, insisting that their guru practiced magic. One reason for her distrust, it seemed, was that too many young girls were joining the order. "They use mantras, say the rosary backwards, etc. . . . They have a big outfit — lots of wealth — and ashrams in every city because they get people to give donations. They persuade virgin girls to join, girls who should be happily married in their own homes. They must have some feelings after all, and these have been suppressed." The idea that young people, especially young girls, should become ascetics in large numbers seemed so wrong as to be sinister. In contemporary Hindu society, female celibacy is a social and conceptual possibility in that women celibates are visible in society, but it seems that they are tolerated, even revered, only as long as they remain exceptions. If women, especially young presexual women, were to begin taking vows of celibacy in large numbers, I believe that the limits of society's tolerance would be reached. Many of the female renouncers I met in Haridwar had taken vows of celibacy in their youth, and most encountered at least some opposition from family, society, and other male ascetics. Anand Mata described her family's reaction to her decision to renounce:

The very idea that [a woman] would do something other than what society expects of her is difficult for people to accept. . . . Being free means "I'll choose my own path and won't put up with any interference from you." For a woman to declare this — and I was a *married* woman — was a real shock to both my parents and of course to my in-laws. A woman's parents will try and understand, but her in-laws never will. They will take it as open revolt.

Once she persuaded her family that she was making the right decision, they were supportive. Baiji described how her request to be initiated provoked such opposition in the renunciant community that her guru, who had earlier agreed to initiate her, changed his mind. Years later, after she was initiated, hostile male ascetics threw stones at her cottage while she was inside meditating. Most female ascetics view themselves as exceptions and do not encourage other women to follow their path (Khandelwal 1996: 129; Ojha 1988: 36). Although I do not think this should necessarily be taken as an indication of sannyasinis' orthodoxy, it does serve to neutralize the threat that they pose to the social order.

The Gendered Meanings of Chastity and Celibacy

In tracing the major nuances of meanings in the ideology and practices of brahmacharya, we can say that it connotes not simply celibacy but a lifestyle of self-control, emotional detachment, and ritual and moral purity. It may be constituted as a temporary stage of life, as an intermittent practice related to some ritual context, as sexual fidelity to one's spouse for the purpose of procreation only, or as a lifelong vow. In whatever context, brahmacharya is assumed to bring power to both men and women.

Brahmanic Hinduism has allowed women intermittent and temporary periods of sexual abstinence, usually performed for the sake of men and children, and has considered lifelong celibacy unthinkable for women. One reason for this disparity between the sexes is that Brahmanic ideas about the dynamics of sexual fluids have given male semen the most powerful and positive role and have assumed that sex involves a net loss for men and a net gain for women.

Although Brahmanic understandings of celibacy are focused on the somatic, alternative understandings of celibacy not only exist but are also less physiological and arguably less androcentric. Even these models, of course, are open to misogynous interpretations: just as women are unable to control their bodily fluids, so they are less capable of controlling their emotions. Unlike models based on semen obsession, however, they have egalitarian potential. A more expansive understanding of brahmacharya focuses on moral as well as ritual purity, a lifestyle of self-restraint, and emotional detachment.

While the somatic models tend to portray women as seducers of celibate men, alternative models may view women as less lustful than men and thus more capable of self-control.[20] One itinerant Dásanāmī sannyasini told me that the renunciant path is easier for women because they have less passion and lust. "Even women have changed in this respect," she said, "but still, in India, women have little passion. I know because women come to me and tell me that for the first couple of years it was OK but now they find [sex] a nuisance." Swami Sivananda has also expressed this view: "Man is the real culprit [in breaking vows of celibacy]; he violates rules and laws. Women have more self-restraint, though the scriptures say that they are eight times more passionate than men" (1987: 212). Gandhi also claimed that control of sexual desire is easier for women. "My wife was never the temptress"; he confessed, "it was my own weak will or lustful attachment that was the obstacle" (1957: 205). Of course, sannyasinis themselves do view women as capable of celibacy, because they understand celibacy as something other than a somatic process.

Even though women may be deemed capable of celibacy, it is not a generally acceptable path for ordinary women. Hindu culture has an ambivalent attitude toward lifelong brahmacharya whether it is undertaken by men or by women; comments about its benefits exist for both men and women alongside attempts to limit its practice to particular contexts. Yet it is clear that there is more at stake for society when women take these vows than when men do. Brahmacharya as sexual abstinence is another matter. Temporary, intermittent, and partial abstinence may be compatible with householder, specifically wifely, ideals, a point which is obscured by translating *brahmacharya* as "celibacy." More ethnographic research on women's attempts to practice brahmacharya, both in the home and in the ashram, will help us confirm the argument made in this chapter. Simply recognizing the wide range of meanings attributed to brahmacharya allows us to consider the possibility that the difference between the celibate ascetic and the chaste woman is a difference of degree rather than kind.

Notes

I thank Ravindra Khare, the editors of this volume, and three anonymous readers for their insightful comments on various drafts of this chapter. Their comments have helped to improve the final product, although I was not able to address every criticism.

1. Very little statistical information is available about Hindu ascetics in general, and even less focuses specifically on female ascetics. Only about 10 percent of the Daśanāmī monasteries visited by Gross in the 1970s had any women residents at all. Among those were some monasteries composed entirely of women, whereas the remaining were mixed (Gross 1992: 142). Ojha reports that sannyasinis can be found in over half of the 10 Daśanāmī orders (1981: 261). Estimates put the number of female ascetics, not renouncers specifically, at 10–15 percent of the entire ascetic population (Denton 1991: 212; Gross 1992: 121; Ojha 1981: 264–265). In contemporary Hinduism there has been a shift away from sectarian cohesiveness toward markedly independent religious entrepreneurial activity and, with this, a rising popularity of unaffiliated charismatic gurus (Gross 1992: 324), many of whom are women. Still, the estimated ratio of female to male ascetics in Hinduism is significantly lower than that reported by Gutschow (this volume) for Buddhist nuns in Zangskar, which may be because Buddhism established institutions for nuns alongside those for monks and because (as Gutschow reports) a family may actually select a daughter for the nunnery.

2. Denton's (1991) study of female ascetics in Varanasi reports that women who become brahmacharinis extend the (ideally adolescent) lifestyle of celibate studentship into a lifelong pursuit. They follow the classical ideal of sexual abstinence, ritual purity, study, and service to the teacher; in contrast with renouncers, then, their lifestyle is one of close supervision and perpetually dependent status (Denton 1991: 222). Here, the distinction I am drawing between temporary and permanent abstinence becomes blurred.

3. Even though other castes may aspire to Brahmanic models by emulating the higher castes (Srinivas 1966: 14–15), this is not always the case; all Hindus do not share the concern with celibacy and ritual purity (Madan 1987: 1–3; Marglin 1985: 18–21; Narayanan 1990; Nichter and Nichter 1989a). For example, one of Daniel's (1984: 171) Tamil informants insisted that too little sex is as bad for a man's health as too much sex. Cohen (1997: 301) speaks of truck drivers who feel that driving a truck builds up heat in the body, which must be expelled through ejaculation. Indeed, the suspicion and humor with which celibate ascetics are often treated in popular expressive traditions is well documented (Bloomfield 1924; Gold 1992: 48–49; Narayan 1988: 155–157).

4. Olivelle (1993: 131) argues that the ashramas were originally seen as four parallel paths leading to the same goal but that in the classical system (beginning with the *Manusmṛti*) they constitute a ladder. Olivelle emphasizes that the system did not reflect social reality, for other sources depict people of all ages, even married men with families, renouncing worldly life (117).

5. Although there is evidence that in ancient India girls were also initiated as brahmacharinis into a period of Vedic study, classical authors assume that only boys are initiated (Olivelle 1993: 81). Young explains that as Vedic ritual became so complex that it required extended training, education shifted from the home of

the family to the home of the guru; girls were kept at home while boys were sent for education. Young maintains that, for all women, chastity became a substitute for knowledge when educational disparities between men and women increased and women as a class came to be associated with ignorance. By the first century B.C.E., for women, the ritual of initiation into a period of Vedic study (*upanayana*) was equated with marriage, and serving the teacher was equated with serving the husband (Young 1987: 66–69).

6. For text-based arguments that place the dialogue between householder and celibate lifestyles at the center of Indian civilization, see Dumont 1980; and Heesterman 1985. For ethnography-based accounts that represent ways in which contemporary Hindus reflect on this debate, see Burghart 1983; Madan 1987; Gold 1992; and Alter 1992.

7. It has already been noted that, according to classical models, a male brahmachari, like a female *kanyā*, is an adolescent who is expected to marry and become sexually active. However, there has always been greater tolerance of a male youth who rejects marriage for a vow of lifelong celibacy than of a young woman who makes the same decision.

8. I found that few sannyasinis were previously widows, and Ojha (1981: 271) reports the same. Courtright (1995) has noted that in the perfect Hindu world, there would be no widows. The widow's option of joining her husband on his funeral pyre (sati) is a way of bypassing the social and ritual marginality of widowhood. Since the practice of widow immolation has been outlawed in India, a tradition has developed in which widows who were prevented by family members from committing sati might choose to live an ascetic lifestyle as "living satis" (Courtright 1995: 188–191). I would add that these satis are seen as pure and extremely powerful; people seek their blessings.

9. Kakar (1989: 20) suggests that there are so many prohibitions on conjugal relations (during the woman's menses, moonless nights, nights of the full moon, festival days for gods and ancestors) that hardly any nights are left for sexual intercourse and that even those are clouded by a general disapproval of the erotic dimension of married life.

10. For more on female saints in legend and history, see Kishwar 1989; Ramanujan 1982; and Ramaswamy 1992.

11. This section is significantly indebted to O'Flaherty's (1980) detailed analysis of male and female sexual fluids in Sanskrit texts.

12. The Upanishadic period, beginning during the seventh and sixth centuries B.C.E., refers to a set of philosophies and texts. Upanishadic thought emphasizes the individual pursuit of liberation from the cycle of birth and death through ascetic practices and knowledge.

13. Daniel (1984: 163) and Trawick (1990: 159, 278) have noted a belief in male and female semen among more mainstream Tamil Hindus, and Marglin (1985: 58) has recorded similar beliefs in Orissa.

14. Caplan writes that it is unclear whether women can build up a storehouse of power by sexual abstinence, as men can, but that some anthropological evidence seems to suggest that this is possible (1987: 283). But Caplan does not offer refer-

ences. So far as I am aware, there is no evidence to support a general belief in women's ability to gain power by accumulating sexual fluids.

15. The difference between a man and a woman, writes philosopher Gandhi, is that "the arousal and fulfillment of her sexual desire does not involve the detachment and loss of any building blocks of life from her body," a condition that makes women less anxious (1988: 216). There is also the hope of having it both ways. Campbell (1976, cited in Bennett 1983: 126) suggests that the patriline's ideal self-image is that of an unbroken line of celibate men, in which sons are produced by a series of miracles rather than through sexual intercourse, thus assuring patrilineal continuity without the loss of purity or power.

16. There may be a parallel here with male arousal in the presence of an attractive woman. Of course, involuntary loss of male semen is devalued, whereas involuntary loss of female milk is highly valued. Also, men are thought to be capable of controlling their loss through ascetic practice.

17. For more on this, see Caplan 1987: 283; Kakar 1989: 20; and Trawick 1990: 278 n. 55. For evidence that women themselves resist the patrilineal forces that devalue conjugal intimacy, see Raheja and Gold 1994.

18. For male ascetics, women represent not just sexual pleasure but also the physical and emotional comforts of home. This is significant because withdrawing semen through brahmacharya should be accompanied by renouncing other comforts, passions, and attachments as well. Women thus become symbols of all that is to be renounced.

19. Mahatma Gandhi commented extensively on his experiments with the effect of diet on sexual control and insisted that a person who has not mastered the palate cannot master carnal desire (Fischer 1963: 243; Gandhi 1957: 210–211).

20. Kakar (1989: 21) reports that most Indian women find sex painful or distasteful or both. Also see Caplan 1987: 292. Kawanami (this volume) discusses a similar duality in female sexuality in Burma, in which women are seen as seducers of celibate men on the one hand and as less lustful than men on the other. While Kawanami seems to view it as the difference between cultural conceptions and social reality, I see this duality in female sexuality in India as expressing two different and contradictory cultural conceptions.

References Cited

Alter, Joseph. 1992. *The Wrestler's Body*. Berkeley: University of California Press.

Alter, Joseph. 1997. Seminal Truth: A Modern Science of Male Celibacy in North India. Medical *Anthropology Quarterly* 11(3): 275–298.

Babb, Lawrence. 1986. *Redemptive Encounters: Three Modern Styles in the Hindu Tradition*. Delhi: Oxford University Press.

Bennett, Lynn. 1983. *Dangerous Wives and Sacred Sisters: Social and Symbolic Roles of High Caste Women in Nepal*. New York: Columbia University Press.

Bloomfield, Maurice. 1924. On False Ascetics and Nuns in Hindu Fiction. *Journal of the American Oriental Society* 44: 202–242.

Burghart, Richard. 1983. Renunciation in the Religious Traditions of South Asia. *Man,* n.s., 18: 635–653.

Campbell, J. Gabriel. 1976. *Saints and Householders: A Study of Hindu Ritual and Myth among the Kangra Rajputs.* Kathmandu: Biblioteca Himalayica, Ratna Pustak Bhandar.

Caplan, Pat. 1987. Celibacy as a Solution? Mahatma Gandhi and *Brahmacharya.* In *The Cultural Construction of Sexuality,* ed. Pat Caplan, 271–295. New York: Tavistock Publications.

Carstairs, G. Morris. 1957. *The Twice-Born: A Study of a Community of High-Caste Hindus.* London: Hogarth.

Cohen, Lawrence. 1997. Semen, Irony, and the Atom Bomb. *Medical Anthropology Quarterly* 11(3): 301–303.

Courtright, Paul B. 1995. Sati, Sacrifice, and Marriage: The Modernity of Tradition. In *From the Margins of Hindu Marriage,* ed. Lindsey Harlan and Paul B. Courtright, 184–203. New York: Oxford University Press.

Daniel, E. V. 1984. *Fluid Signs: Being a Person the Tamil Way.* Berkeley: University of California Press.

Denton, Lynn Teskey. 1991. Varieties of Hindu Female Asceticism. In *Roles and Rituals for Hindu Women,* ed. I. Julia Leslie, 211–231. London: Pinter.

Dumont, Louis. 1980. *Homo Hierarchicus.* Chicago: University of Chicago Press.

Edwards, James W. 1983. Semen Anxiety in South Asian Cultures: Cultural and Transcultural Significance. *Medical Anthropology* 7(3): 51–67.

Fischer, Louis, ed. 1963. *The Essential Gandhi: An Anthology.* London: George Allen and Unwin.

Gandhi, Mohandas K. 1957. *An Autobiography: The Story of My Experiments with Truth.* Boston: Beacon Hill.

Gandhi, Ramachandra. 1988. Brahmacarya. In *Way of Life: King, Householder, Renouncer,* ed. T. N. Madan, 205–221. Delhi: Motilal Banarsidass.

Gold, Ann. 1992. *A Carnival of Parting.* Berkeley: University of California Press.

Gross, Robert L. 1992. *The Sandhus of India.* Jaipur: Rawat Publications.

Hancock, Mary E. 1995. The Dilemmas of Domesticity: Possession and Devotional Experience among Urban Smarta Women. In *From the Margins of Hindu Marriage,* ed. Linsey Harlan and Paul B. Courtright, 60–91. New York Oxford University Press.

Heesterman, J. C. 1985. *The Inner Conflict of Tradition.* Chicago: University of Chicago Press.

Kakar, Sudhir. 1989. *Intimate Relations: Exploring Indian Sexuality.* Delhi: Viking.

Khandelwal, Meena. 1996. Walking a Tightrope: Saintliness, Gender, and Power in an Ethnographic Encounter. *Anthropology and Humanism* 21(2): 111–134.

Khandelwal, Meena. 1997. Ungendered Atma, Masculine Virility and Feminine Compassion: Ambiguities in Renunciant Discourses on Gender. *Contributions to Indian Sociology,* n.s., 31(1): 79–107.

Khare, R. S. 1982. From Kanya to Mata: Aspects of the Cultural Language of Kinship in Northern India. In *Concepts of Person,* ed. Akos Oster, Lina

Fruzzetti, and Steve Barnett, 143–171. Cambridge, Mass.: Harvard University Press.

Kishwar, Madhu. 1989. Introduction. *Manushi: Women Bhakta Poets* 50–52: 3–8.

Leslie, I. Julia. 1989. *The Perfect Wife.* Delhi: Oxford University Press.

Madan, T. N. 1987. *Non-renunciation.* Delhi: Oxford University Press.

Marglin, Frederique Apffel. 1985. *Wives of the God-King: The Rituals of the Devadasis of Puri.* Delhi: Oxford University Press.

McGee, Mary. 1991. Desired Fruits: Motive and Intention in the Votive Rites of Hindu Women. In *Roles and Rituals for Hindu Women,* ed. I. Julia Leslie, 71–88. London: Pinter.

Narayan, Kirin. 1988. *Storytellers, Saints, and Scoundrels: Folk Narrative in Hindu Reliigous Teaching.* Philadelphia: University of Pennsylvania Press.

Narayanan, Vasudha. 1990. Hindu Perceptions of Auspiciousness and Sexuality. In *Women, Religion and Sexuality: Studies on the Impact of Religious Teachings on Women,* ed. Jeanne Becher, 64–92. Geneva: WCC Publications.

Nichter, Mark, and Mimi Nichter. 1989a. Cultural Notions of Fertility in South Asia and Their Impact on Sri Lankan Family Planning Practices. In *Anthropology and International Health: South Asian Case Studies,* ed. Mark Nichter, 7–29. Dordrecht: Kluwer Academic.

Nichter, Mark, and Mimi Nichter. 1989b. Modern Methods of Fertility Regulation: When and for Whom Are They Appropriate? In *Anthropology and International Health: South Asian Case Studies,* ed. Mark Nichter, 57–82. Dordrecht: Kluwer Academic.

O'Flaherty, Wendy Doniger. 1980. *Women, Androgynes, and Other Mystical Beasts.* Chicago: University of Chicago Press.

Ojha, Catherine. 1981. Feminine Asceticism in India: Its Tradition and Present Condition. *Man in India* 61(3): 254–285.

Ojha, Catherine. 1988. Outside the Norms: Women Ascetics in Hindu Society. *Economic and Political Weekly* (April 30): 34–36.

Olivelle, Patrick. 1993. *The Asrama System.* New York: Oxford University Press.

Raheja, Gloria Goodwin, and Ann Grodzins Gold. 1994. *Listen to the Heron's Words.* Berkeley: University of California Press.

Rajayogacharya, Bal-Brahmachari. 1977. *Science of Soul.* Rishikesh: Yoga Niketan Trust.

Ramanujan, A. K. 1982. On Women Saints. In *The Divine Consort,* ed. John Stratton Hawley and Donna Marie Wulff, 316–324. Berkeley: Berkeley Religious Studies Series.

Ramaswamy, Vijaya. 1992. Rebels—Conformists? Women Saints in Medieval South India. *Anthropos* 87: 133–146.

Sivananda, Swami. 1987. *Bhakti-Yoga.* Sivanandanagar: Divine Life Society.

Srinivas, M. N. 1966. *Social Change in Modern India.* Berkeley: University of California Press.

Tapper, Bruce E. 1979. Widows and Goddesses: Female Roles in Deity Symbolism in a South Indian Village. *Contributions to Indian Sociology* 13(1): 1–31.

Toomey, Paul M. 1990. Krishna's Consuming Passions: Food as Metaphor and

Metonym for Emotion at Mount Govardhan. In *Divine Passions,* ed. Owen Lynch, 157–181. Berkeley: University of California Press.

Trawick, Margaret. 1990. *Notes on Love in a Tamil Family.* Berkeley: University of California Press.

van der Veer, Peter. 1989. The Power of Detachment: Disciplines of Body and Mind in the Ramanandi Order. *American Ethnologist* 16(3): 458–470.

Wadley, Susan S. 1983. Vrats: Transformers of Destiny. In *Karma: An Anthropological Inquiry,* ed. E. Valentine Daniel and Charles Keyes, 147–162. Berkeley: University of California Press.

Young, Katherine. 1987. Hinduism. In *Women in World Religions,* ed. Arvind Sharma, 59–103. Albany: State University of New York Press.

9 Mario I. Aguilar

Ritualizing Celibacy
The Poetics of Inversion in Chile and Kenya

We invent tradition by formalizing and ritualizing a practice and imposing its repetition (Hobsbawm 1983: 4). In effect, many of the so-called old practices have been quite recently incorporated as cultural traditions. Sometimes these traditions have been created by interested political and economic elites in the form of discourses that lead to control and social status (Ranger 1983: 252–260), whereas in other situations such processes are part of a dynamic encounter and assimilation that take place between different societies, ethnic groups, and cultures that have been protagonists in the creation and invention of metanarratives (e.g., Lemarchand 1994: 17).

Celibacy is an example of those invented traditions within Christianity. It began as a practice, as a choice, and developed into a habitus, a historical production, that in turn "produces individual and collective practices, and hence history, in accordance with the schemes engendered by history" (Bourdieu 1976: 2). Such is the case of celibacy in the Catholic Church (of the West), whereby a priest must be celibate in order to perform his ritual office.[1] In fact, it was only by the Gregorian reform (ca. 1050–1150) that celibate priests became a norm in the Catholic Church (Coriden 1972: 118–119).[2] Today, it is only the Western (Roman) branch of the Catholic Church that posits celibacy as a condition for ordination.

In fact, most Western Catholics assume priests to be celibate; priests are expected not to contract marriage or to sire children.

Celibacy (i.e., abstention from marriage and procreation) has become a Catholic tradition, even in Latin America and Africa, where people "live in incomplete and mixed times of premodernity, modernity, and postmodernity, each of these linked historically in turn with corresponding cultures that are, or were, epicentres of power" (Calderon 1995: 55). Thus, following processes of "self-ascription" and "ascription by others" (Barth 1969: 13), the Catholic Church requires priests to avoid any emotional and sexual involvement with women. Such involvement could compromise their disavowal of interest in marriage (or procreation) and in any social practice that would in itself create new kin ties.

McBrien (1994: 63, see also p. 14) has distinguished between two kinds of tradition in the context of his discussion of the Catholic Church. *Tradition* with a capital *T* denotes dogmatic and theological understandings that express a cosmological view and promote the notion of a universal community, symbolically constructed. *Tradition* with a lowercase *t* denotes what anthropologists consider custom or practice. While textual scribes within the Catholic community would emphasize celibacy as a "tradition" — that is, a norm and practice — there is still an ambiguous connotation of universal or historical significance in the insider's ascription of such practice. Thus, for most Catholic insiders, celibacy is a "Tradition." In that way, celibacy helps set boundaries and parameters of difference between Catholics and other Christians. In Catholicism, the conferring of such office as priest, then, depends on the acceptance of celibacy as a lifetime practice. This applies to any Catholic community from any culture where the Catholic Church of the West is actually present.

Other cultures, according to the current understanding of the Catholic Church, are subordinated to the conceptual truths expressed by Catholic "culture." In practice, other cultures are ideologically unified by Catholics through the celebration of oppositional rituals of sameness, which confront the otherness of local cultural manifestations. Efforts to appropriate local cultural elements into a European liturgy, following processes known as indigenization, accommodation, adaptation, and inculturation (Shorter 1988: 11), are considered by Catholics as a creative process of diversification (Shorter 1994: 94–95). *Inculturation* refers to the (ecclesial) social recognition that faith (or the gospel) must become culture if it is to be fully received and lived.

Michael Angrosino has criticized the aesthetic emphasis in studies of the development, performance, and cultural significance of ritual. He argues that the culture concept of the Catholic Church has overemphasized ritual as expressive behavior, and therefore has failed to recognize ritual moments as social events that, when analyzed, yield clues about "how people think and feel about the social environment in which ritual is embedded" (1994: 828). Further, in this view there is no room for perceiving ritual as able to alter social reality (Rappaport 1979; see also Angrosino 1994: 828).[3] In social practice what syncretism means is the creative, but complex, relation between a religious tradition and a localized culture, with inculturation as a normative process and a challenge for any fixed tradition, textual or nontextual.

I will argue, on the basis of participant observation, that rituals of ordination communicate ideological messages to those present and that one of them is that Catholic priests are celibate human beings. However, those rituals also create the conditions for some social mobility, a contestation of cultural perceptions by a particular group, and ultimately a gain in status, because of the conferring of office to the priest. I examine rituals of ordination that I witnessed in Chile and Kenya. I will show that, while aesthetic and poetic considerations differed between the two ritual occasions, the actual promise of obedience to the bishop and the promise of celibacy were the key points for empowering those men and for fueling their society's perception of them as "fathers" of many.[4] The person who acquires a ritual office is already related to several groups and networks within the society in which the ritual takes place. The communal perception of priests in the two communities was strongly linked with an offering of their fertility to God, not only by themselves, but also by their kin. Such an offer deserves a reward, not in heaven, but in the social, political, and economic life of the candidates and of their kin. With localized case studies, I argue that while the ritual norms (here, celibacy) become universal, they are locally perceived and constructed according to communal norms.

Aesthetic Similarities

The liturgical reforms initiated with the meeting of all Catholic bishops at the Vatican (Second Vatican Council, 1962–1965) and promulgated in the early 1970s laid out two major ordination rituals: the ordinating to the diaconate (office of deacon) and the ordination to the priesthood. The ritual of ordination to the priesthood represents one of seven communal rituals (sacraments) that can be celebrated by any Catholic. The person to be ordained must be a male (CL 1024), and he must undertake to remain celibate for the rest of his life (CL 1037).

The priesthood ordination takes place in the context of the communal celebration of the Eucharist and consists of a dialogue among the bishop (who ordains the candidate), the candidate, and the participants. The bishop asks the participants if they consider the candidate worthy, after he has been presented by one of his mentors. If the people answer that the candidate is worthy, then the bishop examines the candidate and asks him if he promises obedience to the bishop and his successors After prayers for the Church and the candidate, all priests present lay their hands on the head of the candidate. The candidate is subsequently blessed by the bishop. Then his hands are anointed with oil, he is given the plate and cup in order to preside over the Eucharist, and he is vested with the chasuble in order to preside over the ritual of the Eucharist for the first time, together with the bishop (EVD 1982: 948–953).[5]

I participated in rituals of priestly ordination as a member of the Catholic Church in Chile during 1986–1987 and in Kenya from 1987 to 1990 and in 1992. I knew the candidates well, and I had also taught them during their studies. Therefore, I took part not only in the communal rituals but also in the celebrations that followed at their family homes. During all those occasions the ritual procedure for ordination followed a standard form, and the words used came out of a formula written in a liturgical book. However, the cultural empowerment of different individuals had different meanings and resonance within the two different contexts. Therefore, I would argue that the aesthetics of any ritual of ordination assume signs and symbols chosen by the particular community from which the candidate comes and produce different sets of symbolic constructions and communal understandings. To this end, I compare specific ordination rituals from the two locales.

My example from Chile will be an ordination that took place in Santiago, in the secondary school chapel where the candidate had studied. Hymns known to the school community were sung, and flags and emblems of the school and the particular community of priests that ran the school were predominant in the chapel. The ordaining bishop had been a student in a school run by the same priests. A connection was seen between the priests who had worked in that particular place and the product of their labor, namely, a new priest.

Those elements of social and cultural reproduction were also present in the case of a candidate to the priesthood in Kenya, a man of Boorana ethnic origin who was ordained in the town of Isiolo.[6] Traditional dances, songs, spears, knives, altar cloths, and liturgical vestments distinguished the candidate's lineage within a particular ethnic group, among whom missionaries had begun their work fairly recently. (In the case of the Chilean candidate, the first missionaries had begun their work in that country

in 1541; the Catholic school in question had been founded in 1950 to edu-
cate the children of the country's elite.)

In that realm of comparative aesthetics, where we juxtapose one ordination ritual in Chile with another in Kenya, cultural parameters of localized
songs, dance, and movement represent the diversification of a centralized
ritual that in itself re-creates and reaffirms an already established organic
solidarity. But in the realm of poetics, which entails discourses and perceptions of an actual event by its participants, those rites of ordination remain
unified by the centrality of a normative element: celibacy.

Poetics and the Cultural Expression of Difference

Songs and hymns can be expressions of many types of societal perceptions, such as solidarity as well as dissent and protest. Musicians and sing-
ers have to choose certain songs for a ritual occasion, and in the case of a
priestly ordination they have to balance their choices with those of a local
community. The choirmaster or main singer has to explain some of the
meanings of those songs that are going to be performed in a particular
context. Therefore, a short examination of the motives present in those
songs can elucidate the diversified context and perceptions of our two
rituals.

The Chilean ritual took place at a moment when the community of
priests, having long been established, had already passed on their perceptions of priesthood to their students. Several of those students had been
ordained in the past few years and had left Chile to exercise their ministry
in other countries, often in mission countries, where there were fewer
Catholics and therefore fewer priests than in Chile. The candidate had
received all his primary and secondary education in the same school (for
12 years) and, after studies in Chile and Europe, had returned to the
school chapel to go through his ordination ritual. He was perceived by the
school community not only as a fruit of their own efforts but also as an
affirmation of the good example of teachers and priests in the school, who
had taught and guided him.

The hymns that were used at the ritual expressed that perception of his
journey. It was a journey that others had made before, including the foreign priests from Europe who had founded the school. For example, the
response to the first reading, in which the participants heard how Abraham had left his homeland and marched to another land following God's
invitation, contained the following words,

> The Lord chose his disciples,
> he sent them two by two.

It is lovely to see the peace messengers'
feet coming down the mountain.
The Lord sent them to the towns
and places where he was going.
It is lovely to see the peace messengers'
feet coming down the mountain.
(CVD 1986: 3; my translation).

The chosen hymns provided the bishop with an opportunity to say that, although in Jesus' time his followers were married, Jesus never married, and therefore had the opportunity to lead a community to whom he devoted his full attention and his constant guidance. Jesus' disciples also left their families, according to the bishop, in order to prepare themselves to lead others. They became the first bishops, and they went out of Palestine to found other communities and other churches. The candidate, in the words of the bishop, had followed the same path. He too had left his own family for the seminary, to study and prepare himself to be a leader of communities, to father other people's children. His call was a gift from God, and he was a gift from his family to the Church and to all other families.

The hymn at communion referred to a prophet who could speak a message loudly, and it instructed others, "Leave your brothers, leave your father and mother; leave your house, because the world is suffering" (CVD 1986: 7; my translation). This and the other songs expressed a general call to leave kin and to ignore kinship and social relations. There was a call to serve foreigners and people who express otherness in society, such as the marginalized, the oppressed, and those who are in jail. That call requires an inversion by the prophet that comes close to the attributes expected from a priest: the candidate, ordained as a priest, must assume what would normally be antisocial characteristics in order to be available to all.

The call of a priest to seek the kingdom of God reflects the fact that the kingdom is an invented one with a symbolic boundary. This boundary challenges the human structures of society. Celibacy and the renunciation of marriage and a sexual relationship reflects a challenge to what is considered social. To have a family, to have possessions, to be a good citizen, culturally speaking, is not what is expected of a Catholic priest. As in the case of witches, who constitute an inversion of what is considered social (Evans-Pritchard [1937] 1976: 51–52), the characteristics of a ritual man in Catholicism follow patterns of inversion. Celibacy makes the priest a priest, because it is by leaving the social world related to particular kin that he is able to fulfill the expectation that he will eventually belong to many. If he were to procreate through a wife, his levels of economic and symbolic exchange with his offspring and their mother would interfere with his ideological concern to serve others.

Although in the Chilean ritual, overt stress was put on the fact that the candidate was an only child, it was also suggested that he was leaving family and kin, he was not marrying, in order to be available as a father to a local community anywhere in the world. The particular priest ordained in the particular ritual I write of was a member of a group of missionaries and therefore departing from his home country for another. To that effect, the sending community of his former school, his family of origin, and indeed the country (predominantly Roman Catholic) gained prestige and status within the cultural and symbolic community called the Catholic Church.

The Poetics of African Fertility and Inversion

Emotional difficulties are not absent in the assumption of celibacy as a way of life. Those difficulties relate to the possible loneliness and lack of belonging that some priests experience. The candidates for the priesthood described in these cases I present have to contest and convince other people of the value of celibacy in two different cultural contexts. In Chile, priests are set apart from their families and kin, but cultural parameters of social behavior allow for the existence of single men and bachelors who never marry. Reasons for such a phenomenon are many and include the idea that such people never find a suitable partner to marry or have been too busy pursuing careers to initiate social and emotional commitments. This is not the case in Kenya, where celibacy as a requirement for priestly ordination encounters a form of social stigma attached to renunciation and inversion of a culturally understood social self. From the point of view of some Kenyans, celibacy is required to become like the whites, to become one of them—part of a colonial enterprise understood by Mudimbe, for example, as the conversion of African minds and spaces. Celibate missionaries are perceived by some as envoys of the European God, agents of political empire, and representatives of civilization (Mudimbe 1988: 47).

It is not my intention to expand on the social construction of the emotions; it must suffice to say that as cultures and cultural constructions differ, "the affective life of a South American—his way of feeling and living celibacy—differs from that of an African from Zaire or Senegal" (Otene 1981: 12). The values of fertility, procreation, and fecundity have been fundamental to the cohesion of all African cultures. Celibate persons do exist; however, they are considered anomalies and part of a traditional order. For example, in Boorana (eastern Kenya), collectors of wild plants and roots for medicinal purposes never marry and can have sexual relationships only outside their localized social relations. Their state of singleness reflects Boorana perceptions of the sacred, where the performance of habitual activities, such as sex, can endanger the potency of objects or substances used by ritual specialists in order to link the living and the dead. Such collectors, because they never marry, remain anomalous, and they are not allowed to live in villages. In any case, women build houses, and therefore the celibate Catholic priest could never have his own house or build up a household as an economic or ritual unit (Aguilar 1998: 76–79).

The contextual construction of a celibate person in Boorana society provides the background for understanding another ritual of priestly ordination, one that took place in Booranaland in eastern Kenya during 1991. The first Boorana candidate for the priesthood was ordained then and, like any Catholic priest, pledged obedience to the bishop after having accepted the call to remain celibate in his ordination to the diaconate.

The contextual perception of the ritual was somewhat different from the Chilean one. The politics and poetics of the occasion created the sense that, on the one hand, it was a triumph for the Catholic Church in Kenya. On the other hand, there was general recognition that conflicting schools of missionary strategy had completed a period of community influence, political intrigue, and nationalistic achievement. The candidate came from Merti, an isolated place where most Boorana in the public sphere profess themselves Muslims and are perceived as such by the rest of Kenya (Aguilar 1998: 243–244) after having undergone "Somalization" (Baxter 1966)[7] and "religious diversification" (Aguilar 1995). In the late 1960s though, a Catholic priest from the diocese of Vercelli in Italy, Father Pio Bono, began missionary work in the area, with the conviction that the only way of sustaining converts was by baptizing whole families of Boorana rather than individuals. This mission policy, sustained by the majority of the Italian missionaries, had been recently questioned and criticized by their non-Italian neighboring missionaries, working in the town of Garba Tula (Aguilar 1992; Tablino 1992).

As a result of those challenges, the first ordination of a Boorana as a Catholic priest represented a gain in missionary power for the majority party, a power "presentable to people in such a way that they would gladly submit themselves to social rules and authorities to the extent even of regarding them as desirable" (Parkin 1996: xv–xvi; see also Cohen 1969).[8] The candidate himself was destined to work side by side with an Italian mentor in the parish of Isiolo, where he was ordained, rather than going to foreign lands. He was empowered as a father in the Church on equal terms with other church fathers who had the power of decision, the economic resources, and the rights of elderhood and Europeanhood.

I would argue that there were two different perceptions expressed by participants in that ritual of empowerment. On the one hand, the European priests perceived the Boorana priest as a local and as a sign of the faith and commitment of Africans; on the other hand, local participants in the ritual perceived the newly ordained priest as a European. After all, they said, and more than once, "He is not going to marry, like the European fathers." For the Europeans, the acceptance of celibacy had made the new priest a father who was able to understand and identify with the daily toils of the local people. In the perception of the local population, however, he had gained social status not only because he had a profession, a job, and a future but also because he had been accepted by the Europeans as one of them. He would not experience economic deprivation in the future, nor would he have an immediate family to sustain.

The family of the candidate felt that his mentor, Father Pio, had taken good care of their children, including the candidate, during past famines and times of hardship. The Catholic mission had effectively and regularly fed thousands of people not only through times of famine but indeed throughout the past few years. Children, such as the candidate, had also received free education in the primary and secondary mission schools. It is a fact that education has been accepted in Kenya as a means to acquire national membership in a modern African state. Parents strive to send their children to school, and family networks are used in order to collect enough money to provide secondary school fees, especially for boys. Whatever the implications for the individual life of that Boorana priest, it was clear that he was being subsumed, in the perception of many of his relatives, into another culture, in whose structures and semantics they did not all participate.

Celibacy and Cultural Empowerment

The idea that norms and customs are accepted by people partly in order to belong in a society does not pose any problems for anthropology. After all, human beings acquire culture through their participation in a specific daily social action and not another one (Durkheim 1961: 22). The case of celibacy for priests then, suggests that the Roman Catholic Church has chosen that condition for its ritual leaders and that the practice of celibacy over the centuries has been assumed to be a historical norm and a current mandate.

We might, however, ask, as Meldford Spiro does, "Why is it that religious actors believe in the doctrines that comprise the religious system of their culture?" (1982: 45). Spiro argues that "after all we have for too long — certainly since Durkheim — accepted the coercive power of cultural symbols on the human mind to be a self-evident truth." While his conclusions and methodological suggestions refer to the need to look into the unconscious as well as the conscious, his main assumption is that there are mechanisms of the human mind that tend to search for a kind of infantile gratification, so as to spare society any kind of possible disruption.

Spiro's argument rests on one of the major methodological problems of classification facing any possible representation of processes within the Catholic Church or any other church. In a Durkheimian sense the Catholic Church functions as a body united as an institution through norms. However, one cannot ignore that the empowerment of fathers, as well as any other Catholic officers, requires the mutual participation of communities that are contextually and culturally distinct and that have chosen candidates who have gone through years of individual preparation in order to become empowered.

The case of the Catholic Church as a cultural (or a subcultural) force (depending on the level of social cohesion exhibited by and control exercised over a particular group of people) challenges us to move forward in exploring the idea of the cultural empowerment of chosen individuals. The rituals of ordination (diaconate and priesthood) have the characteristics of rites of passage. They specifically fulfill the general discourse that Turner (1969: 167) produced in relation to the Ndembu concerning "rituals of status elevation," whereby the candidate is irreversibly elevated to a higher position in a ritual system of classification, with churches replacing the seclusion lodge of the Ndembu within complex societies. From that point of view, any interpretation of ritual empowerment of the priest reflects a moment of status elevation that takes place in a liminal place and is irreversible.

The irreversibility of the priest's status elevation is clearly linked to the practice and the norm of celibacy. In some cases, Catholic priests who are tired or sick can take a leave of absence from a parish and remain priests in the perception of that society called the Catholic Church. However, if a priest decides to get married and in practice ends his celibate life, he is suspended from all his duties as a priest. Technically, the act of getting married means an immediate excommunication; there is no reversing one's status to become simply a Church member again.

From an anthropological point of view, I would argue that celibacy as a practice (as a tradition) and celibacy as an ideal are perceived by the Catholic Church as one and the same. That premise would certainly be denied by any informed Catholic who might view celibacy as a norm and practice of the Western Church that can be changed, and indeed that possibility has been discussed in the last 30 years (Hastings 1972). However, celibacy as a requisite for one of the higher ritual roles in such a church is more than a practice. The celibate is associated with the belief that such a person is not in sexual contact with women; therefore, he is pure and as a result closer to God. From a cultural point of view, many societies view sexual intercourse as dangerous and polluting (Douglas 1984: 150–153); from a historical point of view, sex acquired an impure representation in the Catholic Church since the times of Saint Augustine of Hippo (Price 1991). The actual practice of celibacy then is not only a condition for status elevation but also an ideology that developed over many centuries, where rituals of ordination could be described as rituals of separation as well. That particular empowerment requires separation from kin and a reversal of societal perceptions of fertility and fecundity. At the same time, categories of sexual purity express an ideology of permanent separation as necessary to empower individuals to lead communication with the divine and with the spiritual world.

Those rites of empowerment are universal, and men from every culture are empowered as leaders and teachers of Catholic communities in a segmentary fashion, where the center of ideological unity remains in Rome. The ordination ritual expresses an allegiance to Rome, the pope, and his successors. However, anthropological research on particular examples of those rituals of empowerment suggests that there are dissonant culturally constructed perceptions of the condition *sine qua non* for such status elevation. That cultural predicament has been outlined through the case studies in Chile and Kenya. Although a textual formula of empowerment through ordination is unified and universal, the actual condition of celibacy and its implications for family and kin, required of every candidate, are certainly (mis)understood according to the particular context and cultural milieu where the candidate was raised and educated. Thus, the actual relation between the universal and the particular, between Catholic culture and localized societal concerns, could be assessed only by extended periods of research among Catholic communities and their neighbors, so as to provide further ascriptions from within and from without and, indeed, a diachronic perspective on the development of such habitus.

Notes

1. I focus in this chapter on the Catholic priest. However, there are other celibate members of the Catholic Church: the religious (sisters and brothers), monks, hermits, and also laypeople, such as members of secular institutes, and men and women who have pledged virginity and celibacy to their diocesan bishops.

2. As correctly suggested by John Elsner and Simon Coleman (personal communication, 1996), monasticism played an important role in forwarding asceticism and sexual continence; however, there were also critical voices within the Church in the century or two before the Reformation (Lynch 1972).

3. This conception of given truths has also affected social anthropologists, who for the most part perceive Catholic rites as static and repetitive. Indeed, very few anthropological studies of Catholicism have been conducted (but see Turner 1974; and Turner and Turner 1978; also Dahlberg 1991; McKevitt 1991; and Stirrat 1991).

4. Candidates to the Catholic priesthood undergo training and academic studies in colleges known as seminaries, and they go through particular steps of incorporation leading up to ritual ordination as priests. Therefore candidates (seminarians) receive the ministry of lector and acolyte sometime before being ordained as deacons, a ritual that takes place at least six months before the actual ritual of ordination to the priesthood. It is then that celibacy is first formally promised.

5. *Chasuble* is the term used for the outer liturgical vestment worn by the organizer of the Eucharist, from *casula,* or "little house," originally an outer cape or cloak covering the tunic (Stravinskas 1991: 205–206).

6. I have found the spelling "Boorana" closer to the phonetic sound of the word; therefore I have consistently used it since my first explanation of such argument in Aguilar 1993.

7. Paul Baxter (1966) has suggested that the Boorana in eastern Kenya became Muslims because they acquired the cultural traits of the Somali. The Boorana of this region were not the subjects of a preaching crusade but found that it was easier to trade and live with the Somali if they were Muslims. That suggestion would account, in my opinion, for the Somali's becoming distant from the Boorana after independence, when residents of the Waso area of eastern Kenya stressed once again their old ways and old religious practices.

8. A comparable example is described by Mudimbe (1994: 120), when the first indigenous priest of the Belgian Congo (Zaire) was ordained on July 21, 1917, the Belgian Independence Day.

References Cited

Aguilar, Mario I. 1992. A Path of the Gospel in Garba Tulla: An Experience of Dialogue with Boorana Religion. *Seed* 4(10): 10–11.

Aguilar, Mario I. 1993. The Role of the Sarki Dance in Waso Boorana/Somali Symbiosis and Conflict. *Anthropos: International Review of Ethnology and Linguistics* 88: 183–187.

Aguilar, Mario I. 1995. African Conversion from a World Religion: Religious Diversification by the Waso Boorana in Kenya. *Africa* 65: 525–544.

Aguilar, Mario I. 1998. *Being Oromo in Kenya.* Trenton: Africa World.

Angrosino, Michael V. 1994. The Culture Concept and the Mission of the Roman Catholic Church. *American Anthropologist* 96: 824–832.

Barth, Fredrik. 1969. Introduction. In *Ethnic Groups and Boundaries: The Social*

Organization of Culture Difference, ed. Fredrik Barth, 9–38. London: George Allen and Unwin.

Baxter, Paul T. W. 1966. Acceptance and Rejection of Islam among the Boran of the Northern Former District of Kenya. In *Islam in Tropical Africa,* ed. I. M. Lewis, 233–250. London: Oxford University Press for the International African Institute.

Bourdieu, Pierre. 1976. *Outline of a Theory of Practice.* Cambridge: Cambridge University Press.

Calderon, Fernando. 1995. Latin American Identity and Mixed Temporalities; or, How to Be Postmodern and Indian at the Same Time. In *The Postmodern Debate in Latin America,* ed. John Beverley, José Oviedo, and Michael Aronna, 55–64. Durham: Duke University Press.

The Canon Law Society of Great Britain and Ireland (CL). 1983. *The Code of Canon Law in English Translation.* London: Collins.

Cohen, Abner. 1969. Political Anthropology: The Analysis of the Symbolism of Power Relations. *Man,* n.s., 4: 215–235.

Colegio del Verbo Divino (CVD). 1986. Ordenación Sacerdotal del Diácono M.I.A.B. Santiago. Mimeograph.

Coriden, James A. 1972. Celibacy, Canon Law, and Synod 1971. *Concilium* 8(8): 109–124 (issue entitled *Celibacy of the Catholic Priest,* ed. William Bassett and Peter Huizing).

Dahlberg, Andrea. 1991. The Body as Principle of Holism: Three Pilgrimages in Lourdes. In *Contesting the Sacred: The Anthropology of Christian Pilgrimage,* ed. John Eade and Michael J. Sallnow, 30–50. London: Routledge.

Douglas, Mary. 1984. *Purity and Danger: An Analysis of the Concepts of Pollution and Taboo.* Reprint ed. London: Ark Paperbacks. Original publication: London: Ark, 1966.

Durkheim, Émile. 1961. *The Elementary Forms of the Religious Life.* New York: Collier.

Editorial Verbo Divino el alia (EVD). 1982. Misal de la Comunidad III: Ritual de los Sacramentos. Estella, Navarra: Editorial Verbo Divino.

Evans-Pritchard, Edward. [1937] 1976. *Witchcraft, Oracles, and Magic among the Azande.* Abridged ed. with new introduction. Oxford: Clarendon.

Hastings, Adrian. 1972. Celibacy in Africa. *Concilium* 8(8): 151–156 (issue entitled *Celibacy of the Catholic Priest,* ed. William Bassett and Peter Huizing).

Hobsbawm, Eric. 1983. Introduction. In *The Invention of Tradition,* ed. Eric Hobsbawm and Terence Ranger, 1–14. Cambridge: Cambridge University Press.

Lemarchand, René. 1994. *Burundi: Ethnocide as Discourse and Practice.* Washington, D.C.: Woodrow Wilson Center Press and Cambridge University Press.

Lynch, John. 1972. Critique of the Law of Celibacy in the Catholic Church from the Period of the Reform Councils. *Concilium* 8(8): 57–75 (issue entitled *Celibacy of the Catholic Priest,* ed. William Bassett and Peter Huizing).

McBrien, Richard. 1994. *Catholicism.* Reprint ed. London: Geoffrey Chapman. Original publication, 1984.

McKevitt, Christopher. 1991. San Giovanni Rotondo and the Shrine of Padre Pio. In *Contesting the Sacred: The Anthropology of Christian Pilgrimage*, d. John Eade and Michael J. Sallnow, 77–97. London: Routledge.

Mudimbe, Valentin Y. 1988. *The Invention of Africa: Gnosis, Philosophy, and the Order of Knowledge*. Bloomington: Indiana University Press.

Mudimbe, Valentin Y. 1994. *The Idea of Africa*. Bloomington: Indiana University Press.

Otene, Matungulu. 1981. *Celibacy and the African Value of Fecundity*. Eldoret: Gaba Publications.

Parkin, David. 1996. Introduction: The Power of the Bizarre. In *The Politics of Cultural Performance*, ed. David Parkin, Lionel Caplan, and Humphrey Fisher, xv–xl. Providence: Berghahn Books.

Price, Elizabeth. 1991. How the Wine of Cana Became Vinegar. In *Women Experiencing Church*, ed. Dorothea McEwan, 187–198. Leominster, Herefordshire: Gracewing.

Ranger, Terence. 1983. The Invention of Tradition in Colonial Africa. In *The Invention of Tradition*, ed. Eric Hobsbawm and Terence Ranger, 211–262. Cambridge: Cambridge University Press.

Rappaport, Roy. 1979. *Ecology, Meaning, and Religion*. Richmond, Calif.: North Atlantic Books.

Shorter, Aylward. 1988. *Toward a Theology of Inculturation*. London: Geoffrey Chapman.

Shorter, Aylward. 1994. *Evangelization and Culture*. London: Geoffrey Chapman.

Spiro, Meldford E. 1982. Collective Representations and Mental Representations in Religious Symbol Systems. In *On Symbols in Anthropology: Essays in Honor of Harry Hoijer*, ed. Jacques Maquet, 45–72. Malibu: Undena for the University of California at Los Angeles Department of Anthropology.

Stirrat, Richard L. 1991. Place and Person in Sinhala Catholic Pilgrimage. In *Contesting the Sacred: The Anthropology of Christian Pilgrimage*, ed. John Eade and Michael J. Sallnow, 122–136. London: Routledge.

Stravinskas, Peter M. J. 1991. *Catholic Encyclopedia*. Huntington, Ind.: Our Sunday Visitor.

Tablino, Paolo. 1992. An Ignored Church of Northern Kenya. *Seed* 4(6): 23–24.

Turner, Victor. 1969. Humility and Hierarchy: The Liminality of Status Elevation and Reversal. In *The Ritual Process: Structure and Anti-Structure*, 166–203. Ithaca: Cornell University Press.

Turner, Victor. 1974. Pilgrimages as Social Processes. In *Dramas, Fields, and Metaphors: Symbolic Action in Human Society*, 166–230. Ithaca: Cornell University Press.

Turner, Victor, and Edith Turner. 1978. *Image and Pilgrimage in Christian Culture: Anthropological Perspectives*. Oxford: Basil Blackwell.

PART III
CELIBACY, CHOICE, AND CONTROL

10 *Rebecca J. Lester*

Like a Natural Woman
Celibacy and the Embodied Self in Anorexia Nervosa

Anorexic women are notoriously disinterested in sex. The accepted clinical interpretation of this voluntary celibacy is that it is closely associated with the rejection of food. In most understandings, the anorexic's preoccupation with food is interpreted as a sublimation of her sexual conflicts, and her food behaviors are then read as symbolic enactments of sexual fantasies, fears, and aggressions. Because of this, theorists of anorexia generally try to get at the "real" issue (i.e., sex) by starting with the observation and description of "sick" food behaviors and then decoding what these must say about female sexuality and the anorexic's relationship to this standard of health.

In this chapter, I argue that the central contemporary medical and professional understandings of voluntary celibacy in anorexia reflect and reinforce certain constructions of female sexuality that not only efface the anorexic woman's subjective experience of her illness but also may even perpetuate it. Here, I flip the conventional wisdom about anorexia on its head. I consider, in other words, not what it means to be *thin*, to say no to *food*, but rather what it means to be *celibate* and to say no to *sex*. I am particularly interested in what a closer examination of the way his "problem" of celibacy in anorexia is constructed in the literature might tell us about the channeling of female sexuality into culturally appropriate forms contingent on certain understandings about healthy womanhood.

Pathology and Culture

The chapters in this volume consider the voluntary abstention from sex from a variety of perspectives, including its relationship to systems of morality, ritual purity, institutions, and access to the sacred. One of the themes that seems to emerge is that celibacy can be, and often is, used as a means of altering the subjective experience of self, whether this is a personal choice or an institutional mandate. In all cases, the relationships between cultural understandings of sexual behavior and the proper selves allowed in a given context (be it prison, nunnery, or religious community) are central to the practices of celibacy.

Celibacy among anorexic women is no less culturally informed than other forms of celibacy. We must remember that the labeling of any behavior pattern as deviant or pathological is more than a simple description of fact. In the process of identifying the pathological, the cultural norms of health and normalcy and the dominant standards of appropriate living, including sexual life, are reinforced. The designation of dysfunction or pathology can (and often does), then, become a vehicle for moral evaluation. This is perhaps particularly central in the consideration of mental illness, where a disordered or damaged self is often identified as being at the root of the pathology. The treatment of mental illnesses, including anorexia nervosa, often involves such things as lengthy psychotherapy, medication, and behavior modification, all targeted at bringing this fractured or diminished self back in line with the accepted standards of health and proper behavior. The practices and experience of anorexia, then, as well as the dominant understandings of the causes and treatment of the illness, speak not only to individual psychological concerns but also (and perhaps more significantly) to cultural understandings of gender, self, sexuality, and sociability and can serve as a productive window on these issues.

This chapter is meant to be an orientation and a starting point for exploring celibacy within the anorexic condition. It does not attempt to be a comprehensive or extensive discussion of the issues raised. Rather, it is meant to be a first step, a sounding of ideas that require further investigation.

Not Another Bite

Anorexic women certainly appear to be sick and in need of a cure. The anorexic woman denies herself food, suppresses her appetite, and becomes dangerously thin. She is terrified of becoming fat; the thought of gaining even an ounce is unbearable; it is enough to throw her into a deep, and even suicidal, depression. She structures her whole life around food and eating, and she controls, measures, and accounts for every morsel of food and every drop of liquid that enters her body. She views her emaciated frame in the mirror — skin and bones and dull eyes and lifeless hair to those around her — and sees fat: lumpy, bumpy, disgusting, ugly fat. She must become thinner. Streamlined. Strong. Straight. As her illness progresses, she becomes more and more withdrawn and sullen, her zest for life leaving her, until she is a withered, pale, tired creature. This is the daily reality for thousands of women who simply shut off from life and slowly starve themselves to death, all the while protesting that they will be happy, they will be free, they will truly be alive, if only they can lose just five more pounds.

There is an overwhelming abundance of literature on eating disorders. Publications focusing on anorexia and bulimia touch on many aspects of these illnesses and their treatment: drug studies,[1] life histories and personal accounts,[2] therapy techniques,[3] cognitive and psychological profiles,[4] and cultural influences.[5] Despite this diversity of perspectives, a number of general themes emerge — a set of core understandings that appear to cut across these sometimes contradictory viewpoints. These understandings illuminate the continuing influence of the psychoanalytic perspective on the contemporary theorizing of eating disorders and treatment, and they articulate a continued preoccupation with the anorexic's *dislike of sexuality* as the core pathology. Moreover, they reveal key cultural assumptions about voluntary female celibacy.

These basic understandings, as I read them, involve: (1) recognizing that most anorexic women have no desire to be entered by a penis or receive little or no pleasure from heterosexual intercourse and that the construction of this aversion to sex is the central problem of the illness; (2) pathologizing this attitude toward penetration by a penis and assigning the cause of this pathology to ignorance about sexual matters, experiences of sexual abuse, endocrine depletion, immaturity, hormonal imbalance, or some other feature which would explain this otherwise bewildering ambivalence toward the male organ; (3) decoding the anorexic's sick food behaviors as symbolic expressions of this pathological conflict about the penis, behaviors which are read as highly sexualized: food symbolizes the penis or the mother or a baby, the mouth represents the vagina or the anus, eating is either orally sadistic or sexually erotic or both, and the anorexic girl's body is variously the mother or the phallus; and (4) postulating a course of treatment which takes this "stubborn resistance" to penile penetration as its target, reading as evidence of health and recovery the anorexic woman's acceptance of "mature" female sexuality and her embracing of the penis as the source of sexual pleasure.

These understandings of the anorexic woman's relationship to food and sex are rooted in early psychoanalytic conceptualizations of healthy gender development.

Eating Daddy's Baby and Throwing Up Mommy

"We see, then, a syndrome the main symptoms of which represent an elaboration and acting out in the somatic sphere of a specific type of fantasy. The wish to be impregnated through the mouth results, at times, in compulsive eating, and at other times, in guilt and consequent rejection of food, the constipation symbolizing the child in the abdomen and the amenorrhoea as direct psychological repercussion of pregnancy fantasies. This amenorrhoea may also be part of the direct denial of genital sexuality" (Waller, Kaufman, and Deutsch 1940: 15).

When Freud first tackled the enigma of anorexia nervosa in the early part of this century (1918), he proposed a complicated model of oedipal fantasies and forbidden desires which were, he argued, sublimated and articulated in the anorexic girl's bizarre food behaviors. He suggested that little girls live a masculine life until the traumatic and earthshaking discovery that they do not have a penis, that they are mutilated. This discovery leads them to a violent rage against the mother, who has betrayed them by not giving them a penis and by not preparing them for this devastating revelation. Until this time, Freud tells us, the little girl enjoyed a phallic sexuality, with her love object being the mother, and she fantasizes about having a baby by her mother. But the discovering of her lack of penis and the resulting penis envy propel the girl headlong into the oedipal phase, where she seeks refuge with the father and directs hatred at her faithless mother.

In this model, food becomes a powerful symbol for the acting out of oedipal conflicts. Food becomes simultaneously the mother who is being rejected and a symbol of the penis the girl does not have but can "enjoy" (Freud 1918) through sexual intercourse. The anorexic, according to Freud, has fantasies of oral impregnation by her father, and food becomes a sexualized symbol of this wish. At the same time, food represents the poison transmitted to the girl through the (now hated) mother's breast, leading to an ambivalent food relationship and either anorexic or bulimic food behaviors (or both) as the pathological expression of this conflict.

Hilde Bruch summarizes the traditional analytic approach and its articulation in treatment:

One of the first reports of the psychoanalytic treatment of a patient with anorexia nervosa . . . revealed intense father-fixation and the desire for a child from the father; this was looked upon as the psychic motivation for the [patient's] vomiting. The intense food refusal, however, was interpreted as relating to the wish for a penis, something not observed in ordinary neurotic vomiting. The anorexia picture was thus viewed as having developed out of the conflicts between the desire to be a like a man and the desire for a child from the father. (1973: 216)

In other words, the anorexic girl is presented as neurotically fixated on being entered by a penis or, failing this, symbolically enacting her desires through food. She paradoxically desires to be like a man and at the same time wants to have a child from the father, a child who then becomes a substitute for the coveted penis. So great is the girl's envy of the male organ, in fact, that, ironically, even the *rejection* of food is read as the wish for a penis.

Later psychoanalytic thinkers, building upon this idea of food representing the penis, turned the interpretation a bit, reading food refusal not so much as a desire for pregnancy as an expression of infantilism — a rejection of adult sexuality and a desire to return to the idyllic time of childhood. In this understanding, the anorexic woman's refusal of food is read as the attempt to achieve a regressive state in which self-induced starvation — leading to a repression of appetite, sexual drive, and signs of physical maturation — enables her to avoid both the maturational issues of sexual development, independence, and autonomy (and therefore to remove herself from the conflict she encountered in trying to become a woman separate from her mother) *and* the frightening prospect of healthy adult female sexuality. In this perspective, the object symbolized by food is interpreted not only as the penis but also as the mother, and the anorexic's refusal of food (the mother) indicates her struggle to separate from the mother and establish an independent identity. Food in this model represents femininity, nourishment, growth, and feminine sexuality; its rejection represents the anorexic girl's refusal to accept her womanhood.

But on another level food continues, in this model, to represent the penis. The anorexic rejects food, which represents the threat of a penis entering her, and as a result her body loses its feminine contours and she stops menstruating, effectively staving off so-called mature sexuality in favor of an immature, infantile state. This "irrational" fear of sexuality is symbolized in the anorexic woman's food behaviors, her refusal of food expressing an unfounded anxiety about impregnation and an immature response to the natural process of female sexual development.[6]

Although these various articulations of the psychoanalytic perspective on eating disorders may seem somewhat antiquated to the reader, I suggest we must take this traditional construction of anorexia nervosa very seriously. This is suggested not because it is necessarily consistent with the real-life experience of anorexia nervosa but because, despite decades of strong and impassioned feminist critique (e.g., Bordo 1992; Orbach 1978, 1986; Wolf 1991), it remains the core of medical theorizing of anorexia even today. These concerns are clearly articulated in a number of recent works where implicit assumptions attached to the question of celibacy seem to play a central role in the interpretation of anorexic food behaviors. While the pieces I will discuss here may not be strictly representational, neither are they exceptional in their terminology, interpretations, or use of psychoanalytic concepts.

Getting Fixed: Sex Therapy for "Dysfunctional" Anorexics

In their article "Sexual Dysfunction in Married Female Patients with Anorexia and Bulimia Nervosa," Simpson and Ramberg present case studies of five married eating-disordered women who had "a primary diagnosis of sexual aversion along with other psychosexual dysfunctioning" (1992: 44). The husbands of these five patients, the authors observed, showed "remarkable tolerance for their sexual avoidance" but nevertheless were more enthusiastic than their wives at the prospect of intense therapy for their sexual "problems."

The project was to provide intense, in-depth sex therapy to the five eating-disordered women and their husbands. All the women entered into the therapy process, stating that they wanted to be able to stop treatment on demand, a standard therapeutic procedure, which is, interestingly, read by the authors as showing "great resistance" to the therapeutic process (Simpson and Ramberg 1992: 45). Although the authors note that the women "seemed to participate enthusiastically at first," as the therapy sessions proceeded, many of the women reported feeling increasingly anxious.

Two of the five women had been the victims of incest or rape, but all five reported "marked similarity in their approach to sex" (Simpson and Ramberg 1992: 46). They were, the authors tell us, "ignorant of certain basic sexual facts and they found nudity — especially their own — disconcerting and somewhat distasteful." The authors conclude, then, that "their sexual aversion may have been due, in part, to their ignorance," because, "despite their current or former marital status, they all were reluctant to participate fully in intercourse, they all had difficulty responding sexually, and they all were anorgasmic" (p. 46). Since the authors do not compare this sexual "dysfunction" of these women with normal (i.e., non-eating-disordered) women, it is difficult to evaluate just how far outside the realm of so-called average female sexuality these women lie, if indeed, they do. Nevertheless, the reeducation of these women continued, and in four of the five cases the researchers were able to involve the husbands in the therapy. They found that each of the husbands "colluded with his wife to support the wife's dysfunction, exhibiting unparalleled patience with her avoidance" (p. 46).

Through the presentation of the case material, we learn what would seem to be important pieces of information about the women involved in the study. Mrs. A, for example, had been sexually abused by an uncle at the age of 12. The authors describe her present sexual dysfunction as an inability to relax during sex and the continued failure to lubricate when stimulated by her husband, despite the fact that she was able to achieve pleasure through masturbation. Mrs. B described sex as gross, sick, and disgusting and reported that her aversion to sex started as an adolescent, when peers teased her and called her a whore. Mrs. C's "severe sexual aversion" also seems to have links to her childhood. She was raised by grandparents who had instilled in her fear and disgust about anything sexual. One of the hallmarks of Mrs. D's dysfunction was "a frequent fantasy . . . of her being naked and sexually active with an unknown man, not her husband," which was apparently deemed troubling by the researchers (Simpson and Ramberg 1992: 51). And Mrs. E evidenced her dysfunction in having been "promiscuous" in high school, gotten pregnant, had an abortion, and was now timid and inhibited in her sexual relations.

From these five case studies, the authors conclude that, in addition to the primary diagnosis of anorexia and/or bulimia nervosa, "all five also exhibited problematic personality characteristics . . . and strongly entrenched defensive and resistive characteristics. They all knew how to avoid painful introspection, how to resist the therapeutic process, and how to continue in their well-established, self-destructive behavior patterns" (Simpson and Ramberg 1992: 53). These women, the authors clearly suggest, were manipulative (pp. 47, 51), oppositional, resistive, and antagonistic (p. 48), obsessed with controlling themselves and others (p. 49), testy, hostile, angry, anxious, and irritable (p. 49), infantile (p. 50), and oblivious to the way the world "really" works (p. 51). Simpson and Ramberg concluded that these women used their food problems in various ways as excuses for avoiding sex with their husbands and for manipulating others into pampering and indulging them.

Simpson and Ramberg (1992) are representative of much of the new scholarship dealing with a purported sexual dysfunction in women with anorexia or bulimia, and we can see here a number of flaws in their reasoning and the destructive influence of sexual stereotypes on women struggling with eating disorders. First and foremost, it remains unsubstantiated that any of these women even *had* a sexual dysfunction in the first place, and we are continually led to wonder how different from other women these women really were. All reported anxiety and some difficulty lubricating, lack of sexual desire, and failure to be sexually excited by their partners. But is this necessarily dysfunction? And if a woman is not sexually interested in or excited by her partner, are we certain that the problem lies with her?

Clearly, in each case reported by the authors, the so-called dysfunction originates outside the woman herself, and her aversion to sexuality might legitimately be read as a reasonable response to an externally troubling situation. In the case of Mrs. A, we are told that her husband feared her infidelity if she were to enjoy sex — a very traditional conceptualization of female sexuality, which seems to have contributed to the manifestation of hysteria in Victorian times and continues to underpin drastic practices like clitoridectamies and infibulation today. It would seem possible, then, that Mrs. A's dislike of sex may have been, at least in part, a way of preserving her marriage and reassuring her husband of her loyalty. Mrs. B had horrible memories of being called a whore as an adolescent when she began experimenting with sex and so withdrew from her sexuality so she would be seen as a "good girl." Mrs. C was raised by strict grandparents who drove it into her head that sex is bad and dirty and disgusting, and she has yet to be able to shake this association. Mrs. D was clearly unhappy in her marriage, and it is often difficult to find pleasure in the bedroom when the rest of a relationship is falling apart. And Mrs. E sought affection and companionship through sexual promiscuity, a behavior pattern that she recognized as destructive and was trying to mediate through her reluctance to engage in sexual relations when they were unpleasant for her.

This is not to say necessarily that these women are normal, healthy, or untroubled. Obviously, their feelings about sex appear to be unsettling in varying degrees for both them and their partners. But it is obvious from the authors' presentation and their choice of language that they interpret the central problem here as the desire of these women not to have sex with their husbands. They blame the women and paint them as stubborn, childish, manipulative, and controlling, and their poor, deprived husbands are presented as gentle, understanding, and remarkably tolerant (Simpson and Ramberg 1992: 44, 46, 47). This understanding of these women's attitudes toward sex clearly influences not only the interpretations given to their food behaviors, which are reduced to being nothing but clever excuses to avoid "healthy adult female sexuality," but also the therapeutic environment itself. It is, to me, very revealing that all five women terminated the therapy. The authors, of course, present this termination as resistance, manipulation, immaturity, and cowardice.

How Sick Can You Get? Eating Disorders and Sexual "Perversion"

Prophecy Coles articulates in clear and startling form the influence of such interpretations on how eating behaviors are understood and how anorexic and bulimic women are themselves constructed in her 1988 article "Aspects of Perversion in Anorexic/Bulimic Disorders." In this article, Coles categorizes anorexia as a form of sexual perversion and illustrates her point with a colorful comparison between the eating behaviors of an anorexic patient and the cross-dressing and masturbation of a male transvestite. Coles suggests that "the bulimic state seemed to be very similar to a state that a transvestite had described to me when he stood in front of a mirror dressed in women's clothes and masturbating," and she wonders, "Would it make sense to claim that anorexia and bulimia are a form of perversion?" (p. 138).

The core of Coles's theory is that anorexia and bulimia evidence "a primitive sexualisation of the body ego, which was used to ward off psychotic anxieties concerning loss and annihilation" (1988: 139). The parallel with the "perversion" of the transvestite comes in anorexia, she explains, when "the mouth [is] used as compulsively as the genitals" (p. 141) in the pursuit of the phallus, which is, she argues, the "psychic representative of desire and narcissistic completion" and is the same for both sexes (p. 141).

Coles, in line with the psychoanalytic tradition, locates the heart of this perversion in the child's relationship with its mother. "There seems," she writes, "to be evidence that there is a narcissistic mother with strong infantile needs of her own. . . . A narcissistic mother with her own unresolved 'castration' difficulties can use her son in a phallic way . . . whereas a mother is less able to use her daughter in this way, and the daughter can experience her mother's phallic disappointment with her" (1988: 143). The effects of this phallic disappointment are, Coles tells us, devastating for the girl. "The pre-oedipal difficulties seem to prohibit a development towards heterosexual maturity," she clarifies. "Freud . . . spoke of an 'aversion to sexuality' by means of anorexia. I believe that it is not so much an aversion to sexuality as a refusal to give up more infantile forms of sexuality, that 'food and eating become equated with forbidden sexual objects and sexual activities' " (p. 143). In other words, like Simpson and Ramberg (1992), Coles argues that food and eating are symbolic of adult sexuality; and the rejection of food, the expression of the infantile wish to remain a child.

When the girl discovers that she lacks the anatomic penis, Coles tells us, she rejects her "faithless mother" and seeks a "haven of refuge" in her father, a bonding which makes the girl reluctant to surrender her early masculine life in favor of her natural feminine development (1988: 142). Anorexic girls are particularly tenacious in this resistance. "They refuse," Coles continues, "to accept the unpalatable fact of their 'castration' and instead take refuge in an identification *either with the phallic mother or with the father* (p. 142; emphasis in original), and the anorexic girl constructs an "identification of herself as a 'castrated' man" (p. 144) because, in Glasser's (1985) words, she had not been able to identify with "the psychological attributes of the father . . . in her heterosexual need to separate from her mother" (quoted in Coles 1988: 144). Instead, she uses a "phallic identification with her father as a way of attacking her mother, which had at the same time the unwelcome attribute of seeing herself as this hated, ruthless, cold and unfeeling person" (p. 144). Coles adds that the anorexic woman's "failure to negotiate successfully her oedipal difficulties leaves her unable to maintain satisfactory relationships with men" (p. 144).

Perhaps the most revealing section of the article comes when Coles discusses some of the transference and countertransference dynamics of her therapeutic relationship with a young anorexic woman. Coles is perplexed by the woman's having "complained that coming into therapy had made her bingeing worse" (1988: 137), and she tagged this to the client's inappropriate expectations of and feelings toward her, the therapist:

Her rage against me I experienced most vividly at the end of the sessions. . . . as she got up she would swing her body across the room like a fashion model. Her tight jeans revealed her emaciated buttocks as she thrust her flattened stomach forward, and she would bend her stick-like body in a straight and rigid way into her large handbag to look for her car-keys. I had the feeling that she was enacting a primitive phantasy of relating in which her emaciated phallic body entered me (or the handbag) and attacked me for my neglect. The whole enactment seemed highly sexualised as she showed me her slim body. This observation seemed to be confirmed in her constant complaints that she was sexually harassed by men. She would excite and provoke men with these body movements, but she would angrily reject them and turn away. I believe she was repeating the original experience of a mother who provoked her and stimulated her and whom she experienced as rejecting her. (pp. 144–145)

The obvious question here is whether this primitive fantasy and the sexualizing of the interaction are coming from the client or from the therapist herself. It is particularly disturbing that, like Simpson and Ramberg (1992), Coles here presents the anorexic woman as a sort of tease who excites and provokes men with her body movements only to reject them angrily and turn away. Indeed, we are led to wonder if it might be the case that the fantasies and sexual feelings of the *therapist* are being projected onto the anorexic woman, who is then attacked as manipulative and full of rage, the depth of her sexual problems read in the degree of sexual stimulation she excites in her caregiver.

There is more. Coles concludes that this sexualization of the anorexic's body turns back upon itself in an autonomous orgy. Through her anorexia, Coles says,

[Miss B] used her whole body as a phallic object to both attack and impregnate herself in a fantasied coupling which excluded vulnerability and dependence upon other people, in much the same way as the transvestite achieved a self-sufficient intercourse while dressed as a woman. . . . In anorexia and bulimia a primitive and perverse acting out is going on; the whole body is experienced in primitive sexualised images; but because the action takes place principally "inside" the body, the sadism and primitive sexualisation of the ego can be more easily concealed. (1988: 146).

It is clear that her client's eating behaviors and the recounting of these behaviors in the therapy sessions were explicitly sexualized in the mind of the therapist. It is not difficult to see, then, how the client's requests for help and detailed discussion of her bingeing in the pursuit of recovery might be read from this perspective as a form of exhibitionism, a replaying of the fantasied coupling on the therapist's couch. We, of course, have no indication that this elaborate portrait of the anorexic's secret sexual life has anything at all to do with the woman's actual subjective experience of her illness. Regardless, the client is painted as an eminently sexual being, using her sexual powers to control and manipulate others, including her therapist.[7]

The basic interpretations outlined here find expression in countless other contemporary works. Mogul, for example, presents a case study of a woman whose first, aborted pregnancy marked the onset of her anorexia nervosa and whose second, desired pregnancy marked the "recovery from anorexia and the beginning of a happy family" (1989: 65). Identifying the essence of anorexia as a conflict about mothering, Mogul suggests that pregnancy not only offers anorexic women a second chance to repair their own childhood emotional deficits, but also gives them the opportunity for the "significant restructuring of their feminine identities and senses of themselves as separate and worthwhile parents and persons" (p. 72). The anorexic conflict, Mogul seems to suggest, is washed away under a flood of maternal affection and motherly pride. "I have a baby, a house, and a dog," Mogul's client reports, glowing and ecstatic in her "recovery" from anorexia. "I am in love with my husband and enjoy making love. . . . Here I am a housewife; but I know what I'm doing. I'll ask for an academic extension; eventually I'll finish my degree. . . .

I have become normal" (p. 85). Mogul reports that today this client is "at home busy and satisfied caring for their three children" (p. 86) and deems her a true success.

Zerbe (1992b) highlights the fact that, culturally speaking, passivity is valued in women, and uses this to argue that passive, dependent women actually have a *stronger* superego structure than independent, assertive women have. In other words, following Zerbe's logic, dependence and passivity (that is, being in synch with gender expectations) are signs of female health, whereas deviation from the traditional norms (showing strength and independence and, perhaps, resistance to certain therapeutic procedures) is sure evidence of illness. To this premise she adds that, because a woman's genital experience is "diffuse," clitoral, vaginal, and anal sensations are often confused. As a result, "sexual inhibitions may be derived from the linkage of early toilet training practices, anal inhibitions, and their spread to vaginal experience" (p. 60). These "early anal and genital inhibitions to touch," she suggests, might then "spread to the vagina, contributing to the sexual repressions of the girl" (p. 61). This, Zerbe argues, helps to explain the otherwise irrational dislike of penises and penetration expressed by so many anorexic women, and their resistance to the passivity of the female role—a sure indicator of mental illness.

Tuiten and his colleagues refer to the "sexual dysfunction and immaturity" of anorexic women "as manifested in low sexual interest, inhibited sexual behavior, disgust towards sex, and fear of intimacy" (1993: 259). Hardman and Gardner (1986: 55) note that the women they worked with refused to maintain a normal level of sexual activity and that the unrealistic and paranoid fears attached to their anorexia interfered with both physical and emotional intimacy. They characterize these women as throwing temper tantrums as part of a "game to prove themselves superior and special," a project they identify as a "delusional type belief" (p. 58). Andersen (1985: 146–147) includes decreased sexual attractiveness in his list of sexual problems associated with anorexia nervosa. And Schneider identifies bulimic activity as "self-imposed oral rape" (1995: 183).

We can see, then, that in the contemporary literature, the so-called sexual aversion of eating-disordered women is anything but an uncomplicated assessment of an individual's distress. Rather, it is a culturally loaded interpretation of women's sexual feelings and behaviors as measured against some standard of "normal" female sexuality. This avoidance is attributed in the literature to sexual abuse, ignorance, punitive sex education, anal associations, hormonal imbalances—*anything but* a legitimate ambivalence about men or heterosexual sex.

Implications for Treatment: Where Do We Go from Here?

The problems with these constructions of sexuality in anorexia are fairly obvious and need little illuminating. In all these studies, there is a clearly articulated heterosexist formulation of sexuality that is predicated on the penetration of the man's penis into the woman's vagina. If a woman does not want to be penetrated or does not derive pleasure from her partner's penis, she is identified as sexually dysfunctional. If she resists this classification, evidences little enthusiasm over designs to "fix" her condition, or expresses anxiety about aggressive sexual therapy, she is labeled as childish, stubborn, defensive, immature, rebellious, manipulative, and controlling. Once she has been shamed into treatment, she is conditioned to see the mother figure as bad and the penis as good. She is persuaded to give up her immature, childish attachment to the bad mother in favor of a mature and adult attachment to the good penis, which she is then free to enjoy. This thrill at sexual intercourse will be a natural development, it is supposed, once all the pathologies have been resolved and cleared from the path and the woman's true sexuality is allowed to shine through. There are no excuses now. In all these studies, in fact, the implication is that all these women *really* need in order to get well is a good roll in the hay.

This is an extraordinarily troubling situation. If anorexia and bulimia are indeed linked to anxieties about sexuality and ambivalence about developing female bodies and the reactions they draw from others, it would seem that therapeutic environments such as the ones described in these studies are not safe places for these women. Is it any wonder that so many of Simpson and Ramberg's (1992) patients left the treatment or that Coles's (1988) client reported that coming to therapy made her bingeing worse? These women are encouraged — that is, if they *really* want to get well — to submit themselves to the authority of caregivers who take as their central project the reconditioning of these women to fit the traditional construction of femininity *against* which they may be struggling with their anorexia in the first place. But the rub comes in the theoretical subsumation of the anorexia itself into this framework and its interpretation not as resistance to traditional constructions of femininity but as the ultimate expression of it: anorexic women are not strong, independent, and self-possessed; they are childish and immature and controlling. In the meantime, their bodies are always at center stage — talked about, examined, measured, weighed, poked, closely watched by an army of therapists and hospital staff for any sign of change, no matter how small. The femaleness of the anorexic's body — its shapely contours or the lack thereof — is on everybody's mind. In other words, the anorexic woman is caught. She cannot win. She will be forced into a corseted model of femininity regardless of how tight the fit. The choice is laid before her: remain childish and infantile in your illness, or accept our standard of femininity (in which celibacy or the rejection of heterosexual intercourse is not condoned) as the criterion of health. The dominant construction of voluntary celibacy in women with eating disorders, then, has direct implications for treatment, and the prototype of the anorexic woman outlined in this orientation dictates the kind of treatment she receives and the model of "recovery" she is induced to accept.

We must seriously reconsider the way in which these things are talked about and what kind of implications this holds for the way the configuration of behaviors labeled as anorexia is understood. How might a reorientation of our understandings of sexual avoidance in anorexia affect this understanding? What would happen if the anorexic's notorious aversion to sexuality — which she is traditionally conditioned to give up in favor or more mature sexual delights — were read not as expressions of infantilism and immaturity but as part of a larger, sophisticated design to define and preserve a self which is culturally valued and desired? What if, rather than painting sexuality as the core pathology, which is then symbolically expressed in food behaviors, *both* are read as articulations of a more fundamental concern, having to do, for example, with body boundaries and the reshaping of the self (Lester 1995, 1997)? The traditional understandings of anorexia and bulimia would, I suggest, be radically challenged. I suggest that if we look deeply into the traditional models of eating disorders, if we tease out the gendered cultural assumptions imprinted on the very core of these theories, we will be called to significantly reevaluate our received knowledge about this illness and the psychodynamics of those who suffer from it.

Notes

1. See Brewerton et al. 1992; Broocks, Liu, and Pirke 1990; Grignaschi, Mantelli, and Samanin 1993; Hudson et al. 1985, 1989; Leibowitz 1990, 1992; Merola et al. 1994; and Pope et al. 1989.

2. See Chernin 1981; Lawrence 1988; Liu 1979; Messinger 1986; O'Neill 1982; Robertson 1992; and Szekely 1988.

3. See Zerbe 1992a, 1993, 1995; and Yager 1985.

4. See Butow, Buemont, and Touyz 1993; Chernin 1985; Spignesi 1983; Srinivasagam et al. 1995; Striegel-Moore, Silberstein, and Rodin 1993; and Swain, Shisslak, and Crago 1991.

5. See Andersen and DiDomenico 1992; Banks 1992; Brumberg 1989; Ford, Dolan, and Evans 1990; Hall et al. 1991; King and Bhugra 1989; and Waller and Shaw 1992.

6. See, for example, Bruch 1973, 1979; Levenkron 1981; and Woodman 1980, 1982.

7. It is perhaps worth mentioning that this article, which appeared in the prestigious journal *Psychoanalytic Psychotherapy,* is an amended version of a paper that won the 1987 John Kelnar Award offered by the Lincoln Clinic and Institute for Psychotherapy. In other words, Coles's article was judged by a panel of her peers to be exceptional and commendable for articulating current, relevant, and significant research on anorexia and bulimia.

References Cited

Andersen, Arnold E. 1985. *Practical Comprehensive Treatment of Anorexia Nervosa and Bulimia.* London: Edward Arnold.

Andersen, Arnold E., and L. DiDomenico. 1992. Diet vs. Shape Content of Popular Male and Female Magazines: A Dose-Response Relationship to the Incidence of Eating Disorders? *International Journal of Eating Disorders* 11: 283–287.

Banks, Carolyn Giles. 1992. "Culture" in Culture-Bound Syndromes: The Case of Anorexia Nervosa. *Social Science and Medicine* 34: 867–884.

Bordo, Susan. 1992. *Unbearable Weight: Feminism, Western Culture, and the Body.* Berkeley: University of California Press.

Brewerton, Timothy D., et al. 1992. CSF Beta-Endorphin and Dynorphin in Bulimia Nervosa. *American Journal of Psychiatry* 149: 1886–1890.

Broocks, Andreas, J. Liu, and K. M. Pirke. 1990. Semistarvation-Induced Hyperactivity Compensates for Decreased Norepinephrine and Dopamine Turnovers in the Mediobasas Hypothalamus of the Rat. *Journal of Neural Transmission* 79: 113–124.

Bruch, Hilde. 1973. *Eating Disorders.* New York: Basic Books.

Bruch, Hilde. 1979. *The Golden Cage: The Enigma of Anorexia Nervosa.* New York: Vintage Books.

Brumberg, Joan Jacobs. 1989. *Fasting Girls: The History of Anorexia Nervosa.* Cambridge, Mass.: Harvard University Press.

Butow, Phyllis, Pierre Beumont, and Stephen Touyz. 1993. Cognitive Processes in Dieting Disorders. *International Journal of Eating Disorders* 14: 319–329.

Chernin, Kim. 1981. *The Obsession: Reflections on the Tyranny of Slenderness.* New York: Perennial Library.

Chernin, Kim. 1985. *The Hungry Self: Women, Eating and Identity.* New York: Times Books.

Coles, Prophecy. 1988. Aspects of Perversion in Anorexic/Bulimic Disorders. *Psychoanalytic Psychotherapy* 3: 137–147.

Ford, Kathryn A., Bridget Dolan, and Chris Evans. 1990. Culture Factors in the Eating Disorders: A Study of Body Shape Preferences of Arab Students. *Journal of Psychosomatic Research* 34: 501–507.

Freud, Sigmund. 1918. From the History of an Infantile Neuroses. In *The Standard Edition of the Complete Psychological Works of Sigmund Freud.* Vol. 17. London: Hogarth Press.

Glasser, Mervin. 1985. "The Weak Spot" — Some Observations of Male Sexuality. *International Journal of Psycho-Analysis* 66(4): 405–414.

Grignaschi, Giuliano, B. Mantelli, and R. Samanin. 1993. The Hypophagic Effect of Restraint Stress in Rats Can Be Mediated by 5-HT2 Receptors in the Paraventicular Nucleus of the Hypothalamus. *Neuroscience Letters* 152: 103–106.

Hall, Richard, Linda Tice, Thomas Beresford, et al. 1991. Self-Concept and Perception of Attractiveness and Body Size among Mexican-American Mothers and Daughters. *International Journal of Obesity* 15: 567–575.

Hardman, R., and D. Gardner. 1986. Sexual Anorexia: A Look at Inhibited Sexual Desire. *Journal of Sex and Marital Therapy* 12: 55–59.

Hudson, J. I., et al. 1985. Treatment of Anorexia Nervosa with Antidepressants. *Journal of Clinical Psychopharmacology* 5: 17–23.

Hudson, J. I., et al. 1989. Treatment of Bulimia Nervosa with Trazodone: Short-Term Response and Long-Term Follow-Up. *Clinical Neuropharmacology* 1: 38–46.

King, Michael B., and Dinesh Bhugra. 1989. Eating Disorders: Lessons from a Cross-Cultural Study. *Psychological Medicine* 19: 955–958.

Lawrence, Marilyn. 1988. *The Anorexic Experience*. London: Women's Press.

Leibowitz, Sarah F. 1990. The Role of Seratonin in Eating Disorders. *Drugs* 39 (suppl. 3): 33–48.

Leibowitz, Sarah F. 1992. Neurochemical-Neuroendocrine Systems in the Brain Controlling Macronutrient Intake and Metabolism. *Trends in Neurosciences* 15: 491–497.

Lester, Rebecca J. 1995. Embodied Voices: Women's Food Asceticism and the Negotiation of Identity. *Ethos* 23: 187–222.

Lester, Rebecca J. 1997. The (Dis)Embodied Self in Anorexia Nervosa. *Social Science and Medicine* 4: 479–489.

Levenkron, Steven. 1981. *The Best Little Girl in the World*. New York: Warner Books.

Liu, Aimee. 1979. *Solitaire*. New York: Harper and Row.

Merola, B., S. Longobardi, A. Colao, et al. 1994. Hypotalamic-Pituitary-Adrenal Axis in Neuropsychiatric Disorders. *Annals of the New York Academy of Sciences* 7: 263–270.

Messinger, Lisa. 1986. *Biting the Hand That Feeds Me: Days of Binging, Purging and Recovery.* Norato, California: Arena.

Mogul, S. Louis. 1989. Sexuality, Pregnancy, and Parenting in Anorexia Nervosa. *Journal of the American Academy of Psychoanalysis* 17: 65–88.

O'Neill, Cherry B. 1982. *Starving for Attention*. New York: Continuum.

Orbach, Susie. 1978. *Fat Is a Feminist Issue*. New York: Berkeley Publishing Group.

Orbach, Susie. 1986. *Hunger Strike*. New York: W. W. Norton.

Pope, Harrison, Paul Keck, Susan McElroy, and James Hudson. 1989. A Placebo-Controlled Study of Trazodone in Bulimia Nervosa. *Journal of Clinical Psychopharmacology* 9: 254–259.

Robertson, Matra. 1992. *Starving in the Silences: An Exploration of Anorexia Nervosa*. New York: New York University Press.

Schneider, John A. 1995. Eating Disorders, Addictions, and Unconscious Fantasy. *Bulletin of the Menninger Clinic* 59: 177–190.
Simpson, William S., and Joanne A. Ramberg. 1992. Sexual Dysfunction in Married Female Patients with Anorexia and Bulimia Nervosa. *Journal of Sex and Marital Therapy* 18: 44–54.
Spignesi, Angelyn. 1983. *Starving Women: A Psychology of Anorexia Nervosa.* Dallas: Spring Publications.
Srinivasagam, Nalini, et al. 1995. Persistent Perfectionism, Symmetry, and Exactness after Long-Term Recovery from Anorexia Nervosa. *American Journal of Psychiatry* 152: 1630–1634.
Striegel-Moore, Ruth, Lisa Silberstein, and Judith Rodin. 1993. The Social Self in Bulimia Nervosa: Public Self-Consciousness, Social Anxiety, and Perceived Fraudulence. *Journal of Abnormal Psychology* 102: 297–303.
Swain, Barbara, Catherine Shisslak, and Marjorie Crago. 1991. Clinical Features of Eating Disorders and Individual Psychological Functioning. *Journal of Clinical Psychology* 47: 702–708.
Szekely, Eva A. 1988. *Never Too Thin.* Toronto: Women's Press.
Tuiten, Adriaan, et al. 1993. The Paradoxical Nature of Sexuality in Anorexia Nervosa. *Journal of Sex and Marital Therapy* 19: 259–275.
Waller, Glenn, and Julie Shaw. 1992. The Media Influence on Eating Problems. In *Why Women? Gender Issues and Eating Disorders,* ed. Bridget Dolan and Inez Gitzinger, 44–54. London: Anthlone.
Waller, J. V., N. R. Kaufman, and F. Deutsch. 1940. Anorexia Nervosa: A Psychosomatic Entity. *Psychosomatic Medicine* 2: 3–16.
Wolf, Naomi. 1991. *The Beauty Myth: How Images of Beauty Are Used against Women.* New York: William Morrow.
Yager, Joel. 1985. The Outpatient Treatment of Bulimia. *Bulletin of the Menninger Clinic* 49: 203–236.
Zerbe, Kathryn J. 1992a. Eating Disorders in the 1990s: Clinical Challenges and Treatment Implications. *Bulletin of the Menninger Clinic* 56: 167–187.
Zerbe, Kathryn J. 1992b. Why Eating-Disordered Patients Resist Sex Therapy: A Response to Simpson and Ramberg. *Journal of Sex and Marital Therapy* 18: 55–64.
Zerbe, Kathryn J. 1993. Whose Body Is It Anyway? Understanding and Treating the Psychosomatic Aspects of Eating Disorders. *Bulletin of the Menninger Clinic* 57: 191–197.
Zerbe, Kathryn J. 1995. Integrating Feminist and Psychodynamic Principles in the Treatment of an Eating Disorder Patient: Implications for Using Countertransference Responses. *Bulletin of the Menninger Clinic* 59: 160–176.

11 *Victor C. de Munck*

Cultural Schemas of Celibacy

Jeremy, a male virgin and a 21-year-old student at the University of New Hampshire, has coined the slogan "To be celibate is to be alive." He is celibate neither for religious reasons nor for fear of being infected by a sexually transmitted disease. Jeremy has had girlfriends whom he has kissed and even slept with. However, he states that he does not like to kiss and that he retreats from any attempt at sexual intimacy. The one time he slept (fully clothed) with a female student who was attracted to him, he broke off the relationship. He readily states that he becomes sexually aroused and develops deep crushes on women, yet he is adamant about remaining a celibate and a virgin for the rest of his life.

Another student, Mark (20 years old), met his current girlfriend, Christine, at a University of New Hampshire Christian Fellowship meeting. They are in love and he expects to marry her. They do not kiss on the lips, and they take precautions to avoid situations or activities that are potentially arousing.

Rachelle is a University of New Hampshire student who turned 21 during the course of the research. She says that she has never been in love and would engage in sexual intercourse only if she were to have a boyfriend and they were in love with each other. All the men she has known have been found deficient in one way or another.

Gwen is 22; she has just graduated from the University of New Hamp-

shire and is a virgin. She has been proud of her celibacy, but since graduation she says it has become a burden, and she wants to find the right guy to
"get it over with." She states that he does not have to be the love of her
life, just a nice guy.

During the 1995–96 academic year I interviewed Jeremy, Mark, Rachelle, and Gwen as part of a research project on romantic love. Each
informant was interviewed three times, and each interview lasted one to
two hours and was tape-recorded with the consent of the informant. In
this chapter, I explore two questions: What do these informants mean by
celibacy? How do they explain their own decision to be celibate?

I will use schema theory to explore both of these questions. The assumption underlying schema theory is that meaning is constructed through a
process of mapping one's experiences onto culturally conventionalized
(i.e., prototypical) knowledge. The task of the researcher is to discover
the schemas that underlie and frame what people say. Recent advances in
schema theory demonstrate that schemas are not only used to interpret
the world but also have a motivational force (D'Andrade 1992, 1995;
Kronenfeld 1996; Strauss 1992a; Strauss and Quinn 1997).

I will show that informants' celibacy schemas vary along dimensions of
meanings that extend from the Euro-American prototype of celibacy, the
monk. I begin with a brief introduction to schema theory followed by a
prototype-schema analysis of what informants mean by *celibacy*. I then
apply schema analysis to informant narratives in order to explain their
motivations for choosing to be celibate at this stage in their lives.

A Schema Approach to Defining Celibacy

Fillmore (1977: 77) said that the meaning of *bachelor* cannot be found in a
dictionary "checklist of properties"; instead, it is encapsulated in a "simplified world view" that relates *bachelor* to cultural norms regarding marriage (Sweetser 1987: 44). For example, although my *American College
Encyclopedia Dictionary* (6th ed.) defines *bachelor* as "an unmarried man
of any age," we do not typically think of boys, the pope, divorcees, or
widowers as bachelors. To understand what *bachelor* means, we rely on a
cultural prototype of the term. I imagine an adult male in his 30s, living in
a messy house, drinking too much, posturing as a bit of a playboy, referring to women as ladies or dolls, and looking a bit like William Powell.

In the 1970s, Rosch (1978) and her collaborators (e.g., Rosch and
Mervis 1975) showed that people organize their perceptions, thoughts,
and even behaviors in terms of prototypes. A prototype is a generic model
constructed of the most common and distinctive features we use to identify an object, activity, or event. For example, our concept of fish is con-

structed from salient features: size, shape, scales, gills, fins, and habita-
tion in water. Our prototypical fish is something like a trout or salmon in
size, shape, and features. The more a water animal looks like a trout, the
quicker and easier it is for us to identify it as a fish. We can mentally
extend these features from their prototype so that size, overall shape,
scales, fin shapes, and such can vary along a continuum. The more features a creature has that resemble the prototype, the more quickly and
more certain we are that it is a fish. By mapping an animal's family resem-
blance to the prototype, we cognitively judge some animals to be more
fishlike than others. Thus, while we know that porpoises, alligators,
shrimp, and squid are not fish, we also are more likely to classify porpoises as more fishlike than shrimp and definitely more fishlike than alligators. Understanding *fish* in terms of a prototype rather than a dictionary
definition allows us to be very flexible and dynamic in the way we process
and interpret what we are confronted with.

To understand how schemas motivate behavior, schema theorists focus
on the hierarchic relations among schemas. The idea of meaning being
organized as a network of schemas is a fairly recent innovation in schema
theory (Quinn 1996; Strauss 1992b; Strauss and Quinn 1997).

D'Andrade (1992: 39; 1995: 232) refers to top-level schemas as "master
motives" that instigate lower-level schemas. A master motive is one that
is not derived from other motives and is thought of as a natural motivation
or goal for human beings. Love is an example of a master motive: we seldom question the naturalness of love, and we do not require a reason to
love. But we usually need love as a reason to marry. In this instance, marriage is a secondary, or "basic-level," schema that is motivated by love.
Dating and phoning someone up for a date are examples of lower-level
schemas. The phoning-up schema is motivated by the dating schema,
which in turn may be motivated by a marriage or love schema. The motivation to enact a lower-level schema is derived from higher-level schemas.

Strauss (1992b: 211) notes that hierarchic and associational connections among schemas "excite," or motivate, a person. She refers to these
associations of schemas as "personal semantic networks. For example,
love, marriage and dating are schemas that are strongly associated with
each other." For practicing Christians, celibacy may be positively associated with the above triad, whereas for others it is either negatively associated or simply absent from their personal semantic networks.

What Is Celibacy?

Southgate (this volume) provides an "official" Catholic answer to the
question, What is celibacy? He writes that the Catholic Church defines it

(as my dictionary does) as an unmarried state and that it is not, strictly speaking, equivalent to virginity. However, within the Catholic world view, celibacy also entails virginity (and chastity) because sexual activity is proper only within the context of marriage. Southgate notes that a priest's "motivation for celibacy . . . signifies his total dedication to the service of God and humanity." In other words, celibacy is a basic-level schema motivated by the master-level schema: to serve God and humanity. We will see that my informants use the same hierarchic structure of motivations to describe their reasons for being celibate.

Though only Gwen was born a Catholic (she is not a practicing Catholic), all my informants invoked the prototype of a monk in our discussions on what celibacy means. Jeremy said that celibacy is "sort of like being a monk. I don't think you are celibate unless you have chosen to be that way." Here, Jeremy identifies volition as a prototypical feature of celibacy. To support this, he further points out that a prisoner is, "technically speaking," not celibate.

Similar to both Southgate's and Khandelwal's explanations (each this volume) for celibacy among Catholic priests and Hindu ascetics, respectively, my informants view celibacy as a volitional act done for a greater good. The "greater good" varies across informants: for Mark it is part of being a Christian; for Rachelle and Gwen it is love; and for Jeremy it is "freedom."

Time is a core feature of the monk prototype my informants hold for celibacy. The monk volitionally takes a vow of lifetime celibacy. Only Jeremy, among my informants, explicitly wishes to remain celibate for life, arguing that "pure" celibacy is a permanent condition, it is a "life choice." Mark takes the lay Christian position that celibacy is the proper moral condition for unmarried men and women. All the informants agree that celibacy implies that a person is sexually abstinent for a long period of time. Gwen noted that one person's "dry spell" could be another person's celibacy, depending on how each of them defines that period of time. Volition and time are separate but interdependent dimensions of celibacy: celibacy must be a long-term choice.

A third issue raised by the informants is the degree of sexual intimacy allowed. Jeremy again takes the most prototypical position; he stated that celibacy is "complete uninvolvement with anyone at all, and if I think of it any longer I just sort of define it as not having sex. Pure celibacy is not being involved in any way physical with anyone, like not kissing." Gwen said, "Celibacy is abstaining from sexual [long pause] — abstaining from intercourse or abstaining from anything beyond kissing and fooling around a little bit." Rachelle considers oral sex the critical act that differentiates noncelibates from celibates; kissing and fondling are "border-

line" acts but do not, in themselves, push a person into the noncelibate
category. Mark noted that kissing is fine but that it "inflames the passions," and therefore, to maintain celibacy, he and his girlfriend refrain
from kissing. But they do hold hands and hug. For Mark, the key issue is
the intent of the act; acts thought to inflame the passions exist on the
borderline of celibacy and should be avoided so that sexual desires can be
quelled. He said, "If you know that and put a halt to it, then it's okay. You
have to show her respect and love, and that means not thinking of her like
that until after you are married. If you keep getting physical, then you are
not really celibate."

My informants understand celibacy as a graded category or semantic
continua (Kronenfeld 1996: 148) composed of three dimensions: volition,
time, and sexual intimacy. The prototypical (celibate) monk chooses celibacy, is expected to be celibate for his lifetime, and abstains from all
behaviors that are ordinarily construed as sexual. All my informants are
volitional celibates, but they vary in the temporal and sexual intimacy
dimensions. The celibacy schema does not simply denote the state of
being unmarried; it evokes a whole "simplified world view" (Sweetser
1987: 44).

Being celibate is not the same as being in love, being successful, or
serving God; the last three are master motives that need not justification
in themselves, whereas celibacy is always justified and explained in terms
of a higher-level motive. In the next section, I will examine why these
informants choose to be celibate and recall the notion of a greater good.
As we proceed, you will note that the more closely a person's self-understanding of celibacy fits the prototype, the more his or her motives are
likely to correspond to those of the monk or Catholic priest as described
by Southgate (this volume).

Motives for Choosing Celibacy

I will discuss each informant in turn. Brief excerpts from the interviews
are presented, and from these I extrapolate the schemas represented. Because we are investigating motivations, I am particularly concerned with
the hierarchic and associational linkages between schemas (D'Andrade
1992). As noted before, celibacy is rarely its own motivation; people
choose to be celibate for a reason. Thus, my main analytic strategy is,
first, to search for the higher-level reasons or schemas that motivate each
informant to be celibate and, second, to search for the schema that contrasts with celibacy. The motive to be celibate and the force, or valence,
of that motive should be a result of the pattern of hierarchic and hori-
zontal relations in which the celibacy schema is embedded. These rela-

tions, which I call vectors of motivation, include the master-level schema, the contrasting basic-level schema, and the network of associational schemas.

Mark's Story: Single and Christian

Mark's father is a minister and selectman (like a town council member), and eventually Mark wants to go into politics. Mark has long, wavy, blond hair and looks and dresses a bit like James Dean, who is one of his heroes. Though a devout Christian, Mark states that he is drawn to rebels, and he has his own Harley-Davidson, which he is expert at repairing and customizing. He and his girlfriend, Christine, have been dating exclusively for six months. When I asked Mark what was most important in his life, he replied: "Basically I have my sights set more on heaven than on my earthly family, except my earthly family is Christian as well. They all are a part of the heavenly family which we will become someday. So basically I consider everybody else who is Christian as well to be my brother and sister in Christ, because we will all be part of the same family someday in heaven." Clearly, Christianity is the master motive for Mark. He states that he is a virgin and has had romantic desires but has managed to control them.

Mark met Christine at a Christian meeting at school, and they started going out. I inquired about his relation with her:

VICTOR: Did you kiss her that night [after the first date]?
MARK: Oh, no, I didn't kiss her.
VICTOR: Would you have?
MARK: I don't kiss her now, in fact. We try to keep away from physicality because we are afraid we'd be inflamed in the passion of the moment — break into sexual immorality before marriage.
VICTOR: Wow, that's pretty intense.
MARK: Yeah [smiles at me].
VICTOR: So you don't hold hands?
MARK: We hold hands, yeah, and give each other hugs and whatnot.
VICTOR: So you have never kissed her.
MARK: The first week we were going out we kissed — short little pecks, you know.
VICTOR: On the lips?
MARK: Right — before I'd leave. I'd give her a quick kiss and leave. But, I don't know, I guess we decided that we probably should stop that because of the consequences that could result from one kiss — you want to give another one. So, yeah, it was more [that] she was the one who brought up the idea of laying off the physicality. I guess it was harder for her than it was for me; she tended to focus on the kiss more than I did, I guess. Yeah, she was the one who brought it up, and she asked me what my feelings were about it. I didn't really have a problem with it. I kind of liked kissing in fact, but I took her point of view from it, and I wanted to

meet her needs, so I decided to stop kissing her because that's what she wanted. I respected her opinion.

For Mark and Christine, there is a triad of schemas that regulate their courtship behavior: Christianity, celibacy, and marriage. For both, Christianity is the master-level schema, and celibacy is a basic-level schema motivated by their adherence to Christian principles. Christianity provides a courtship "script" which they follow: courtship is exclusive and is expected to end in marriage, and expressions of passion should be held in check and limited to public displays of polite affection (e.g., handholding and hugs). This courtship script is intended to ensure celibacy (including virginity) and is, therefore, informed by subordinate-level schemas of the basic-level celibacy schema. Basic- and subordinate-level schemas are directed toward a Christian world view of marriage and courtship, in which sex is legitimate only in the context of marriage and courtship involves a commitment to marriage.

Rules for the physical expression of affection becomes more refined and restrictive as the relationship progresses. Thus, as romantic commitment increases, the couple become more vigilant in monitoring and inhibiting contexts or acts that may "inflame their passions." Mark mentioned that when they visit each other in their respective dorm rooms, they make sure that the door is always open, the lights on, and that they do not touch, nor do they sit on the bed together. Hugs are permitted for greetings and good-byes, but they should be relatively brief.

Celibacy is a temporary condition terminating with marriage, but it is a positively valued condition. According to Mark, neither he nor Christine is ambivalent about being celibate; both perceive premarital celibacy as virtuous. Their relationship to their faith motivates them to adopt celibacy as a necessary condition for maintaining and developing their own relationship.

Rachelle's Story: Love Is Serious Business

Rachelle's celibacy narrative is based on her central proposition: "Without love, I will not engage in sex." Rachelle said that she has never been in love but that she has had crushes on boys since the fifth grade. In the first interview, we discussed the difference between love and crushes.

Victor: How can you tell if it's a crush or love?
Rachelle: Love is a big concept; love is serious, and whatever I was feeling about people wasn't that serious, because it never developed far enough. I was never into a "relationship" [she gestures quotation marks]. It was just hanging out, and, you know, it was fun, and I didn't take it very seriously.

VICTOR: Uh huh.
RACHELLE: I just remember seeing people that were going out and not feeling like I could do that.

In the second interview, Rachelle described a time the lines seemed blurred momentarily; this helped her to describe the importance of the distinction to me.

RACHELLE: My roommate one time said to me, "Oh you are falling in love with him!" And I was like, "No, I'm not!" and thinking, Oh my gosh, am I? is that what this is? And just thinking that what I was thinking was too superficial to be love. I hated people throwing that around like, "Oh, I love you" and "I'm in love." I thought people took that too casually and was determined that I wasn't going to be one of those people, like, "Oh I love you," [when] they've only known each other for a month or something. I've never had a boyfriend; [I've] just been "this is the one person I'm with" and just kind of moved around and got to know people and saw people. Once I see people for a while, you sort of come to a point where it either has to move on or stop; and I never really moved on because there's always things about the person that — I don't know — there's always something that I'm, like, well, this isn't really what I want.
VICTOR: So you didn't like the way other people used the word *love?*
RACHELLE: Yeah. I think it was too casual. I think love is something more serious. I've heard my mother say that you can think you love someone when you marry, but you find yourself loving them so much more than you did before when you thought you couldn't ever love them more than you did. The more you get to know someone, you lose the chemistry and butterflies in your stomach, but it develops into something that's — love. It's not all those feelings but just all that person, and there's nothing you wouldn't do for them. The depth of your emotion isn't superficial — "they're cute" and stuff like that. I've always had this idea that love was something deep and big and powerful and really friendship-based — that kind of way rather than just lust and feeling excited about someone.

Rachelle distinguishes between love and sex. Love is her master mo-tive and sex a basic-level schema that is legitimate only when motivated by love. However, sex and deep sexual desires may also be motivated by "chemistry." Thus, it is often difficult to figure out if sexual attraction is caused by the legitimate master-level motive (romantic love) or by its biological — and, for Rachelle, improper — counterpart (chemistry). Both chemistry and romantic love can trigger the same basic-level feel-ings, so it is easy for people to be deceived into thinking that they are in love when in fact they are only "in lust." Rachelle describes how she has, herself, been fooled. Two prototypical features of her love schema, "seri-ous" and "deep," contrast with the "fun" and "superficial" features of her crush schema. She also notes that most of her peers confuse chemistry for love, a problem she profoundly wants to avoid. But why is this so important to her in the first place? The most obvious answer is that she is striving for romantic love, and celibacy is a means to assure that her sexual feelings are genuinely derived from her master motive and not its false twin.

She elaborates further on her ideas about romantic love in her discussion of the "perfect couple." She describes how she had a crush on the most popular boy in high school but that he was so "unreachable" for her that she could not even imagine him being interested in her. Both parties of the perfect couple, by definition, have no personality deficits or physical defects; each partner is complete. If the ideal of romantic love entails one's being half of a perfect couple, then one constantly has to strive toward perfection. Indeed, Rachelle states that she is constantly dieting and exercising, even though, as a self-professed feminist, she hates the fact that she is so concerned about her physical appearance.

Experientially, she and the males she dates come up short of the cultural prototype — the "myth model" (Obeyesekere 1981: 99–102) — of romance. Hence, Rachelle constantly doubts that her own feelings are genuine, and simultaneously she must doubt that she is worthy of love, given that she is imperfect. The very grandiosity of Rachelle's love schema, its fairy-tale perfection, makes love both a buried treasure worth singularly pursuing and one that is impossible to find.

Gwen's Story: Too Shy and Insecure to Be Loved

In our first interview Gwen emphasized her fear of boys while growing up. She did not date during high school and says that she actively avoided socializing with boys. During high school, she was active in the local chapter of Amnesty International, and her career goal is to help improve the living conditions of the poor. Below are excerpts from my interviews with Gwen:

VICTOR: Why have you been celibate?
GWEN: For the most part, well, I haven't had the opportunity until very recently; basically until I got to college, the opportunity didn't présent itself, although I could have gone out and found it. I didn't date in high school. I was really shy; I didn't give off signals to guys to ask me on a date. I was very shy, not very confident, so I didn't date much and therefore didn't have much of an opportunity to have sex. Although, I could have gone up to any guy and hit on him, you know what I mean.
VICTOR: Right.
GWEN: So technically, yes, I could have [long pause] — like the opportunities were there but not realistically for me.
VICTOR: Because?

GWEN: I wouldn't have felt comfortable doing it. Since I've come to college, I've become more confident and I have dated a little more, so the opportunity has presented itself to me, but I didn't feel comfortable enough with the person to do it. So that's why I think it's more involved, it's more of a conscious decision for me since I came to college, whereas in high school it wasn't even an issue really. Do you understand?

VICTOR: Yes. Totally. How do you feel about being celibate?

GWEN: I find it frustrating. Actually, I didn't use to, but I do now. What I ideally would like — I don't want to have sex until I feel comfortable with someone. For me, that would probably mean being in love with them, although not for everyone but for me, or almost in love with them, or really comfortable because I am a good friend, you know, childhood kind of thing. What was your question?

VICTOR: So do you feel comfortable?

GWEN: Oh right. It's kind of like a cross to bear lately. I am kind of self-conscious about being a 22-year-old virgin, because I have a lot of desires. I can tell that I am a passionate person. I can tell that I would enjoy having sex a *lot,* but — so that's frustrating for me. It's frustrating not having met someone yet that I feel comfortable doing that with.

Gwen's reasons for being celibate are an outcome of her master-level self schema, in which she sees herself as fundamentally different from her peers. She attributes her celibacy to a lack of opportunities, being shy and insecure, and her discomfort around males. Celibacy is part of a more global peer-avoidance strategy that, she said, has allowed her to cope with her fellow students both in high school and at the university. Gwen's motives for being celibate are based on negative self-perceptions and deep feelings of social inadequacy. Like Rachelle, she is also motivated to be celibate because she wants sexual intercourse to occur within the context of romantic love. But for Gwen the sex-only-in-the-context-of-love schema is a preference, a basic-level schema, and not a master motive.

As she became more confident and began to date, her attitudes about her own celibacy changed. Without a master motive and in the absence of cultural sanctions against premarital sex, there are few reasons for students to opt for celibacy (which, in Gwen's terminology, signifies penetrative-receptive sex). Gwen lacks such a master-level motive and now portrays her celibacy in terms of a prototypical Christian image of suffering: as "a cross to bear." Like Rachelle, she believes that sex is best in the context of a love relationship, but she does not negate the possibility of enjoyably engaging in sex outside such a relationship. She does not have a biochemical master-level schema that stands in symbolic opposition to romantic love, Rachelle does.

Gwen is the only informant who identifies herself as a passionate person and who desires to experience sexual pleasure for its own sake. She expresses what the others leave implicit: that celibacy and sex not only are contrasting basic-level schemas but also are inversely related, so that as the motivation valence of one schema increases, that of the other decreases. The folk theory of the relationship of sex and celibacy is evident in Gwen's affirmation of her sexuality in the absence of a master motive that justifies her remaining celibate.

Jeremy's Story: "To Be Celibate Is to Be Alive"

Unlike Mark, Rachelle, and Gwen, Jeremy embraces celibacy as a permanent condition. Jeremy was also the only informant that expressly likened his celibacy to that of a monk. Jeremy utterly rejects sexual-romantic love as a viable option for him:

Seeing the way love is used in other contexts — I never had a context like that, my life is not that way. It doesn't *fit*. It doesn't translate itself. I don't know, it just gets used a lot, and it's all sort of happy and no troubles; happy is better than no troubles and — I don't know. A lot of it comes down to television and media-type stuff. I have all these images in my head of lovey-dovey cheesy stuff, and most people just seem to think that love is. And I've known people claiming to be in love for years and years. They all say they are in love, and it never seems to last. And it never seems to be anything all that profound, and it seems to me that love is supposed to be profound. And I think that love and lust get confused.

Like Gwen, Jeremy views celibacy as a basic-level schema that differentiates and isolates him from his peers. That process of differentiation entails, for Jeremy, a full-scale rejection of the popular culture he attributes to his peers and the adoption of a complex of schemas that contrast with those of his peer group. But his adoption of alternative, contrasting schemas is not just reactionary, it is also pro-active.

Before I explain this, let me summarize excerpts from interviews where Jeremy describes his experiences in junior high (13–15 years of age) and high school (16–18 years of age). Junior high and high school were very traumatic for Jeremy. He states that he felt like nothing around his peers, and they were mean to him, calling him pond scum and other names. He hated his classmates and their value system. But, he says, "I loved my parents," and he couldn't imagine being rebellious toward them, as his classmates were with their parents. When he was 13, their house caught fire, and Jeremy and his family were fortunate to escape without injury. Jeremy says: "After we had the house fire I was really scared about my parents dying. I used to call my dad from school. When I went to school every day, I brought lots of change with me so that I could call him at the office and make sure he got to the office okay. And every time I'd leave, I'd state exactly when I was going to see him next." He notes with evident scorn that his classmates were "so disrespectful to their parents."

During his adolescent years, Jeremy said, his experiences with his peers were horrible; at the same time, his attachment to his family was intensified by the house fire. Jeremy's family-attachment schema is a master schema that contrasts with his perception of his peers' family-attachment schema. He stated that he *loves* his parents, semantically differentiating familial love from his peers' version of love. In contrast with his peers' love schema, which he perceives to be fueled by lust and derived from popular culture, his basic-level schema of family love is asexual and private. It seems the seeds for an affirmation of celibacy were sown during his formative years, when he rejected the world of his peers and intensified his attachment to his nuclear family. His master-level schema includes a desexualized, familial-type love, which, in turn and in contrast with his perceptions of his peers' sexualized master motive, entails a basic-level celibacy schema.

Jeremy graduated summa cum laude from the University of New Hampshire in three and a half years, and during that time he had deep, obsessive crushes on two women at different times. He said that he hated fantasizing about them but could not stop. Tennov (1980: 21–25) coined the term *limerence* to describe obsessive fantasizing love that is seldom communicated to or realized with the "limerent object." She argues that, because it is reported by so many people in very similar terms, limerence has a neurophysiological base. Limerent fantasies seldom include explicitly sexual imagery, though romantic scenarios are frequently evoked (i.e., handholding, loving embraces). Oftentimes, limerent individuals have idealized the limerent object to the point that they fear communicating with that person and prefer to avoid face-to-face encounters. Jeremy's crushes seem to have been of this nature. Though he fantasized about the two women he had crushes on, his fantasies never included sexual imagery, and he stated that he hated thinking about them but just could not stop himself. After graduation, Jeremy said that his celibacy became "purer" because he thinks that he has put an end to crushes. Hence, he has begun to celebrate his celibacy.

[My friend and I, we] came up with a little slogan: "To be celibate is to be alive" [he laughs]. It's just sort of — to make a choice to be celibate seems to be like transcending a lot of junk that a lot of people are caught up in. And it seems to me that if you just don't care anymore — like you know, it was this great source of angst for me, the fact that I couldn't have a relationship, that I couldn't find someone who was, you know, who I could even start having a relationship with. But if that ceases to matter to you, it frees up your life in a lot of ways; it opens up a lot of — it's a type of freedom, to simply not care, at least for me coming from a background where it was this big weight on my shoulders. I felt like a loser because no one I liked liked me back then and [laughs], like, I couldn't talk to girls and all sorts of stuff like that, and then suddenly just to throw it off.

Jeremy explicitly contrasts his celibacy schema with a limerence schema (or what Rachelle referred to as chemistry and crushes), and to the extent that he eliminates (or suppresses) romantic-sexual desires, he affirms his desire to be permanently celibate. That he was, at one time, motivated to have a relationship is implied in the phrase "I couldn't find someone." Unlike Rachelle and Gwen, Jeremy has not internalized a romantic love schema that has motivational force; instead, he has a familial love schema. Hence, the schema complex of limerence versus love was a "great source of angst" for Jeremy, and by eliminating it as a motivational force in his life, he has freed himself from "a lot of junk."

Jeremy embraces celibacy and, unlike Gwen, associates celibacy with a positive master motive he calls freedom, by which he means a monastic withdrawal from the social world. Celibacy, in both its denotative sense of being unmarried and its connotative sense of abstaining from sexual activity (and involvements), is a necessary if not a sufficient means to accomplish this goal. Celibacy became a necessary condition for freedom because, as he said half facetiously, "girls drag you down."

Through a personal vow of lifetime celibacy, Jeremy has put himself at the service of a cultural concept and master motive that are unified and in some ways as grand and mysterious as God: freedom. At the same time this master motive articulates with his other master motive — attachment to his family — although Jeremy speaks of celibacy at times as if it were a master-level motive in its own right. In his slogan "To be celibate is to be alive," celibacy is presented as a valued end in itself; it is equated with living and not a means to attain some other goal.

Variations on a Prototype Schema

Netting reports 1990 rates of college student celibacy at 32 percent for single students, with 36 percent of them having had "previous sexual experiences but no sexual partners in the preceding year and 64% of them being virgins" (1992: 970). These figures are consistent with my own findings. In Netting's sample of 32 celibate female students, the four main reasons for celibacy were: "waiting for love" (25 percent), "personal morality" (18.8 percent), "fear of pregnancy" (15.6 percent), and "religion" (12.6 percent). The four main reasons for celibacy among male students were: "no opportunity" (29.3 percent); "religion" (17.5 percent); "fear of AIDS" (14.6 percent); and "waiting for love" and "personal morality" (each at 12.2 percent) (p. 971). Religion and AIDS are frequently mentioned as the reasons that students choose celibacy. Sprecher (1994: 4–5) notes that fear of AIDS has influenced student sexual patterns in three ways: by reducing the number of partners, by reducing the frequency of sex, and by motivating people to stay with a current relationship longer than they might have otherwise. None of my four informants gave fear of AIDS as a reason for choosing to be celibate.

Focus on the Families, Project Respect, and True Love Waits are among the many Christian-based programs that target adolescents and young adults, urging them to remain virgins. The success of these programs is due, in part, to their ability to formulate and advocate a schema complex of romantic love and Christian ethics that contrasts with the schema complex of chemistry and lust, articulated by Rachelle and Jeremy. Organizations that advocate celibacy further stigmatize adoption of a schema complex of chemistry and lust by noting their causal link to HIV/ AIDS and other sexually transmitted diseases.

Although only Mark mentioned religion as the primary reason for remaining celibate, all the informants use a variant of the religious prototype for celibacy to explain their reasons for being celibate. For each, celibacy is both a means to a higher end (e.g., love, freedom, marriage, and family) and a kind of self-indicator of their own morality in contrast with that of their noncelibate peers, who are constantly confusing lust with love. As in the "simplified world view" (Sweetser 1987: 44) of the monk, celibacy allows the informant to distinguish himself or herself from the masses and, in that act, to give meaning to his or her life. Whether with conscious intent or not, the schema that motivates monks to be celibate provides these four informants with a model for explaining their motives for choosing celibacy.

Celibacy, like any concept, is interpreted in the light of a culturally shaped prototype. Schema theory provides a strategy for analyzing intracultural (or interpersonal) variations in motivations. Despite the variety of explanations for celibacy, all four informants use the same hierarchic structure of motivations to explain why they are celibate. In addition, each informant contrasts celibacy with the basic-level schema of sex. Schema analysis illuminates and shows how people use similar cultural templates to organize and make sense of their experiences and their feelings about those experiences.

References Cited

D'Andrade, Roy. 1992. Schemas and Motivations. In *Human Motives and Cultural Models,* ed. Roy D'Andrade and Claudia Strauss, 23–44. Cambridge: Cambridge University Press.

D'Andrade, Roy. 1995. *The Development of Cognitive Anthropology.* Cambridge: Cambridge University Press.

Fillmore, Charles. 1977. Topics in Lexical Semantics. In *Current Issues in Linguistic Theory,* ed. Robert Cole, 76–138. Bloomington: Indiana University Press.

Kronenfeld, David B. 1996. *Plastic Glasses and Church Fathers: Semantic Extension from the Ethnoscience Tradition.* New York: Oxford University Press.

Netting, Nancy S. 1992. Sexuality in Youth Culture: Identity and Change. *Adolescence* 27: 961–976.

Obeyesekere, Gananath. 1981. *Medusa's Hair.* Chicago: University of Chicago Press.

Quinn, Naomi. 1996. Culture and Contradiction: The Case of Americans Reasoning about Marriage. *Ethos* 24(5): 391–425.

Rosch, Eleanor. 1978. Principles of Categorization. In *Cognition and Categorization,* ed. E. Rosch and B. Lloyd, 104–146. Hillsdale, N.J.: Erlbaum.

Rosch, Eleanor, and C. B. Mervis. 1975. Family Resemblances: Studies in the Internal Structure of Categories. *Cognitive Psychology* 5: 573–605.

Sprecher, Susan. 1991. The Impact of the Threat of AIDS on Heterosexual Dating Relationships. *Journal of Psychology and Human Sexuality* 3: 3–23.

Strauss, Claudia. 1992a. Models and Motives. In *Human Motives and Cultural Models,* ed. Roy D'Andrade and C. Strauss, 1–20. Cambridge: Cambridge University Press.

Strauss, Claudia. 1992b. What Makes Tony Run? In *Human Motives and Cultural Models,* ed. Roy D'Andrade and C. Strauss, 191–224. Cambridge: Cambridge University Press.

Strauss, Claudia, and Naomi Quinn. 1997. *A Cognitive Theory of Cultural Meaning.* Cambridge: Cambridge University Press.

Sweetser, Eve E. 1987. The Definition of *Lie:* An Examination of the Folk Models Underlying a Semantic Prototype. In *Cultural Models in Language and Thought,* ed. D. Holland and N. Quinn, 43–66. Cambridge: Cambridge University Press.

Tennov, Dorothy. 1980. *Love and Limerence.* New York: Stein and Day.

12 *Mark S. Fleisher and John R. Shaw*

Celibacy in American Prisons
Legal and Interpretive Perspectives

In much of this book, authors examine issues surrounding consensual celibacy choices; however, criminal incarceration raises a set of issues centered on the proposition that celibacy is officially imposed on inmates in American prisons as a consequence of imprisonment. In this chapter, we examine the historical, legal, practical, and moral issues faced by correctional administrators in developing and implementing policies of enforced celibacy in American prisons. We also discuss inmates' violation of the celibacy policy and that violation's factual and folkloric consequences.

Historical Perspective

Modern American prisons with an emphasis on crime control, societal protection, and rehabilitation originated some 200 years ago with the Quakers (Jacobs and Steele 1977). A central theme in the Quaker approach to prisoners' social and moral rehabilitation was the doctrine that explicitly banned all inmate sexual behavior, including masturbation (Jacobs and Steele 1977: 291) — an approach that seemed rational then (see Barnes and Teeters 1968; Gray [1847] 1973). Two hundred years later, the Federal Bureau of Prisons, the correctional agency of United States government, now housing more than 100,00 male and female inmates in approximately 100 prisons, still lists masturbation as a prohibited behavior for inmates (Code of Federal Regulations 1992: 1110–1144).

Until the twentieth century, prisoners were denied the rights of free citizens (*Wali v. Coughlin,* 754 F.2d 1015, 1028–1029 [2d Cir. 1985]). The Bill of Rights was held not to apply to prisoners, who, by virtue of violating the law, forfeited liberty and personal rights as well (*Ruffin v. Commonwealth,* 62 Va. [21 Gratt.] 790, 796 [1891]). With the loss of personal rights, inmates lost the right to engage in sex with legal spouses and lovers. In 1998, 123,041 federal and 1,178,978 state inmates, of whom 6.5 percent were women (Beck and Mumola 1999: 1), were disallowed same-sex relations with one another as well.

Whether to allow inmates to have heterosexual sex, and, if so, with whom and how often, is a decision courts have relegated to prison administrators. Despite this local control, all federal prisoners and the overwhelming majority of state prisoners are prohibited from engaging in sexual contact with spouses during visits.

Constitutional Basis for Celibacy

The courts, under the guidance of the U.S. Supreme Court, have increasingly found that prison administrators must be accorded great deference when making the very difficult and myriad decisions regarding the operation of penal institutions (see *Jones v. North Carolina Prisoner's Union,* 433 U.S. 119, 128 [1977]). However, while the Constitution "does not mandate comfortable prisons" (*Rhodes v. Chapman,* 452 U.S. 337 [1981]), "neither does it permit inhumane ones" (*Farmer v. Brennan,* 511 U.S. 825 [1994]). Thus, treatment of prisoners is subject to scrutiny under the Eighth Amendment's cruel and inhumane punishment clause. In addition, over the years the Supreme Court has found that many other constitutional protections, such as freedom of speech and religion (First Amendment), the right to be free from unreasonable searches (Fifth Amendment), the right to due process of law before being deprived of liberty or property (Fifth and Fourteenth Amendments), and the right to equal protection under the law (Fifth and Fourteenth Amendments), do reach over the prison walls and are applicable to prisoners, thus restraining the conduct of prison officials. However, the related cases are careful to point out that constitutional protections expected and demanded in the "free world" are limited in the prison context. A prisoner retains only those rights that "are not inconsistent with his status as a prisoner or with the legitimate penological objectives of the corrections system" (*Turner v. Safley,* 482 U.S. 78 [1987]). Thus, when a "prison regulation impinges on inmates' constitutional rights, the regulation is valid if it is reasonably related to legitimate penological interests" (p. 89). The reasonableness of a regulation or practice is to be determined by consideration of a number of factors and use of a "balancing" test, that is, weighing the right of the prisoner to the constitutional protection involved, on one hand, against the governmental interest in restricting the right, on the other. In general, the courts will defer to the prison authorities once they have articulated a rational basis for the decision to restrict the right involved. Thus, it is established that constitutional protections survive incarceration. In addition, many states and the federal government have articulated mandates for the operation of their prisons through statutorily created provisions. These laws may provide an avenue of relief for prisoners in the courts if they are not followed by correctional administrators. Finally, alleged violations of regulation or policy may trigger judicial review under a "state created right" analysis, but under a recent Supreme Court decision this approach is now in great doubt as a viable course of action.

Is Celibacy Subject to Judicial Intervention?

Within the above framework, let us examine enforced celibacy in prisons. Can such a policy be subject to judicial scrutiny? To answer this question, we must remember that the courts have limited review authority over prison administrators. The policy decision must involve a constitutionally protected right or a statutorily created one before a court can entertain review of the matter. The interest must constitute more than an "abstract need or desire" (*Board of Regents v. Roth*, 408 U.S. 564, 577 [1972]), and the individual claiming the right must have a legitimate entitlement to it (see *Kentucky Dept. of Corrections v. Thompson*, 490 U.S. 454, 460 [1989]). If it could be successfully argued that the right to sexual freedom is contained in the Constitution (or perhaps in statutory form), then the courts would be placed in a position of having to weigh the competing interests to determine if the proscription is justified. No doubt the courts would be inundated with claims of various rights by heterosexual and homosexual prisoners to engage in constitutionally protected sexual relations.

The easier task in this analysis is to determine if there are any United States jurisdictions that recognize in statutory provision the right to sexual freedom in prison. We have found no state or federal statute that confers such a right. Thus, the argument is closed regarding a statutory right to engage in sex while incarcerated, except perhaps with regard to conjugal visitation programs.

Let us now turn to whether there is a constitutional basis for the proposition that the right to private sexual relations survives incarceration. However, before a balancing test is employed to determine if the proscription is reasonable, it must first be determined whether any constitutional right is even involved because, in the absence of constitutionality, the courts lack a basis to review the matter. In order to answer whether a constitutional issue is at hand, we must briefly review the origins of the right to certain personal or fundamental liberties not specifically found in the Constitution.

The notion that the Constitution includes the right to personal privacy did not come to the forefront of judicial analysis until 1965 with the landmark case of *Griswold v. Connecticut* (381 U.S. 429). In that case the Supreme Court established the existence of certain rights to "privacy" in the United States Constitution's Bill of Rights, although these rights are not specifically articulated in the first 10 amendments. In *Griswold*, the Court found, under several constitutional amendment theories, that there is a "zone of privacy" protecting individuals against governmental intrusion, at least regarding certain marital and familial decisions, such as whether or not to bear children. Over the ensuing years, the Supreme Court expanded the breadth of the privacy zone first articulated by Justice Douglas, in *Griswold.*

Eight years after *Griswold v. Connecticut,* the Supreme Court extended the right to privacy to include a woman's decision to terminate a pregnancy (*Roe v. Wade,* 410 U.S. 113 [1973]). However, Justice Blackmun cautioned a limitation to the privacy zone the Court had formulated, concluding: "The Court has recognized that a right of personal privacy, or a guarantee of certain areas or zones of privacy, does exist under the Constitution. . . . These decisions make it clear that only personal rights that can be deemed 'fundamental' or 'implicit in the concept of ordered liberty' . . . are included in this guarantee of personal privacy" (p. 207). Justice Blackmun listed at least some of the areas the Court had identified as being within zones of privacy protected by the Constitution, including contraception, abortion, activities relating to marriage, procreation, family relationships, child rearing, and education.

During the several decades following *Griswold v. Connecticut,* it became increasingly clear that the Court should rule in regard to the outer boundaries of its private decisions. In particular, the pressing question was whether the *Griswold* and *Roe* series of cases extend the right of privacy to sexual behavior between consenting adults. The issue was considered and not decided by the Court for more than a decade after *Griswold.* Finally, the Court addressed the issue head on in the case of *Bowers v. Hardwick* 478 U.S. 186 [1986]. Hardwick, an adult male, was charged with violating Georgia's sodomy law by committing a sexual act with another adult male in his own bedroom. The Georgia law defined sodomy as committing or submitting to "any sexual act involving the sex organs of one person and the mouth or anus of another."[1]

In *Bowers v. Hardwick* the Court stressed that it was not required to decide "whether laws against sodomy between consenting adults in general, or homosexuals in particular, were wise or desirable" (p. 190). Rather, the issue presented was "whether the Federal Constitution confers a fundamental right upon homosexuals to engage in sodomy" (p. 190) and thus invalidates the laws of many states making such conduct illegal. The Court, by a narrow majority, answered in the negative. Writing for the Court, Justice White emphasized that the previous cases establishing privacy rights involved family, marriage, or procreation. The Court was "quite unwilling" to pronounce that there is a fundamental right to engage in homosexual sodomy. Justice White noted that sodomy as a crime has ancient roots and was an offense under common law and under the laws of the original 13 states when they ratified the Bill of Rights. Thus, the Court concluded that, against this background, to claim that a right to engage in such conduct is "deeply rooted in this Nation's history and tradition . . . [or] implicit in the concept of ordered liberty is, at best, facetious" (pp. 191–194).

On the basis of the Supreme Court's refusal to expand constitutional protections to private, consensual sex in the free world, it is not surprising that *no cases have held that there is any right for incarcerated individuals to engage in sexual activity within the confines of the nation's prisons.* Even if there were such a right, the many important governmental interests that could be asserted by prison administrators regarding jeopardy to the safe and secure operation of prisons would no doubt defeat any inmate claims to exercise this particular right.

Sex as a Prison Management Tool

Most state and federal correctional officials would likely argue that, for the most part, inmates' same-sex relations are disruptive and threaten the safety and orderly operation of a prison. Inmates argue, however, that revoking the celibacy policy and permitting conjugal visits would lower rates of inmate homosexual contact, which would then lower rates of inmate violence, as well.[2] Fleisher (1989) reports conversations with prisoners at the United States Penitentiary (USP) at Lompoc, California, a high-security prison housing approximately 1,200 inmates, 98 percent with violent criminal histories, who alleged that the penitentiary's violence was directly attributable to sex among inmates and that the violence would end if the federal prison system were to allow conjugal visiting. In 14 months of penitentiary life, from August 1995 to the end of September 1996, there were, in fact, no sexual assaults, no inmate-on-inmate rapes, and no murders attributable to homosexuality (see Fleisher 1989 for a full discussion of cellhouse sex at USP Lompoc). The serious violent incidents at USP Lompoc were motivated by drug deals, prison gang retaliation, and gambling debts, not by sex.

Since the inception of the Federal Bureau of Prisons (BOP) in 1930, the agency has implemented the policy of inmate celibacy as well as a policy of denying inmates sexual access to a spouse on prison grounds (the Bureau of Prisons has, like most state correctional agencies, an inmate furlough program for qualified inmates). Why has the federal agency done that? The answer lies in part in the *Federal Prison Service Task Force Report on Family Visitation* (Bureau of Prisons 1980), a BOP-commissioned study of state-prison conjugal visiting programs, which was conducted as part of an effort to prepare national prison and jail standards (Goetting 1982). In addition to reviewing then current literature, federal prison officials conducted on-site visits to state prisons.

The federal *Task Force Report on Family Visitation* found a number of problems with conjugal programs; in summary, they follow: Conjugal programs were, in general, poorly run and involved a very small number of prisoners. There was a lack of internal management review, as well as uncritical support, of conjugal programs and of conjugal programs as a substitute for furlough programs. There were no data to demonstrate that conjugal programs met stated institution objectives. Senior prison administrators failed to be aware of difficulties with conjugal programs. Long-term inmates had less access than short-term offenders to the conjugal programs, because long-term inmates abused these programs more often than others, thus losing access to privileges. Line staffers had generally negative opinions about the conjugal programs and senior administrators' oversight of them. There were no data to support prison administrators' claims that the conjugal programs promoted good institutional behavior. Inmates using the conjugal programs were often aggressive toward staff and visitors and made sexually obscene comments to female visitors. Inmates were more interested in sexual gratification than in promoting the conjugal programs' goal of family support. Finally, the smuggling of contraband (drugs, weapons) through the facilities of the conjugal programs caused a serious security problem. In the end, the federal prison system concluded that conjugal visiting led to more prisoner misconduct than it precluded or resolved.

To date there is no prison research to support the following assumptions: Long-term conjugal visiting programs have lowered rates of inmate-on-inmate violence. Consensual, same-sex inmate relations would, if endorsed by prison policy, contribute to a safer quality of life inside men's prisons by reducing nonconsensual same-sex relations. State prisons with conjugal programs have lower rates of same-sex inmate contact and institutional violence than similar prisons without such programs. And, conjugal visiting programs have had a measurable positive effect on inmates' readjustment to community life. Additionally, the literature on men's prisons shows few references to how inmate same-sex relations are affected by the race or ethnicity of individual inmates. Generally speaking, then, research on the sexual behavior of inmates in men's prisons as it relates to race, ethnicity, and the lives of inmates prior to and following imprisonment is virtually absent (an exception is Fleisher 1998, which discusses in detail the sexual lives of African American, Mexican, and white, gang-involved adolescents and examines the links between sexual behavior and street violence).

Government Morality

Correctional organizations are government agencies. Prison officials are state or federal government employees whose salary and benefits depend on retaining employment. When elected officials rail against homosexuality in the free community, wardens are expected to enforce a celibacy policy. To lift the celibacy policy would signal to the public that elected officials and prison officials condone and promote homosexual enjoyment among convicted felons, paid for with tax dollars on government property.

To be sure, the link between sex and government standards of morality extends to staffers as well, as shown by the following incident. An unmarried man and woman, both staffers in their 30s, shared the same bed on federal government housing reservation adjoining a prison complex. When this couple's "dating" caught the attention of the warden, each party was reprimanded for "immoral" behavior on federal property. In the federal government, simply the appearance of impropriety, however it is defined by an agent of the government (here, the warden), is sufficient to engender difficulties for staffers, as well as for inmates.

State government standards of morality influence conjugal programs in state prisons where, for instance, prisoners may spend the night with legal spouses but not with common-law spouses or lovers. These are discretionary decisions made by prison administrators, who may be exercising power over inmates on a sensitive topic (Jacobs and Steele 1977). There is another view, as well. A prison visiting program, whether it is conjugal or (nonsexual) family visiting, is a so-called public program. Such programs

allow free citizens on prison grounds, and, in the case of conjugal programs, outsiders are permitted to spend the night with convicted felons.
However, the stated purpose of these overnight visits is not sex; rather, it
is to preserve the inmates' families. In the context of correctional culture,
family preservation is a form of rehabilitation; sex is not.

Deterrence Theory

Deterrence theory was first fully developed by the University of Chicago's
Nobel laureate Gary Becker (1968). Deterrence is an economic theory
predicated on the notion that offenders make rational decisions about
their behavior and weigh the consequences of punishment against the
benefits of crime. Thus according to deterrence theory, inmates who are
punished severely will decide that the cost of crime outweighs its benefits
and will then choose lawful lifestyles. To impose a higher cost of imprisonment, prison officials would be forced to toughen prison conditions,
which may violate state and federal case law on conditions of inmate confinement and/or modern practices in correctional management. The riots
at Attica and Santa Fe taught correctional administrators a harsh lesson
about the link between poor prison conditions and cellhouse violence (see
Goodstein and MacKenzie 1989).

Conventional notions of punishment conflict with modern principals of
prison management. In a recent strategic planning document, the Federal
Bureau of Prisons (1995) stated that inmates are incarcerated in federal
institutions *as* punishment but not *for* punishment. Thus, inherent in the
federal notion of imprisonment is the organizational belief that inmates
are to be well treated in federal custody and that the removal of and constraints on specific constitutional rights are the very nature of punishment
brought by imprisonment to once-free citizens.

State and federal research on prisons suggests that in well-managed
institutions inmates' quality of life is high, with an emphasis on education
and vocational training programs, dental and medical care, treatment for
alcohol and other drug abuse, and safety for staff and inmates (Fleisher
1989; 1995: chap. 4; Fleisher and Rison 1997). In a modern correctional
setting, safety is interpreted as the assurance that inmates are physically
and emotionally undamaged by prisons' physical and social conditions. If
an inmate were injured during sex and a prison warden and other correctional officials had known that dangerous conditions existed and still did
nothing to remedy those conditions, the injury might be taken as proof of
a violation of an inmate's right to be free from cruel and unusual punishment (see *Bivens v. Six Unknown Named Agents of the Federal Bureau of
Narcotics* 403 U.S. 388 [1971]).

Correctional officials cannot toughen a prison's environment in ways that materially exceed management boundaries specified by courts; however, all federal and nearly all state prison officials have removed from the array of authorized prison programs one of the activities that inmates truly want: permission to have heterosexual sex with visitors. If the celibacy policy makes inmates' lives in prison tougher, then it will likely remain in force for a long time.

Violating the Celibacy Policy

Classic studies of prison sex have been carried out (Clemmer 1940; Sykes 1958), and subsequent studies have been conducted inside maximum-security prisons (Earley 1992; Fleisher 1989; Lockwood 1980, 1985; Nacci and Kane 1984; Wooden and Parker 1982) or have used a sampling procedure that included data from maximum-security prisons (Naaci and Kane 1982, 1984).[3] Maximum-security prisons house the most violent criminal offenders (those convicted of sexual offenses, for instance), and if sex-related violence among inmates occurs at all, research shows that it happens most often in high-security cellhouses.

Every American prison has a policy prohibiting sex among inmates. But inside cellhouses, heterosexual celibacy is a matter of inmate choice. The general nature of prison life offers male and female inmates opportunities to break the celibacy policy with male and female staffers. Inmates wanting the pleasure of opposite-sex relations simply have to find the right man or woman. Many prison staff members (personal communication, 1991) told Fleisher that in the late 1980s, one of America's largest state correctional agencies faced the serious management problem of a growing number of women staffers who were having sex with male inmates.

Davidson's (1974: 110) research at California's San Quentin prison found that some inmates had sex with a nurse in the prison hospital. At the Washington State Penitentiary between 1979 and 1984, Fleisher's research with prisoners and their wives and girlfriends showed the ease with which inmates had unsanctioned sex with women. In those years, the penitentiary was unaffected by modern correctional management. There was no staff-training academy, and new correctional officers were posted for on-the-job training in one of the two visiting rooms. In both visiting rooms, Fleisher watched female visitors performing fellatio on male inmates and inmates engaging in sexual intercourse with female partners in full view of adult and child visitors and prison guards (Fleisher 1981, 1982, 1985; see also Fishman 1990 in regard to prison visitations, women's relationships with inmates, and subsequent problems). One of the two visiting rooms had men's and women's washrooms. A guard was posted outside these rooms to prevent an inmate and his visitor from hopping inside to be alone. But instead of preventing inmate–visitor trysts, guards sold access to these rooms by the minute. Inmates and guards called it toilet time. Roaming the visiting room were children called bathroom babies, who had been conceived inside these washrooms.

In the early 1980s Washington State Penitentiary's staff corruption, coupled with egregious levels of inmate violence, resulted in a number of inmate-initiated federal law suits (Stastny and Tyrnauer 1983). Under the watchful eye of a federal judge, Washington State spent 60 million dollars to remodel the prison. In an attempt to reduce inmate levels of violence, a conjugal program had been established in 1980. Fleisher knew many legally married inmates who, to the chagrin of their wives, refused conjugal visits. Some inmates said they were afraid "it [their penis] would fall off" because it had been so long since they had had sexual intercourse with a women. Others said they were afraid to have sex in a private place; and still others said their "pipes were rusty" and they would not be able to "get it up [have an erection] for a woman." Years later Fleisher recorded similar remarks from male street criminals (Fleisher 1995: 165–166) who said they felt comfortable engaging in sex with women only when they and their sexual partners were high on drugs and alcohol or subsequent to incidents of interpartner violence. How drugs, alcohol, sex, and power are interrelated in the sociosexual world of male street criminals and their partners deserves much greater systematic study.

Cases such as those in California and Washington embarrass correctional agencies. Prison officials believe this conduct reflects poorly on the correctional agency as a government organization. Every year, an undisclosed number of men and women are dismissed or resign from prison employment and then continue to "date" inmates. Prison officials believe these staff–inmate affairs endanger prison security, largely because staffers understand institutional security precautions and can find ways to circumvent these precautions and smuggle drugs and weapons to inmate-lovers. However, there is no publicly available research to show these former prison staffers who become inmates' lovers do, in fact, endanger prison security more than other staff members do.

Prison Sex Roles

Sykes's (1958) study of the maximum-security Rahway state penitentiary in the 1950s showed the deprivations of prison life and alleged that male inmates had sex with one another because they did not have access to women. By contrast, anthropological studies of male sexuality have shown that male–male sex is common even when women are available (Harris 1989: 98–115; Herdt and Boxer 1995). Fleisher (1995: 165) has shown that male street criminals choose sex with men over women, even if women are easily accessible. No prison studies have shown that inmates who engaged in conjugal programs desist from same-sex relations inside cellhouses.

Harris (1989: 236–237) notes that among the world's cultures sexual "preferences do not necessarily entail avoidances" (p. 236). A male inmate may prefer sex with a woman, but if one is not available, sex with a man is an acceptable substitute. Same-sex encounters in prison represent the flexibility of the male sexual appetite rather than being "unnatural" behaviors caused by a harsh environment.

Like the Azande, Papua New Guineans, and the Greeks (Harris 1989: 242), prisoners assign a special status to differentiate the "insertee" from the "insertor." In prison, an insertor is an aggressor, and within inmate culture, he is not classified as a homosexual; however, the insertee is known as a fag, punk, or bitch. Some inmates switch roles, acting as the insertor on some occasions, the insertee on others (Fleisher 1989: 156–157).

Consensual sex among male inmates is common in cellhouses and to some degree establishes social role relations among these inmates. Often these roles mirror stereotypic free-world gender roles (Gagnon and Simon 1968). "Husbands" work; "wives" cook, clean, iron, shop, and offer sex on demand. But often these relationships include unsavory elements, such as a husband giving his wife to other men to do chores or perform sex acts in exchange for cash, drugs, or cigarettes or as repayment for a debt. In this way, sex obtains value within a cellhouse's informal economy. A man may order his cellhouse wife, known also as his bitch, to work as a prostitute. In such relationships, a husband gives at most a minimum of the property or cash gained through prostitution; if the wife refuses, he may be beaten or killed. A cellhouse husband's ability to control his quality of life depends in large part on his ability to control his wife's work (informally with chores and sex and formally as income through a legitimate prison job). On the other hand, a cellhouse wife uses the husband–wife relationship as protection against potential violent sexual assaults from the queue of men who want the wife's sexual favors. Such a cellhouse sexual arrangement is typical of street-level pimp–prostitute relationships.

When a cellhouse wife refuses to work or works without his husband's permission, the outcome may be violent. Every inmate in the closed social world of a cellhouse knows such refusals. Inmates may tease a man, saying that he cannot control his bitch. At this point, a husband's honor is at stake, and his inability to control his wife is interpreted by inmates as weakness, and with weakness comes a loss of respect among inmates. Weakness signifies to other inmates a man's vulnerability. If a disrespected husband does not gain respect, he will lose his bitch and his earning potential to someone else. Often the only way to regain respect is by severely beating or killing his wife.

Sex and violence are linked to social control mechanisms within imprisoned street gang members. Older, experienced street gang members exploit young members of their own gang by forcing them to work as cellhouse prostitutes. Gang leaders send these "fish" (new inmates) to "work" the cellhouse under the watchful eye of a gang pimp. Prostitution earns gang leaders and senior members cash, property, and drugs; however, a sexually abused young inmate receives nothing. A refusal to work as a prostitute leads first to a serious beating, then to death. Punched in the face and head, a young man's lips, cheeks, eyes swell. He is then called a pumpkin head. Gangs parade a pumpkin head on the prison yard. Accurate and publicly available data on such incidents are at best difficult to obtain.

Cellhouse Sex Folklore and the Politics of Power

The push-and-pull between inmates' demands for more freedom and prison officials' resistance to those demands is the central dynamic in prison life. Today the prisoner–correctional agency dynamic is being played out symbolically in a number of challenges to prison management issues, such as sexual parity (Fleisher, Rison, and Hellman 1997) and the allegation that the celibacy policy causes inmate homosexuality, homosexual rape, and contributes to increased levels of prison violence. Such claims notwithstanding, federal prison research has shown that incidents of nonconsensual sex occur at an extremely low frequency (Nacci and Kane 1982).

Extract the legal interventions of the 1960s, 1970s, and 1980s from prison case law, and prison life would likely resemble the civil rights nightmares of decades ago. Specific issues such as those noted above reached courtrooms, and decisions favorable to inmates changed prison environments. In the conservative political climate of the 1990s, however, inmates' complaints about poor food quality, lack of education programs, and so on would not likely raise public support for inmates' causes. But allegations of inmates raping inmates on government property get the attention of the American Civil Liberties Union, the Human Rights Watch, and inmate support groups.

To file a federal law suit against a warden and a correctional agency requires only allegations of sexual violence (see *Farmer v. Brennan,* 825).[4] Inmates' allegations of sexual violence have become part of a substantial body of prison sex-and-violence folklore. *Folklore* simply means the things people say, in this case, stories about sex and violence that have not been verified (Fleisher 1989 discusses inmates' and staffers' folklore and how it is integrated into prison culture). Earley's popular account of inmate life inside the federal high-security penitentiary at Leavenworth, Kansas, claimed to have found evidence for inmates' reports of sexual aggression in this statement: "There is a saying . . . 'Every convict has three choices. He can fight [for his life], he can hit the fence [try to escape], or he can fuck [for protection]' " (1992: 55–56). In fact, high-security federal penitentiaries, including USP Leavenworth, have relatively low rates of armed and unarmed inmate-on-inmate assaults (Fleisher 1989: 200; Fleisher and Jacobs 1998). Notwithstanding, in the early 1970s at the Washington State Penitentiary, Fleisher heard the same aphorism Earley reported. During his 14 months of work inside USP Lompoc's cellhouses, there were no reported inmate-on-inmate rapes.

Prison talk about "punks," "fags," "fuck boys," "bitches," "blowjobs," and violent sex is a popular way to pass the time in prison cellhouses (Fleisher 1989; Rideau and Wikberg 1992; Wooden and Parker 1982), and equivalent talk occurs on the street among adolescent male and female gang members (Fleisher 1998). Cellhouse sex talk extends to folkloric street characters, such as Big Dick Bob, who, according to an inmate at a medium-security Illinois state prison, "takes care of [our] old ladies while we're doing time."

In the absence of data on consensual and nonconsensual violent inmate-on-inmate sexual encounters, prison researchers have relegated such tales to the category of bogeyman stories. In state and federal prisons, sex-and-violence folklore is learned and repeated by generations of prison inmates; however, in the litigious world of American corrections, sexual bogeyman stories can be used as powerful tools in inmates' arsenal of legal weapons against correctional administrators.

Celibacy, Sex, and Violence

Centuries ago, U.S. society enforced a celibacy policy as a way to punish inmates and impose standards of morality on them. Today's prison authorities use celibacy as a management mechanism, which is designed to forestall disorder by controlling a behavior (sex) that has been closely linked to violence inside prisons. Prisoners say, however, that celibacy leads to more serious violence. Prison administrators retort that the social and emotional complexities effected by same-sex relations are, along with

drug distribution, the primary contributors to inmate-on-inmate violence, especially within medium- and high-security prisons. Inmate
advocates, often inmates' wives and girlfriends as well as former inmates,
argue that freely available heterosexual relations implemented with conjugal visiting programs would maintain unity within prisoners' families
and improve inmates' reentry into their communities. Despite such
claims on both sides of the argument, one thing is well known: prison
researchers know little about the role of celibacy and conjugal visiting on
inmates' in-prison conduct and former inmates' postprison community
lives. There is no research suggesting that inmates who have participated
in conjugal visiting programs have stronger families, fewer divorces,
lower rates of domestic or child abuse, or recidivism than inmates who
have not participated in such programs.

Decades of prison research have identified risk factors that contribute
to prison violence. Most notably these include the illegal activities of
street and prison gangs, including drug smuggling, in-prison drug distribution, and drug and gambling debts, as well as interracial hostilities reminis-
cent of societal race conflicts and violent forms of retribution and retaliation between prison gangs and street gangs. Teasing out the affect that
celibacy might have on inmate violence, as compared with other well-
known risk factors, is a difficult, and yet unaccomplished, task.

Most research on prison celibacy and other violence-related issues has
been conducted in men's high- and medium-security prisons. Such institutions house the most violent inmates. These are offenders whose violent
criminal histories indicate a lack of compliant behavior inside as well as
outside prison. In these prisons, violent behavior is expected and is usually linked to drugs, gambling, and street and prison gangs. To posit that
inmates with violent criminal histories would be nonviolent or less violent
if they were permitted to have sex with women overlooks these same
inmates' violence when on the street, even with wives and girlfriends.
Also, street ethnography shows that adult male criminals participate in
same-sex relations on the street even when women are accessible and that
male street criminals are likely to use violence in same-sex and cross-sex
social and sexual relations (Fleisher 1995: 165–166 and *passim*).

Prison- and community-based research on inmate and former inmate
behavior does not support the assertion that heterosexual celibacy causes
inmates irreparable harm by inflicting on them a level of punishment ex-
ceeding normal expectations of imprisonment. To be sure, if offering violent criminals heterosexual sex would effect compliant, nonviolent behavior inside and outside prison, America's quest for a rehabilitative panacea
would be practical and relatively inexpensive. Prison research has not
demonstrated that cross-sex abstinence motivates prisoners to behave

more violently than they would if policy were to permit cross-sex relations. Publicly available data show that some New York, Texas, and California prisons with well-established conjugal visiting programs are among the country's most violent institutions (Maguire and Pastore 1995: 585). Without strong research based on sound methods and accurate data, current prison celibacy policies will most certainly remain enforced.

Notes

1. Almost all sodomy statutes define the offense in similar terms. The obvious implication in the prison setting is that all consensual sexual activity among inmates will meet the definition of sodomy.

2. Prisoners and their spouses have attempted to utilize the sometimes sweeping and inconsistent language in the Supreme Court's line of privacy cases to argue that the right of marital privacy jumps the prison wall and requires prison officials to grant conjugal visits to them; however, it has long been held that there is no right to contact visitation in America's jails and prisons (see *Block v. Rutherford*, 468 U.S. 576 [1984]). Likewise, while there have been only a few cases on the issue, the courts have been consistent in holding that there is no constitutional right of prisoners or their spouses to conjugal visits (e.g., *Hernandez v. Coughlin*, 18 F.3d 133 [2d Cir. 1994]). In *Turner v. Safley*, the U.S. Supreme Court recognized that at least some of the rights of marriage survive incarceration, but that decision has not swayed other courts to order conjugal visits as a matter of constitutional right. The *Turner* Court noted that "the right to marriage, like many other rights, is subject to substantial restrictions as a result of incarceration" (*Turner v. Safley*, 95). In fact, while listing the "attributes" of marriage which survive incarceration, the Court declined to mention the right to procreation or sexual relations. Instead, the Court stated that prisoners retain the "expectation that the marriage may someday be fully consummated" (p. 96). Finally, it should be noted that none of the reported cases found any solace for prisoners or their spouses in statutory language authorizing conjugal visits. The states have been careful in drafting language implementing a family visitation program to ensure that final decisions are left to the discretion of prison authorities and not subject to judicial intervention.

3. A jail is a correctional facility that, for the most part, houses men and women awaiting trial. Many of America's megajails in Los Angeles, New York, and Chicago are enormous warehouses, some holding 10,000 offenders at any time, and during the course of a year, hundreds of thousands of offenders are arrested and released while other are detained and processed for trial. The effect of celibacy on jail inmates or on jail management has not been studied. By contrast, prisons house inmates convicted of a felony and serving sentences in excess of a year. Prisons are classified by security levels, including minimum, low, medium, high, and super-maximum.

4. The Centers for Disease Control and Prevention developed an HIV/AIDS program to be used in a California state prison. Inmates uninfected by HIV were

having sex with inmates known to be HIV positive. Rather than distribute condoms, the state agency resorted to an education program to alter inmates' sexual behavior. A one-time classroom education program is cheaper and easier for a correctional agency to implement than a condom distribution and collection program funded with taxpayers' dollars. The state agency is less vulnerable to legal acts by inmates who received the education and, despite it, persist in engaging in high-risk sex.

References Cited

Barnes, Harry, and Negley Teeters. 1968. *New Horizons in Criminology.* 3d ed. New York: Prentice-Hall. Original publication, 1927.

Beck, Allen J., and Christopher J. Mumola. 1979. *Prisoners in 1998.* Washington, D.C.: U.S. Department of Justice, Bureau of Justice Statistics.

Becker, Gary S. 1968. Crime and Punishment: An Econometric Approach. *Journal of Political Economy* 76(2): 169–217.

Clemmer, Donald. 1940. *The Prison Community.* New York: Holt, Rinehart and Winston.

Code of Federal Regulations. 1992. Inmate Disciple and Special Housing Units. In *Judicial Administration,* vol. 28. Washington, D.C.: National Archives and Records Administration.

Davidson, Theodore. 1974. *Chicano Prisoners: The Key to San Quentin.* New York: Holt, Rinehart and Winston.

Earley, Pete. 1992. *The Hot House: Life inside Leavenworth.* New York: Bantam Books.

Federal Bureau of Prisons. 1980. *Federal Prison Service Task Force Report on Family Visitation.* Washington, D.C.: U.S. Department of Justice, Bureau of Prisons.

Federal Bureau of Prisons. 1995. *Bureau of Prisons: GOALS for 1995 . . . and Beyond.* Washington, D.C.: U.S. Department of Justice, Bureau of Prisons.

Fishman, Laura. 1990. *Women at the Wall: A Study of Prisoners' Wives Doing Time on the Outside.* Albany: State University of New York Press.

Fleisher, Mark S. 1981. The Psychosocial Dynamics of Prison Inmate Families. Paper presented at the 80th Annual Meetings of the American Anthropological Association, Chicago.

Fleisher, Mark S. 1982. The Socialization of Women and Children into Prison Society. Paper presented at the 81st Annual Meetings of the American Anthropological Association, Los Angeles.

Fleisher, Mark S. 1985. Learning Whose Rules? Strategies of Married Life in a Maximum Security Prison. Paper presented at the 84th Annual Meetings of the American Anthropological Association, Washington, D.C.

Fleisher, Mark S. 1989. *Warehousing Violence.* Newbury Park, Calif.: Sage.

Fleisher, Mark S. 1995. *Beggars and Thieves.* Madison: University of Wisconsin Press.

Fleisher, Mark S. 1998. *Dead End Kids: Gang Girls and the Boys They Know.* Madison: University of Wisconsin Press.

FLEISHER AND SHAW: *Celibacy in American Prisons*   245

Fleisher, Mark S., and James B. Jacobs. 1998. The Federal Bureau of Prisons, 1989–1998. Paper presented at the 12th World Congress of Criminology, Seoul, Korea.

Fleisher, Mark S., and Richard H. Rison. 1997. Health Care in the Federal Bureau of Prisons. In *Classical and Contemporary Issues in Corrections,* ed. James Marquart and Jon Sorsensen, 347–354. Los Angeles: Roxbury.

Fleisher, Mark S., Richard H. Rison, David W. Helman. 1997. Female Inmates: A Growing Constituency in the Federal Bureau of Prisons. *Corrections Management Quarterly* 1(4): 28–35.

Gagnon, John H., and William Simon. 1968. The Social Meaning of Prison Homosexuality. *Federal Probation* 32 (March): 23–29.

Goetting, Ann. 1982. Conjugal Association in Prison. *New England Journal on Prison Law* 8(1): 141–154.

Goodstein, Lynne, and Doris MacKenzie, eds. 1989. *The American Prison: Issues in Research and Policy.* New York: Plenum.

Gray, Francis. [1847] 1973. *Prison Discipline in America.* Reprint ed. Montclair, N.J.: Patterson Smith.

Harris, Marvin. 1989. *Our Kind.* New York: Harper and Row.

Herdt, Gilbert, and Andrew Boxer. 1995. Bisexuality. In *Conceiving Sexuality,* ed. Richard G. Parker and John H. Gagnon, 69–83. New York: Routledge.

Jacobs, James B., and Eric H. Steele. 1977. Sexual Deprivation and Penal Policy. *Cornell Law Review* 62(2): 289–312.

Lockwood, Daniel. 1980. *Prison Sexual Violence.* New York: Elsevier.

Lockwood, Daniel. 1985. Issues in Prison Sexual Violence. In *Prison Violence in America,* ed. Michael Braswell, Steven Dillingham, and Reid Montgomery, 89–96. Cincinnati: Anderson.

Maguire, Kathleen, and Ann L. Pastore, eds. 1995. *Sourcebook of Criminal Justice Statistics 1994.* U.S. Department of Justice, Bureau of Justice Statistics. Washington, D.C.: United States Government Publications Office.

Nacci, Peter L., and Thomas R. Kane. 1982. *Sex and Sexual Aggression in Federal Prisons.* Progress Report 1(1). Washington, D.C.: U.S. Department of Justice, Federal Prison System.

Nacci, Peter L., and Thomas R. Kane. 1984. Sex and Sexual Aggression in Federal Prisons. *Federal Probation* 8 (March): 46–53.

Rideau, Wilbert, and Ron Wikberg. 1992. *Life Sentences.* New York: Time Books.

Stastny, C., and G. Tyrnauer. 1983. *Who Rules the Joint? The Changing Political Culture of Maximum-Security Prisons in America.* Lexington, Mass.: Lexington Books.

Sykes, Gresham. 1958. *Society of Captives: A Study of Maximum Security Prison.* Princeton: Princeton University Press.

Wooden, W. S., and J. Parker. 1982. *Men behind Bars: Sexual Exploitation in Prison.* New York: Plenum.

13 *Paul Southgate*

A Swallow in Winter
A Catholic Priesthood Viewpoint

People live a celibacy life-style for different reasons. This chapter is an attempt to give some insight into the motivation that persuades a Catholic priest to submit to mandatory celibacy. It is neither an attack on nor a defense of the practice. It will explain the language of celibacy as it applies to the Catholic priest and then consider some of the influences that have formed the Church's understanding and practice of celibacy. It will not refer to celibacy among women.[1]

There are a number of participant observers of celibacy but few observing participants. This chapter presents a view from one of the few. I am a Roman Catholic priest. Celibacy for me is not a continuously serene condition of life: sometimes I rejoice in it, sometimes I am angry about it, sometimes I grieve over it. It is the subject of an ongoing argument, within myself and with my friends, in which celibacy is sometimes winning and at other times losing. During my 20 years of priesthood I have changed my mind about mandatory celibacy and now feel that it should be optional. Quite possibly, I might change my mind back again. We, the Church and I, are still trying to figure out sexuality.

If I were not a priest, or if I were permitted as a priest to do so, I would certainly marry. Celibacy is a challenge and often a struggle, accepted willingly in order to enter the priesthood. Having accepted it for life, I can say that I am still learning to live with it as a fruitful, if not always comfortable bedmate. I would rather be its hero than its victim.

Mandatory celibacy has been proposed and challenged from within the Catholic Church almost since its inception. It is this creative dialectic, which is both personal and institutional, that opens the way to new discoveries. Even the discouraging of debate, which is attempted from time to time by those in power, plays its part in this vital process. The explanation for celibacy that I put forward here is given from a religious perspective. Celibacy, as it has been understood and practiced in the Catholic Church, is not beyond the hermeneutics of suspicion inherent in anthropological inquiry into religion, but there is more to religious celibacy than meets the scientific eye.

Why Choose Celibacy?

As I wrote the first draft of this chapter, a fellow priest of my diocese was imprisoned for abusing children and exporting pornography on the Internet. He may have been exceptional, but we all feel more tarnished and less trusted as a result and perhaps a little less convinced about the sign-value of our celibacy. This is demonstrated in the angle taken by Sky Television in reporting the story, which centered on the easy availability of pornography on the Internet. The priestly identity of the abuser was no longer of primary interest, presumably because abuse was no longer so shockingly unusual. Indeed, a few months prior to the event, a Scottish bishop eloped with a divorcee and resigned from the active priesthood amid great publicity. "So what do you think about celibacy, then?" had already become a choice chat-up line in pubs throughout the nation.

There is no denying that there is a crisis of celibacy in the Catholic Church today that touches the life of every priest and every Catholic. What are its roots? Theologian Karl Rahner explains:

There are [reasons] which lie in the modern social situation, those which emerge from the mentality of modern man, those which have their cause in the change of attitude to ecclesiastical authority on the part of the individual Christian, those which are connected with the nature of sexually conditioned human relationships and of celibacy itself. But if we are not deceiving ourselves, we must see that the ultimate reason for the crisis by and large is to be found in the present-day lack of faith. We are living at a time when the reality of God and eternal life can be appreciated by man only with difficulty. We are living at a time which is characterized by catchwords like demythologization and secularization and by the tendency to reduce the whole of Christianity to purely human relationships. (1974: 148)

And this is precisely the point: my life would be radically different if I did not believe in God, in eternal life, and in the teachings of the Catholic Church. In other words, the Christian faith that I profess makes a practical daily difference to my life and relationships. Celibacy is one way of expressing and living out that faith. If this faith turns out to be deceptive, then my loss is profound: no wife, no children, no family, no sexual ecstasy.

American theologian Daniel Berrigan once graphically remarked: "Your faith is rarely where your head is at, just as it is rarely where your heart is at. Your faith is where your ass is at!" (as cited in Rolheiser 1995: 163). What you are actually doing reveals what you believe. Celibacy helps me to do my job as a Catholic priest: to bear witness for Jesus Christ, for the eternal dimension in human life, and for the presence of God in the world; that is why I choose it.

Celibacy and Chastity

The word *celibacy* comes from the Latin *caelebs,* which means "alone" or "single," and thus stands in relation to *monk* and *hermit.* I am neither monk nor hermit, however, but a secular priest. A *secular* priest usually lives alone, but not isolated, among the people in the world, as opposed to a *religious* priest, who is a member of a religious community such as a monastery. My secular position influences my view on celibacy. My bishop, who happens to be a Benedictine monk, would doubtless write differently about the topic.

Celibacy is understood in the Roman Catholic tradition in the limited sense of the commitment to remain unmarried rather than in the broader modern secular sense of a voluntary renunciation of genital sex. This is an important distinction, because a priest's primary renunciation is of a wife, children, and family rather than of genital activity, although the latter follows from Catholic teaching about chastity.

Celibacy and chastity are not the same thing. Celibacy is a discipline; chastity is a virtue. A person who is celibate is not by the fact chaste. In effect, though, the obligation to celibacy is an obligation to maintain perfect (that is, completely continent) chastity, because chastity is expected of all Christians. Chastity is the virtue of excluding or regulating the use of the sexual faculty according to the particular state of a person. For celibate people and for those simply not married this means abstaining from sexual activity because, according to Catholic teaching, sex is proper only within marriage. For married people, chastity means engaging in sex only within the marriage partnership.

A secular priest makes two promises to his bishop at his ordination to the deaconate (which usually takes place one year before his ordination to the priesthood): he promises to be obedient to his bishop and to remain celibate.[2] He is required to sign a declaration and take an oath to the effect that he does in fact realize what is involved and that he does act freely, without force, fear, or ignorance. His promise to embrace celibacy is strengthened by invoking God as a witness of, and security for the fulfillment of, that promise.[3]

A Question of Culture

While some religions and cultures esteem the observance of celibacy (e.g., Buddhism, Hinduism, and Christianity), others do not. Celibacy is alien to Muslims, abnormal to Jews. In the course of my missionary work, I found it impossible in Kikuyu thought (see Nelson 1995: 221) and sinful among the Masai. In all cases celibacy raises significant cultural and religious questions, and often the answers for one group contradict those for another. In Christian belief there is no physiological explanation for the benefits of celibacy as there is, for example, in the Hindu practice of brahmacharya (see Caplan 1995). For the Christian, celibacy has a more optional, spiritualized character. For the Catholic priest celibacy is not the *sine qua non* for salvation but a contributory factor to attaining salvation both for the priests who observe it and for the people whom they serve. It is a way of putting human sexuality — for celibacy is a form of sexuality — at the service of God, the person, and the community.

Sometimes this is easier said than done. "What a waste!" is a familiar exclamation one hears in England from people, usually women, who are confronted by a young celibate priest. As a young priest, I used to sense a wistful humor in those words. However, when I moved to Kenya (and into middle age) to work among the Masai and Kikuyu peoples, the same remark was no longer humorous but accusatory. That I, an only son (albeit with two married sisters), would deliberately refuse to keep my family alive by marrying a wife and siring children was both incomprehensible and reprehensible in their view. Dutch priest J. Donders explains why:

The flow of life is a necessary condition of our being able to live. But to receive life is not sufficient to live. Really to live we in our turn must pass on life. It is in the stream that one lives. If we did not pass on life we would be stagnant pools, and not really living links in the life chain. This necessary element in life makes any appreciation for celibacy practically impossible. It is in the African vision, not only abnormal not to pass on life; it is also just plain bad. It is a refusal to use God's most important gift to humankind. (1985: 12)

Being considered stagnant, half dead, abnormal, irresponsible, and just plain bad was not a view of celibacy I had encountered before. In the Catholic milieu in which I was brought up in the 1950s and 1960s, celibacy was seen as spiritually potent, admirable, and heroic. This was what made Catholic priests different. It came as quite a shock to me to encounter an aggressively opposite view. So much for the universality of the sign-value of celibacy! In these circumstances it is remarkable that the African peoples produce any priests at all, since the Church does not relax the rule of celibacy for them and I am not sure that they find the Roman Church's spiritual explanation completely satisfactory. Yet their seminaries (literally, "seed beds" where men train to be priests) are full (see Aguilar, this volume).

Scripture

Christians appeal to two scriptures in support of celibacy: Matthew's Gospel 19:10–12, and Saint Paul's first letter to the Corinthians (1 Cor. 7:25–38). In the Old Testament, where childlessness is a sign of God's disfavor, only the prophet Jeremiah chose celibacy (Jer. 16:1–4). The Church does not usually appeal to this text, however, since celibacy in Jeremiah's case was a prophetic response to a particular set of historical circumstances in which God was understood to be threatening to withdraw from disobedient Israelites his gifts to them of life and health, grace and future — a threat of extinction, which is quite the opposite of what the Christian celibate seeks to signify by his way of life.[4]

In the Gospel of Matthew in the New Testament, Jesus commends those who can remain celibate ("make themselves eunuchs") for the sake of the kingdom of God, although biblical exegetes question whether Jesus was referring to celibates or to those who were considering remarriage after the divorce or death of a spouse. Saint Paul, believing the end of the world to be near, reasoned that marriage was losing much of its point and that celibacy was therefore better (see 1 Cor. 7:31). It is from this perspective that he says, "I should like everyone to be like me" (1 Cor. 7:7).[5] He commends celibacy because it encourages holiness in body and spirit, and it focuses attention on the Lord.

History

The obligation of celibacy among Catholic clergy arises neither from divine law nor from the nature of priesthood but from Church law. It is a discipline of the Church in response to historical experience. The Church now welcomes married former Anglican clergy into the Catholic priesthood, for instance, without expecting them to observe celibacy. It nevertheless insists that should their spouses die these priests must not remarry. This points to the important fact that there are different kinds of celibates: those who have the personal charism (a special grace given by God) of celibacy,[6] and those who do not. The latter include those who take a promise of celibacy because it is the only way they can become priests. It also includes some who are uncomfortable about relationships with women or with intimacy and some who seek power under the pretense of priesthood. Plainly, married former Anglican clergy do not have the charism of celibacy.

Sandra Schneiders explains the nature of charismatic celibacy:

Celibacy is not a personal achievement, an act of the heroic will, a statement of affective invulnerability, or a declaration of psychological independence. *A fortiori* it is not a means of control, of or by oneself or someone else. It is not an entrance requirement to an elite organization, the ascetic discipline of the morally superior, a noble sacrifice, or a way of building *esprit de corps* in a group. It cannot be imposed, commanded or required. As a charism celibacy is the public face of contemplative experience making visible in this world the absolute freedom, the captivating beauty, the supreme generosity, and the ultimate fidelity of that divine "love that moves the sun and the other stars." (1993: 24)

In fact, celibacy has been and is all of these. It is both required for priests and a means of control. Schneiders is talking about celibacy as a charism as opposed to a Catholic discipline.

As celibacy is of negligible interest to scriptural authors and nonessential to the nature of priesthood, where does this discipline come from? During 2,000 years of Christianity, many influences have impacted upon the practice and meaning of celibacy: culture and society, politics and economics, theology and philosophy, and, I would have to say above all, the grace of God. In the first three centuries of Christianity, no law required celibacy as a matter of obligation, and the renunciation of marriage was left to individuals. Marriage was generally held to be the norm for all Christians, although virginity for both the male and female was esteemed. Virginity did not imply that sexuality was sinful (that came later); rather, it was the dedication of one's whole self, sexuality included, to God's service.

Laws concerning clerical continence were originally enacted in a climate ill disposed to thinking of sexual love in marriage as a beautiful gift from God. Christian priesthood adopted the Old Testament concept of cultic purity, especially the idea of ritual uncleanness caused by sexual activity, so that priests were expected to abstain from sex before celebrating the eucharistic ritual.[7] This was not yet mandatory celibacy, however, and marriage remained the norm for priests.

In the fourth century, laws were issued in some local churches, such as the Council of Elvira in Spain in 306, which forbade not only the marriage of clerics but also the use of marriage already entered into. This was not a universally accepted position, and at the Council of Nicea in 326 it was rebuffed as a bad idea, but a compromise was reached by which priests were forbidden to marry after ordination. The die was cast.

A Question of Perfection: Monasticism

Following the era of persecution in the Roman Empire, and after Christianity became the official religion of the empire, martyrdom (literally, "witness") was substituted by monasticism and virginity as the highest Christian ideals.[8] In North Africa, some Christians retreated into the desert in order to devote their entire lives to God, and so the monastic movement began whose asceticism quickly captured the imagination of the marketplace. Virginity was a cornerstone of this ascetic approach to religion.

At this time in North Africa there were strong undercurrents of thought, such as Neoplatonism, Gnosticism, and Manichaeism, which regarded the physical as corrupt, evil, and the source of temptation, and only the spirit as pure and good. The body and emotions were considered hostile to the spirit. This was especially true of sexuality. The idea grew in Christianity that sexual intercourse tainted one's relationship with God and that ministers of the altar in particular were defiled by sexual intercourse. Somehow sex affronted God's holiness. Sexual intercourse was regarded as a necessary evil to propagate the human race. This negative view of sex was propounded by the main patristic writers of the period: Ambrose, Jerome, Chrysostom, and Augustine.

Augustine, a North African, had been a Manichaean before his conversion to Christianity, and he carried some of its skepticism about sex into his new religion. Louis Bouyer writes of him:

Undoubtedly, St. Augustine himself failed, in spite of the sincere attempts he made, to arrive at a vindication of the sanctity of marriage. In spite of his assertions to the contrary, he could only see it as a kind of permission or toleration of sin. However holy he proclaimed marriage to be in principle, he was always unable to admit, as a fact, the possibility of a use which was not intrinsically wrong. (1960: 73)

A Question of Power and Property: The Gregorian Reforms

The second major period of legislation concerning celibacy arose out of the struggle between popes and emperors in the eleventh and twelfth centuries and was aimed at controlling Church resources, namely, its personnel and possessions. By reserving to itself alone the power to make clerical appointments, the papacy stemmed the influence of imperial power and lay lords and countered the practice of simony (buying or selling a spiritual reality, or the temporal reality — such as benefice — joined to that spiritual reality, for a temporal price). The hemorrhage of Church property into private hands was staunched by forbidding priests to marry, so that there were no families to inherit.

In the eleventh century the popes, especially Gregory VII, barred married priests from performing ritual acts of worship, living on Church property, and drawing upon ecclesiastic funds. The laity were prohibited from attending Mass celebrated by a married priest, so he received no sustenance from them. Effectively the married priest was denied his priesthood and home, his employment and financial support. The Second Lateran Council in 1139 passed the first universal law of celibacy, stating not only that priests must give up intercourse and cohabitation with women but also that their marriages were null and void. Rome had succeeded in its aim of centralizing Church power.

In the sixteenth century, the practice of mandatory celibacy was reasserted at the Council of Trent, which successfully sought to produce a new kind of semiotically sealed priest: one who was separated from the laity, educated in a seminary, clothed in a cassock, tonsured, later collared and called Father — one easily recognized for the highly trained professional cleric he would become.[9] It was once even considered a sin for a priest to take off his cassock in front of a lay person. Today, since the Second Vatican Council, the term *Tridentine* (literally, "of Trent") tends to mean "old-fashioned," traditional, a regime that has had its day. The culture of separation is being gradually dismantled, and the new catchphrase in Catholic circles is *collaborative ministry,* which means that the laity are being encouraged once again to take on their rightful responsibilities in the Church and to do many of the things formerly reserved to the priest. Frazee notes the change:

More enlightened attitudes towards sexuality and marriage have destroyed the primitive connection between sexual abstinence and ritual purity, and the alienation of church property is no longer a threat. Moreover there has been a general disenchantment among the secular clergy with ascetic ideals born of the monastic life during periods of extreme fervor. The popes and bishops generally resist change, still fearing that a married priesthood would diminish their power, an opinion which they have in common with their twelfth-century predecessors. (1988: 126)

It is evident that mandatory celibacy is far more favored by pope and bishops than by priests and lay people. In November 1996, the Catholic bishops of England and Wales wrote to the pope endorsing mandatory celibacy, though they candidly acknowledged "the shortcomings in the living out of the obligations of priestly celibacy in our dioceses. This is indeed a calling which is not easily understood by our contemporaries, and yet it is a witness sorely needed in our society" (*Tablet* 1996: 1560).

Celibacy and Marriage

The issue of celibacy therefore begs the question, Does choosing celibacy imply that marriage is regarded as a lesser good? This seems to have been Paul's conviction, influenced by his expectation of an imminent end to the world and in response to unrecorded questions from the Christian community at Corinth.[10] He held that "the man who sees that his daughter is married has done a good thing but the man who keeps his daughter unmarried has done something even better" (1 Cor. 7:38). He considered celibacy the better choice "in these times of stress" but did not legislate about it. On the contrary, the whole tenor of his discussion is one of proposing, rather than imposing, celibacy as a better way of life for those who have been gifted by God to embrace it. On the other hand, Pope John Paul II chose to use the language of mutuality rather than comparison when speaking of marriage and celibacy: "When marriage is not esteemed, neither can consecrated celibacy exist; when human sexuality is not regarded as a great value given by the Creator, the renunciation of it for the sake of the Kingdom of Heaven loses its meaning" (1982: 826).

Why Celibacy Today?

A priest should not, as in previous eras, choose celibacy because he despises sex or fears women, or "through any proud desire to be different from the rest of men, or to withdraw himself from common responsibilities, or to alienate himself from his brothers, or to show contempt for the world" (Pope Paul VI 1982: 301). This historic continuity notwithstanding, Church documents since the Second Vatican Council reveal the different mentality of contemporary Catholicism where the reasons *for* celibacy are concerned. What was once a pragmatically imposed condition is now an elected one, and it is elected for reasons having less to do with logic and more to do with faith.

The Christian faith teaches that God wants us to love Him and our neighbor as Jesus did. The commandment of Jesus, given in John's Gospel, is "Love one another as I have loved you" (15:12). Celibacy is one dimension of that way of loving. The Greeks had several words to describe different kinds of love: for example, *philia* (friendship), *eros* (erotic love), *storge* (affection), and *agape* (charity or unconditional love). It is this last way of loving above all, *agape,* that the Christian strives to practice, and celibacy is one way of doing this. Pope Paul VI wrote: "The free choice of sacred celibacy has always been considered by the Church as a badge of charity, an encouragement to charity: it signifies a love without reservations, it stimulates to a charity which is open to all" (1982: 292). Contemporary clerics have found that celibacy is a means to far more than the original ends for which it was instituted.

The first motivation for celibacy today is the desire to share with Christ his very condition of living, the better to "be in your minds the same as Christ Jesus,"[11] to have an undivided heart, to be completely at his service. The lifelong celibacy of Jesus Christ is significant:[12] it signifies his total dedication to the service of God and humanity. Celibacy is a striving after God, a choosing of God first. It focuses on the goal of Christian life: union with God. The celibate directs his generative energy to the daily seeking of this goal through prayer, ministering to his community, and nurturing his friendships. Without these his celibacy ceases to be passionate, energetic, and potent and ends up being sterile, nonpersuasive, and confused. The disciplined living of these three activities — prayer, ministry, and friendship — gives him the sense of belonging, of doing something worthwhile, of having something to contribute — the tripod upon which rests his sense of identity, fulfillment, and meaning.

Why My Celibacy?

Who can plumb completely his or her own life decisions? Reasoning finally fails. There is a cloud of unknowing within us, lacunae that we cannot penetrate with the eyes of reason, nonrational (I do not say irrational) drives whose origins we cannot fathom. Yet this 45-year-old priest never stops trying to understand why the 10-year-old boy inside him told his bishop 35 years ago that he wanted to be a priest "to give God the biggest thing I can." Let me fall back on paraphrasing a well-known story — my personal celibacy myth — to illustrate the point; it is "The Happy Prince" by Oscar Wilde:

The Happy Prince was a statue gilded over with gold leaf and perched high above the city, a statue whose eyes shone with rare bright sapphires and whose sword glowed with a ruby. The townspeople below thought him beautiful. One night a small weary Swallow, heading south for the warmth of Egypt, alighted between the Prince's feet to rest. He found the Happy Prince weeping because of the poverty and misery continually before his eyes. The Prince begged the Swallow to stay and help. The Swallow reluctantly agreed, for it was becoming colder in this place and he needed the sun for his very survival. The Prince asked the Swallow to take the ruby from the sword and his sapphire eyes to some poor and desperate people.

"It is very cold here," said the Swallow, "but I will do as you ask." He flew back to the Happy Prince, saying, "It is curious, but I feel quite warm now, although it is so cold." When day broke he flew down to the river for a bath. "What a remarkable phenomenon," said the Professor of Ornithology, "a swallow in winter!" And he wrote a long letter about it to the local newspaper. Everyone quoted it; it was full of so many words that they could not understand.

At this point the Swallow knew that he could not leave the blind Prince alone and so stayed to keep him company and to act as his eyes. He told the Prince of all the poor, hungry, hurting people he spied as he flew about the city, and the Prince told him to peel off all the gold leaf and give it to them. Finally, after the snow and frost, the Prince was completely stripped of all his riches. The Swallow grew colder and colder, but he would not leave the Prince, for he loved him too well. He picked up crumbs outside the baker's door when the baker was not looking and tried to keep himself warm by flapping his wings. The bitter cold that he should have left long ago got to him, and at last he knew he was going to die. In one last supreme effort he flew upwards, kissed the Happy Prince on the lips, and then fell down dead at his feet. At that moment, the leaden heart of the Happy Prince snapped in two. Finally, the townspeople, disgusted at the shabby statue, tore it down and melted it in a furnace. But curiously the broken lead heart would not melt, so the townspeople threw it on a dustheap where the dead Swallow was also lying.

God, thinking them the most precious things on earth, sent one of his angels to bring the Happy Prince's broken heart and the dead bird to the warm garden of Paradise, where the Prince praised God and the little bird sang forevermore.[13]

This wonderful story sums up my personal motivation for celibacy, and this is also the first reason that the Church is motivated to require it. It is rooted in love and is the biggest sacrifice I can make, a way of life chosen for the sake of doing God's will (being a celibate for the sake of the kingdom of God); it allows me to be available to God and to the people I serve; it is a renunciation of the warmth of a wife and family even though I die (father no children) as a result; and it is at the service of God's love for his people. Being celibate is the only way open to me as a Catholic if I want to mediate between Christ and his people, to offer his sacrifice (to offer his body for the people) in the ritual of the Mass. The conclusion of the story carries the eschatological assurance that God will reward the faithful servant by giving him his life back in a more abundant way.

No Marriage in Heaven

A second motive for celibacy is eschatological witness: Christ spoke of the coming reign, or kingdom, of God at the end of time.[14] The primary eschatological sign in the New Testament is childbirth; for example, in his letter to the Romans, Saint Paul imagines the end-time in terms of the eager waiting, the groaning, the revealing, the setting free: "From the beginning till now the entire creation, as we know, has been groaning in one great act of giving birth" (Rom. 8:22). So Janette Gray asserts: "Celibacy is not a concern for the Johannine community. To the Gospel community a woman in childbirth is the eschatological sign, not celibacy as traditionally assumed by the Church" (1995: 50). Yet celibacy is a secondary sign, for Jesus taught that in heaven there will be no marriage (see Luke 20:35). The celibate witnesses to the reality of God's reign, to that kingdom where we shall see God face to face and become like him. The Second Vatican Council identifies celibacy as "a living sign of that world to come . . . in which the children of the resurrection shall neither be married nor take wives" (Vatican Council II 1975: 893). The priest does not, of course, witness to celibacy, but celibacy enables him to witness to something else. The witness is the way the celibate lives the celibate life.

Practicality on Top of Personal Reward

Third, celibacy has an enabling purpose, albeit one quite different from the concrete end of keeping Church property intact. It is not only God-directed; it also serves humanity and frees the celibate to reach out in love, giving him greater flexibility in serving and being available for people, because he is not bound by the ties and responsibilities of marriage or family. Pope Paul VI wrote that celibacy gives to the priest "the maximum efficiency and the best disposition of mind, psychologically and affectively, for the continuous exercise of a perfect charity. This charity will permit him to spend himself wholly for the welfare of all, in a fuller and more concrete way" (1982: 294).

Celibacy lends a certain character to the relationship that exists between the priest and his people. The Catholic priest is experienced by his people as belonging to them in a special way. The point of his celibacy is not just that he has given up a wife but that he has given up a wife in order to commit himself in love to them. This brings out another dynamic of celibacy, namely, that the secular priest cannot live his celibacy alone but needs his people to help him and to respond in love to the gift he is giving them of himself. In other words, celibacy is for the sake of the people, not for the priest alone.

Protest

Fourth, the celibate can be motivated by protest: celibacy signifies a different set of values from those often espoused by the prevailing culture. The priest understands his celibacy in terms of fasting in solidarity with the oppressed. The very "foolishness" of celibacy, being a clown of God, has a prophetic dimension. Matthew Fox sees the joke: "In many respects a celibate is a sexual fool — all dressed up with no place to go. To introduce humor into human sexuality is a prophetic dimension in an era when sexuality has lost its sense of play" (1987: 22). Where society considers sex as the keystone of relationships, celibacy proclaims the possibility of acting out of unconditional love. Where society marginalizes the weak, sick, and aged and glorifies youth and physical health, celibacy points to the primacy of spiritual health regardless of physical condition. Donald Goergan notes that celibacy witnesses to God as a source of motivation:

Celibacy points towards another value system than the one society endorses; it has social and political implications as well as religious ones. Celibacy becomes an invitation to understand life differently. Celibacy is an invitation to a society where love and not orgasm is the goal of sexuality and God not comfort is the goal of man. This is not to say that there is anything wrong with orgasm or . . . comfort; it is simply to say that there is more to life than these. (1974: 113)

Training

Twenty years ago, training for celibacy in seminaries was not a high priority. One simply got on with it. Local clergy recount the story of the seminary rector who was asked how he dealt with students' emotions, which were bound to surface in an enclosed all-male environment: "Crush them!" was his terse reply. The story suggests the presence of some homosexual activity, though I hardly encountered it during my 13 years of training. Men with a homosexual orientation are not by that fact debarred from the priesthood, but they are required to observe chastity and continence.

Following the rash of scandals in recent years, seminaries are engaged in serious self-examination regarding the way they train students for the priesthood. Their approach is now more holistic with greater emphasis on emotional and psychosexual development, and the motives of aspirants to the priesthood are examined more thoroughly. There are signs of greater cognizance of actual human experience, since married men (although so far only married convert Anglican clergymen) are being admitted into the Catholic priesthood.

There are still anomalies in the way the seminarian is trained for the celibate way of life before ordination and the way he practices it afterward. Trained to live in the close supportive community of the seminary, he is soon appointed to a parish where he will live alone and apart. Taught that his celibacy will help him to share the very condition of Christ, who had nowhere to lay his head, he is sent to live as the sole occupant of a roomy house, where he must learn to combat selfishness and loneliness. This does nothing to dispel the idea of religion as eccentric, private, individualistic, and yes, in our day, suspicious. It would seem that the way forward is to have communities of priests living together who would mutually support one another in serving a large area.

The Future

There is a sense today among Catholics that our Church is treading water over the issue of mandatory celibacy. The value of priestly celibacy does not appear to be an issue among either proponents or opponents of mandatory celibacy in the Catholic Church, although, as I have indicated, in Africa even its value is reasonably contested. Church officials are quite comfortable talking about the value of celibacy, but they become less than articulate when invited to justify its necessity. The arguments used in the past to justify mandatory celibacy are no longer admissible today, and most priests would simply not recognize themselves in the ancient rationales used to justify it: cultic purity, the sinfulness of sex, simony, and control of Church property. For example, as Michael Winter points out, the Vatican published a booklet in 1994 entitled *Directory on the Ministry and Life of Priests,* which still draws upon conciliar and patristic texts to support the case for mandatory celibacy based upon the concept of ritual purity. He concludes:

If the Vatican wishes to base its law of mandatory celibacy, for the priests of the Latin rite, on arguments such as these, then presumably they have their reasons for doing so. However, on the basis of the evidence presented in this Directory, they can hardly hope to inspire confidence and command assent from the generality of the Church. Still less can they expect intelligent young men to make a great and lifelong sacrifice on such an unsatisfactory basis. (1996: 432)

A recent poll indicated that over two-thirds of the laity support a return to optional celibacy (McGrandle 1996). Can mandatory celibacy survive? If it is having a negative impact upon recruitment to the priesthood, can it be justified when half the world's billion Catholics have only rare access to the Eucharist, which is the heart of their worship, and to the sacraments of reconciliation and anointing of the sick, which only priests are allowed to administer? In view of the many scandals, is celibacy still a compelling witness in society? Should the Church relax the rules in cultures where celibacy has a negative sign-value? Does the present crisis reveal "a power system using celibacy for the domination and control of others," as Sipe (1995: 163) maintains?[15] The double standards of insisting upon celibacy for Latin-rite priests and tolerating an exodus of priests who wish to marry (estimated at 100,000 worldwide, three of whom live in my parish), while admitting married men into the priesthood, is unintelligible to many people, whatever the arguments from Church law.

Moreover, if we allow for Karl Rahner's view that "the Holy Spirit must not always and necessarily be on the side of a purely numerical majority" (1974: 165), does the lack of support for mandatory celibacy suggest a defect in the priest–laity mutuality required for celibacy to function effectively in the Church? Gallagher and Vandenberg perceive a "fatal flaw":

Celibacy is a charism of the Spirit that invites a priest to enter into a covenant relationship with the Body of Christ [that is, the whole Church]. . . . But . . . few of the faithful had any inkling of being party to such a covenant with their priests. By default, priests were and are sentenced to live celibacy alone. In this we find the fatal flaw in celibacy as it is being lived today. It will no more work than a marriage will when only one party is committed to the marital covenant. The nature of celibacy, like the nature of marriage, requires mutuality of commitment to the covenant. (1988: 94)

On the other hand, might we not be on the verge of another half-millennial reform? Rahner (1974: 164) posits a future in which a completely new understanding of celibacy might emerge, a nonconformist decision taken by the young in response to a secularized society, a protest against materialism and convention. Mary Douglas (1996: 161–192) sees the pursuit of purity and abstinence as common themes running through the third-century Christian reformist movement, when young people embraced asceticism in defiance of the irrelevant values of the older generation, Ghandi's movement in protest against British rule in India, and the contemporary Green movement to protect the environment. Asceticism is not dead, though it takes different forms. Perhaps the world will finally heed the warning element of Jeremiah's celibacy after all. In an age of environmental pollution, genetic engineering, divorce, abortion, and euthanasia — which Pope John Paul II calls "a culture of death" — we are caught up in fearful, dangerous, holy areas. We need to take off our shoes as we approach the holy. Maybe priestly celibacy can speak to such contemporary issues as these.

Notes

1. There are no Catholic women priests. Janette Gray (1995) offers an excellent consideration of Christian women's celibacy.

2. The two promises are distinct from vows to observe a particular lifestyle, which are taken by members of religious orders but not by secular priests.

3. An oath is a calling upon God, who is Truth itself, as a witness to some truth.

4. Jeremiah lived through the catastrophic events that befell the kingdom of Judah in the sixth century B.C. The Chaldean armies invaded Jerusalem twice and deported its inhabitants. Jeremiah had accused the kingdom of rebelling against God and embracing policies that would destroy its land, people, and society. Gray shows how Jeremiah's celibacy fit the situation: "His lack of generativity indicates the full tragedy of the community's sin and its consequences. Jeremiah embodies the desolation of the environment, the hopelessness of relationships, the isolation and loneliness of being friendless among enemies, the pathos of the self-destructing community" (1995: 57).

5. All biblical quotations in this chapter are from the Jerusalem Bible.

6. *Charism* refers, theologically, to a specific gift or talent. Some other charisms are listed by Saint Paul in 1 Corinthians 12:8–10, for example, wisdom in preaching and teaching, and gifts of healing and prophecy.

7. See, for example, Leviticus 21:16–24.

8. A martyr is a witness for Christ. Originally *martyr* referred to those who distinguished themselves in the service of Christ, then to those who suffered persecution for Christ, and by the third century it was a title reserved to those who actually died for Christ.

9. The title "Father" for secular priests is a fairly recent form of address in England. Until the 1880s priests were invariably spoken of as Mr. So-and-So and addressed as Sir. There was some opposition to the innovation, in the north of England, for example, but after the emigration from Ireland, the established Irish custom of referring to priests as Father prevailed. The title suggests spiritual kinship and generativity. Referring to the appropriateness of celibacy for priests, the Second Vatican Council stated that it makes them "less encumbered in their service of [Christ's] kingdom and of the task of heavenly generation. In this way they become better fitted for a broader acceptance of fatherhood in Christ" (Vatican Council II 1975: 893).

10. Saint Paul's first letter to the Christians at Corinth, Greece, was evidently his response to moral questions and problems that had arisen in that community

and had been put to him by a Corinthian delegation. One can infer from the text that these included questions about marriage, scandals, and the relationship between Christians and pagans.

11. See Saint Paul's letter to the Philippians (Phil. 2:1–5).

12. This has been the constant teaching of the Catholic Church, reiterated, for example, by Pope Paul VI (1982: 291).

13. The unabridged story can be found in Wilde 1995.

14. *Eschatology* (from the Greek *ta eschata,* "last things") means the study of what happens to people as they die and after they die, including the consideration of heaven and hell, resurrection, and the end of the world.

15. Sipe's (1995) thesis is that celibacy (as understood and lived in the way this chapter presents it, for example) is not itself the reason for the crisis in the Church today but rather its use as a tool of domination—economic, social, political, or sexual—in the name of religion. Analyzing the structure of the celibate/sexual system in the Catholic Church, he identifies seven elements underpinning the crisis: the equation of women, sin, and sex; the superiority of males; the restriction of power to celibate males; the subjugation of women by those in power; the idea that this is God's will; behavior condemned in the general populace being tolerated in the select; and the toleration of violence to retain the system.

References Cited

Buoyer, Louis. 1960. *Woman and Man with God.* London: Darton, Longman and Todd.

Caplan, Pat. 1995. Celibacy as a Solution? Mahatma Gandhi and *Brahmacharya.* In *The Cultural Construction of Sexuality,* ed. Pat Caplan, 271–295. London: Routledge.

Donders, Joseph. 1985. *Non-bourgeois Theology.* Maryknoll, N.Y.: Orbis.

Douglas, Mary. 1996. *Thought Styles.* London: Sage.

Fox, Matthew. 1987. A Deep and Sacred Mystery. *Creation* 3(2): 20–22.

Frazee, Charles A. 1988. The Origins of Clerical Celibacy in the Western Church. *Church History, Centennial Issue* (American Society of Church History) 57: 108–126.

Gallagher, Charles A., and Thomas L. Vandenberg. 1988. *The Celibacy Myth.* Slough: St. Paul's.

Goergan, Donald. 1974. *The Sexual Celibate.* New York: Seabury.

Gray, Janette. 1995. *Neither Escaping nor Exploiting Sex.* Slough: St. Paul's.

The Jerusalem Bible. 1966. Alexander Jones, general ed. London: Darton, Longman and Todd.

John Paul II. 1982. *Familiaris consortio,* 22 November 1981. In *Vatican Council II: More Post Conciliar Documents,* ed. Austin Flannery, 815–898. Leominster: Fowler Wright.

McGrandle, Piers. 1996. Laity Overwhelmingly Back an End to Celibacy. *Catholic Herald,* Nov. 1, p. 3.

Nelson, Nici. 1995. "Selling Her Kiosk": Kikuyu Notions of Sexuality and Sex for

Sale in Mathare Valley, Kenya. In *The Cultural Construction of Sexuality*, ed. Pat Caplan, 217–239. London: Routledge.

Paul VI. 1982. *Sacerdotalis caelibatus*, 24 June 1967. In *Vatican Council II: More Post Conciliar Documents*, ed. Austin Flannery, 285–317. Leominster: Fowler Wright.

Rahner, Karl. 1974. *Opportunities for Faith*. London: SPCK (Society for Promoting Christian Knowledge).

Rolheiser, Ronald. 1995. *Against an Infinite Horizon*. London: Hodder Stoughton.

Schneiders, Sandra M. 1993. Celibacy as Charism. *The Way Supplement* 77: 13–25.

Sipe, A. W. Richard. 1995. *Sex, Priests and Power*. London: Cassell.

Tablet (London). 1996. The Bishops Write to Pope John Paul. November 23, 1560.

Vatican Council II. 1975. Presbyterum Ordinis, December 7, 1965. In *Vatican Council II: The Conciliar and Post Consiliar Documents*, ed. Austin Flannery, 893. Dublin: Costello.

Wilde, Oscar. 1995. The Happy Prince. In *The Complete Shorter Fiction of Oscar Wilde*, ed. Isobel Murray, 95–103. Oxford: Oxford University Press.

Winter, Michael. 1996. A New Twist to the Celibacy Debate. *Priests and People* 10(11): 428–432.

Contributors

Index

Contributors

MARIO I. AGUILAR is chair of ritual studies of the American Academy of Religion and lectures at the School of Divinity at the University of St. Andrews, Scotland. He is the author of *Being Oromo in Kenya* (1998), *The Rwanda Genocide* (1998), *Dios en Africa: Elementos para una antropología de la religión* (1997), and *Ministry to Social and Religious Outcasts in Africa* (1995), and the volume editor of a collection, *The Politics of Age and Gerontocracy in Africa: Ethnographies of the Past and Memories of the Present* (1998).

SANDRA BELL is lecturer in anthropology at the University of Durham, England. Under her maiden name, McDermott, she wrote *Female Sexuality: Its Nature and Conflict* (1969, 1970). She has published papers on the expansion and development of Buddhism in the West in *Journal of Contemporary Religion; Novo Religio: The Journal of Alternative and Emergent Religions;* and other academic journals. She has also written on gender and sexuality in Theravada Buddhism. With Simon Coleman, she is coeditor of a forthcoming volume, *The Anthropology of Friendship* (2000).

MICHAEL CARRITHERS is professor of anthropology at the University of Durham, England. He is the author of *The Forest Monks of Sri Lanka* (1983), *The Buddha* (1983), and *Why Humans Have Cultures* (1992), and an editor of *The Category of the Person* (1985) and *The Assembly of Listeners: Jains in Society* (1991). He is presently researching personhood and the construction of publics in the former East Germany.

PETER COLLINS is a social anthropologist at the University of Durham, England. His doctoral research was on British Quakerism. Articles on this subject have appeared in *Auto/Biography, Architecture and Design, Journal of Contemporary Religion, Worship,* and *Journal of Quaker Studies.* His current interests include the uses and abuses of narrative analysis in the social sciences and in folk definitions of *stress* and *coping.*

VICTOR C. DE MUNCK is assistant professor of anthropology at the State University of New York, New Paltz. He is also the editor of *Reviews in Anthropology.* He is a cognitive and political anthropologist and conducted fieldwork in Sri Lanka on local patterns of conflict and cooperation in the context of cultural change. He has published articles on Sufism, orthodox Islamic movements, agricultural development, the changing culture of work, constructions of the self, gender, exorcism, household disputes, methods, marriage, romantic love, and micro-macro theory. He has published an ethnography on Sri Lanka titled *Seasonal Cycles* (1993), edited a volume titled *Romantic Love and Sexual Practices* (1988), and coedited a volume on methods titled *Using Methods in the Field* (1998). His current research is on romantic love and capitalism.

MICHAEL DUKE carried out his dissertation research in the Sierra Mazateca region of Oaxaca, Mexico, and is currently a research anthropologist with the Hispanic Health Council, where he is exploring the political economy of violence and drug use among the Puerto Rican community of Hartford, Connecticut. In addition, he is a consultant on Mesoamerican ethnology for the Library of Congress, a contributing editor for the *Handbook of Latin American Studies,* and a lecturer at Trinity College.

MARK S. FLEISHER is a cultural anthropologist, a former administrator in the U.S. Department of Justice, Federal Bureau of Prisons, and a professor of criminal justice sciences at Illinois State University. He is the author of *Warehousing Violence* (1989) and the two award-winning books *Beggars and Thieves: Lives of Urban Street Criminals* (1995) and *Dead End Kids: Gang Girls and the Boys They Know* (1998).

KIM GUTSCHOW is Mellon Fellow at Brandeis University. Her dissertation was on the performance of gender and sexuality within Buddhist monasticism. She has published on Buddhist merit making, Tibetan medicine, irrigation, and settlement processes, as well as worked on an award-winning documentary film, *Behind the Ice Wall,* shot in Indian Kashmir.

HIROKO KAWANAMI has done extensive fieldwork in Burma and Thailand. During her first fieldwork in Burma, she lived as a Buddhist nun for 16 months. Her interests focus on gender and Buddhism and new Buddhist movements in Southeast Asia. She is currently lecturer at the Department of Religious Studies at Lancaster University.

MEENA KHANDELWAL conducted her dissertation research, which was supported by grants from the American Institute of Indian Studies and from Fulbright-Hays, on female Hindu renouncers. She spent 18 months in Haridwar, North India, from 1989 to 1991. Her most recent publication is in *Contributions to Indian Sociology.* She currently teaches at Denison University in Ohio.

REBECCA J. LESTER conducted her dissertation research in a Mexican convent, where she investigated the cultivation of a specific, gendered religious sensibility among the nuns as a response to a burgeoning nationalist discourse of modernity.

Her work has appeared in *Ethos* and *Social Science and Medicine*. She is presently a postdoctoral fellow with the Committee on Human Development at the University of Chicago.

PETER PHILLIMORE lectures in social anthropology at the University of Newcastle, England. He received his Ph.D. on the basis of fieldwork in Himachal Pradesh, India. His recent research has focused on northeast England, concentrating on health and inequality, environmental health, and politics of industrial pollution. He has published widely on these topics.

HECTOR N. QIRKO is assistant professor of anthropology at the University of Tennessee, Knoxville. His primary research interest is the relationship between human-evolved psychology and cultural practices. Related papers have appeared in the *American Journal of Human Biology* and the *Annals of the Southeastern Council on Latin American Studies*.

ALICE SCHLEGEL is professor of anthropology at the University of Arizona. Her theoretical interests are social organization, gender, and human development. She has pursued these interests in such books as *Sexual Stratification* (1977) and *Adolescence: An Anthropological Inquiry* (with Herbert Barry as coauthor, 1991) and in numerous articles and book chapters. After some years of research on Hopi society and culture, she is now doing research in western Europe. Her latest project there was a study of German adolescent industrial apprentices. She is currently writing another book on adolescence.

JOHN R. SHAW is an attorney and has practiced correctional law in the U.S. Department of Justice, Federal Bureau of Prisons, for more than 20 years, as regional counsel in the western and north-central regions. He is licensed to practice law in South Carolina and California, has been invited to speak at criminology and law conferences throughout the United States, and has served as correctional law consultant to European countries.

ELISA J. SOBO is trauma research scientist at Children's Hospital and Health Center in San Diego, California. She has published numerous journal articles and several books, including *One Blood: The Jamaican Body* (1993), *Choosing Unsafe Sex: AIDS-Risk Denial among Disadvantaged Women* (1995), *The Cultural Context of Health, Illness, and Medicine* (coauthored with M. Loustaunau, 1997), and *The Endangered Self: Managing the Social Risks of HIV* (coauthored with G. Green, 2000). Other, coedited books are *Using Methods in the Field* (with V. de Munck, 1998) and *Contraception across Cultures: Technologies, Choices, Constraints* (with A. Russell and M. Thompson, forthcoming). She is on the editorial boards of *Anthropology & Medicine* and *Reviews in Anthropology*.

PAUL SOUTHGATE began studying for the priesthood at the age of 11. He was ordained a priest in 1977, serving in both England and Kenya. He is presently parish priest at Whitley Bay in England.

Index

abuse, 52–54, 107, 199, 202, 203, 237. *See also* rape
adolescence, 18–19, 87–102 *passim*; and homosexuality, 96–98; relations with parents, 95–96, 98–99 *passim*; relations with peers, 96
adolescent subfecundity, 100. *See also* adolescence
Africa, 181
AIDS, fear of, 226
Alter, J., 15, 17
altruism, 67, 68; biological, 68, 69; induced or manipulated, 66, 69, 71, 79; psychological, 69, 70; reciprocal, 68–71; terminal, 71, 79
America, in the 1950s, 93–96
androgyny, 36
anorexia, 8, 13, 198–99
apyo-gyi, 146. *See also* virgin
asceticism, 10, 29–43 *passim*, 157, 173, 174*n1*; Catholic, 251–53, 260; practice of, 163, 169
asexuality, 12, 37, 47, 115
ashrama, 160, 174*n4*
association, 71–73, 75–76, 79
attachment, 72, 74

bachelor, 215
Balch, S. H., 68, 72, 77
Balkans, 20
basic-level schema. *See* schema: basic-level
Bible, 250, 261*nn4, 10*
body, 199, 209, 210. *See also* master motives
Boorana, 183, 187, 188
Bowers v. Hardwick, 232–33
brahmacharya, 29, 34, 42–44, 152, 157, 158, 166

Brahman: caste, 41; influence of, 139; priest, 34. *See also* Hinduism
bridewealth, 89; service, 98
Bruch, H., 200
Buddhism: in Kangra, 36; Theravada, 7, 16, 100, 137–40; Tibetan, 47–59 *passim*, 67. *See also* Eight Chief Rules; *jomo*; monks: Buddhist; nuns: Buddhist
Burma. *See* Myanmar
Bynum, C. W., 15

Cassian, J., 14
caste, 30. *See also* Brahman; Hinduism
Catholicism, 8, 10, 13, 16, 112, 180–90 *passim*, 216–17; as asceticism, 251–53, 260; as charism, 251, 260, 261*n6*; and chastity, 248; crisis of celibacy, 247, 260, 262*n15*; and cultic purity, 251–53, 259; as discipline, 248, 251; future of celibacy, 259–61; history of celibacy, 250–54 *passim*; as mandatory, 246–48, 250, 252–54, 259–60; and monasticism, 252–53; as power and control, 251, 253–54, 259–60, 262*n15*; practicality of celibacy, 257–58; priests' training for celibacy, 258–59; as protest and prophecy, 250, 258, 260; ritual, 182; sign-value of celibacy, 247–48, 250, 254–55, 257, 260; and virginity, 251, 252
celibacy: and agriculture, 126; and Christianity, 76–78, 217; and cleanliness, 125–26, 131–34; as communication, 7–9; and curing rituals, 127–28; and desire, 11–12; and diet, 127; and evolution, 22; female, 19–22, 41, 151; as graded category or semantic continua, 218; as greater good, 217; and history